ap advantage™

U.S. History

Skillbook

D1567148

MICHAEL

HENRY

ap advantage™

Editorial and Production

Publisher: Tom Maksym

Executive Editor: Steven Jay Griffel

Vice President, Production and Manufacturing: Doreen Smith

Creative Director/Assistant Vice President: Amy Rosen

Project Manager: Steven Genzano

Production Editor: Carol Deckert

Designer: Amy Rosen

Copy Editor: Michael O'Neill

Cover Design: Pronk & Associates

Permissions Manager: Kristine Liebman

Photo Research: Pat Smith, Robert E. Lee

To my wife Ann and my daughter Kimberly

* AP is a registered trademark of the College Board, which was not involved in the production of, and does not endorse, this book.

ISBN 1-4138-0493-4

Printed in the United States of America.

10 9 8 7 6 5 4

Table of Contents

PREFACE

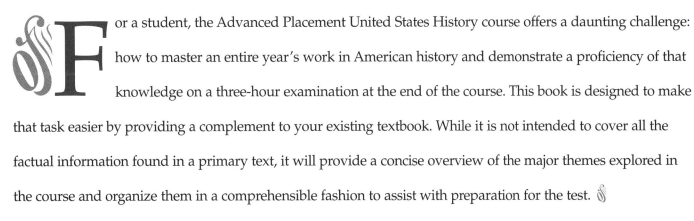

For a student, the Advanced Placement United States History course offers a daunting challenge: how to master an entire year's work in American history and demonstrate a proficiency of that knowledge on a three-hour examination at the end of the course. This book is designed to make that task easier by providing a complement to your existing textbook. While it is not intended to cover all the factual information found in a primary text, it will provide a concise overview of the major themes explored in the course and organize them in a comprehensible fashion to assist with preparation for the test.

As the chapters examine the chronological periods of United States history, they outline major trends, provide a conceptual summary, and highlight important terms, people, and events associated with each era. In addition, the book develops writing and primary source skills necessary to succeed on the examination. The early chapters address basic skills such as what a question is asking, and what a document is saying. Progressing through the book, you will be introduced to increasingly complex skills so that by the last chapters, you can write analytical essays and sophisticated document-based essays.

This book has several instructional applications. It can serve in classrooms as a companion to the textbook and reading book used in the Advanced Placement course. With this arrangement, you can review content and build writing and analytical skills as you progress through the course. The book can also serve as a writing and skill tutorial, helping to prepare you for your work on primary sources as you move toward writing Document-Based Questions (DBQ).

You may want to form study groups and work through the materials in an extracurricular fashion. This will structure review sessions as the exam approaches. For an individual student, the book is useful to review content you have forgotten and to reinforce essay writing and primary source analytical skills. Overall, the book offers a fresh and concise perspective on the knowledge presented in the course and strengthens historical thinking and writing skills. In short, it is an excellent means to enhance content and skills performance in Advanced Placement United States History.

Introduction to the Advanced Placement Program

What Is AP?

The Advanced Placement program is an educational testing program that offers college-level curricula to secondary school students. It is based on a fundamental premise: Motivated high school students are capable of doing college-level work while still attending high school. The program also grew from the belief that students were not being sufficiently challenged academically, especially in their last years of high school.

Advanced Placement (AP) officially started in 1955. Beginning with eleven subjects (United States History was not one of the originals), 1229 students took the first AP tests in May 1956. The exams are constructed and administered by Educational Testing Service (ETS) under the aegis of the College Board. The exams define the knowledge and skills of a freshman-level college course. Students who qualify on the exam (scoring three or better on a five-point scale) are recommended for college credit and placement. The final decision on awarding credit or placement rests with the college or university that the test taker plans to attend, however. The College Board reports the scores and makes its recommendations, but the Board cannot offer college credit or placement itself. Worldwide, over twenty-nine hundred colleges and universities have AP credit and placement policies.

As it approaches its fiftieth anniversary, AP has become the standard of excellence for American secondary education. In 2003 there were thirty-four AP courses and students took 1,737,231 million exams worldwide. Over fourteen thousand high schools participate in the AP program, with 60 percent of all U.S. high schools offering at least one AP class.

What Benefits Does AP Offer Students?

AP classes offer students many benefits and opportunities. First, and most importantly, AP is an outstanding educational program that introduces college courses into high schools. Students are given instruction in content and skill development that they would normally receive only in their first year of college. AP courses go into greater depth and detail than regular high school courses as they offer more stimulating and challenging curricula. In short, AP provides high school students with a superior academic experience.

Other benefits include:

- By qualifying on the end-of-the-year exam, students can receive college credit and placement while still in high school.

- With sufficient numbers of AP courses and qualifying scores, students can earn sophomore standing at over fourteen hundred colleges and universities. This can be a substantial tuition savings. (Mom and Dad really like this one.)

- Students can exempt introductory college courses and begin studying in their major field of interest earlier and/or they can explore other academic areas of interest.

- With AP credits, students increase their opportunity for double majors and to participate in off-campus programs without jeopardizing their timely progress towards college graduation.

- On a transcript, AP courses serve as an indicator to college admission officers that students are dedicated and willing to accept challenges in their education.

- AP courses provide students with a national standard by which to measure their academic progress.

- AP offers the opportunity for self-discovery. Through the AP challenge, students can better define their scholarly strengths and weaknesses and see themselves more clearly in comparison to other students around the country and the world.

What Are Student Expectations of the Class?

An AP history class is an intensive study of the history of the United States from 1600–1985. It makes the same academic demands that both parts of a college survey class would involve.

In general, you will be asked to:

- read thirty to sixty pages from a college-level, history textbook per week;

- outline or take reading notes from the textbook assignments;

- establish relationships among facts and be able to formulate concepts and generalizations about events, people, and ideas in American history;

- take notes from classroom lectures;

- understand and analyze primary sources including documents, cartoons, charts, and graphs;

- think historically—that is, determine validity, point of view, and bias; weigh evidence; evaluate conflicting positions; and make inferences;

- write coherent, persuasive, analytical essay answers about historical problems;

- utilize primary source materials along with relevant outside information and write analytical essays about historical problems.

How Does a Student Succeed in the Course?

A simple truth exists about AP United States History: There are no shortcuts or "magic bullets" that lead to a good grade or a qualifying score on the test. In order to succeed, a student must commit to a year-long protocol of nightly study, periodic review, and intense application of the content and skills taught in the course.

The most important path to success is to stay current with the reading and complete all assignments in a timely fashion. Cramming will not work in AP United States History. You should allocate at least one to two hours of preparation for your AP history class per night.

On a regular basis, you must write in-class essays on significant history problems. In addition, you must write document-based essays. All writing must have a strong thesis that is thoughtfully developed and defended. Students must heed the advice of their teacher to improve and strengthen their writing skills.

A consistent and regular review schedule should be established. You should periodically look back on previous materials and relate them to current classroom work. The creation of outlines, charts, and other graphic organizers is an excellent means of review. Review of content should not be left until the end of the year, as the exam approaches. It must be a regular weekly or biweekly activity during the year. The formation of a study group is an excellent means to structure a review program. The group should meet at least once a month in the first semester and twice a month as the exam approaches.

The AP exam consists of two sections: a multiple-choice section and an essay section, which is divided into two parts. The first segment of the essay section requires students to write a Document-Based Question (DBQ), and the other part consists of choosing between two sets of essays and answering one question from each set.

Each part of the exam will be described in the pages that follow.

The Multiple-Choice Section

Mastery of the multiple-choice questions is critical to qualifying on the AP exam. The section consists of eighty items that are given in the first fifty-five minutes of the testing session. This part of the test counts 50 percent of a student's grade. Further, there is a positive correlation between scores on the multiple-choice portion of the exam and the essay sections. Often, a student who scores high on the multiple-choice will score high on the essays. Beyond the statistics, this makes sense. The essays require strong factual support for competent answers. Thus, a student who knows details should be able to answer multiple-choice questions and write convincing essay answers as well.

The multiple-choice questions will ask you to identify trends, causes, results, and relationships between events. There are few questions that test simple recall of people, events, or dates. In addition, less than 15 percent of the questions are negative types of questions (e.g., "which was NOT" or "all of the following EXCEPT"). Such questions can be daunting to answer even when you know the topic, but they do not predominate on the test.

In general, a student who answers 50–60 percent of the multiple-choice questions correctly and does reasonably well on the three essays (a score of five or better on a nine point scale) is likely to qualify on the test. For example, on the 2001 examination, there was a 77.2 percent probability that students with multiple-choice scores between 34 and 44 would receive a 3, 4, or 5 grade on the overall test. In contrast, students with scores of 15 to 33 had only a 12.2 percent probability of qualifying.

In its course description of United States History, the College Board offers the following breakdown of the chronological eras and content areas on the AP United States History exam:

17 percent of the multiple-choice questions deal with the years 1607–1789.

50 percent of the multiple-choice questions deal with the years 1790–1914.

33 percent of the multiple-choice questions deal with the years 1915–present.

In addition,

35 percent of the questions address political institutions and behavior.

35 percent of the questions are concerned with social change.

15 percent of the questions are about diplomatic events.

10 percent of the questions test economic issues.

5 percent of the questions deal with cultural/intellectual topics.

This breakdown suggests that the multiple-choice section focuses on political and social relationships from the establishment of nation under George Washington to the eve of the Great War in Europe. While mastery of this material alone will not guarantee success on the exam, these are the areas of greatest emphasis on the test and the foundation upon which competency must be built.

Two other questions concerning the multiple-choice section often arise:

1. Should the course begin with 1763, ignoring the colonial period?

2. Should the course deal with the most recent political and social events by the date of the test?

Looking at the two most recently published tests (1996, 2001) for answers, we find that among the 160 multiple-choice items, 8.1 percent (13/160) came from the years 1607–1763 and 5.6 percent (8/160) of the questions were about events after 1968. This suggests that excluding the colonial period would not be wise, since one of every twelve questions comes from this era. Thus, colonial topics such as Jamestown, Bacon's Rebellion, the Mayflower Compact, and the Great Awakening should be an important part of your review.

At the other end of the course, you will be well-prepared for most of the multiple-choice questions if you finish the 1960s or early 1970s by test day. Very few questions are asked about the last quarter of the twentieth century. After the test, students often recall those few questions they had not studied and exaggerate their numbers. You may hear there are many questions on Jimmy Carter or Ronald Reagan on the multiple-choice section. This is simply not accurate. There will be only two or three questions at most about events in the post-1975 era.

Another issue that arises concerning the multiple-choice section is whether you should try to finish the entire eighty questions. The multiple-choice questions will become increasingly difficult as you proceed through the test. For example, the first ten multiple-choice questions on the 2001 exam had a 75.3 percent rate of correct response, while the last ten questions had 35.9 percent rate. However, you should make sure to look at every question on the test. You should not simply decide to do only the first sixty questions because they are easy and ignore the last twenty because they are likely to be too hard. We will examine the issue of guessing and omitting questions later. For now, however, make sure that you look carefully at every multiple-choice question on the examination.

Types of Questions

An alternative categorization system of the multiple-choice questions offers trends and patterns slightly different from those presented in the College Board course description book. As part of a study, I examined the multiple-choice section of the test from 1960 to 1983. I also used the published exams in 1984, 1988, 1996, and 2001 in a long-range search for trends in the multiple-choice section in the last four decades.

In my analysis, I divided the multiple-choice into six categories:

1. Primary-documents questions, which were based on reading passages from diaries, state and national laws, speeches, court rulings, and government documents. Students were asked to identify the speaker, point of view, or significance of the source.

2. Historiographic questions, which asked students about the history of history as well as schools of historical interpretation

3. Symbolic representation questions, which asked students to interpret cartoons, graphs, and maps

4. Arts and humanities questions, which asked students about literature, architecture, painting, and sculpture

5. Social science questions, which were not based on reading passages, maps, graphs, or cartoons and asked students about social history involving economics, labor relations, minority groups, women, Native Americans, and monetary policy

6. Traditional questions, which were not based on reading passages, maps, cartoons, or graphs and asked students about political parties, legislation, presidential administrations, armed conflicts, and foreign relations

Table 1. Distribution of Multiple-Choice Questions, 1960–2001

Years	Total No. of Questions	Primary Documents	Historiographic	Social Science	Arts/ Humanities	Symbolic Representation	Traditional Questions
1960–1964	300	118 (39.2%)	2 (1.0%)	43 (14.2%)	4 (1.3%)	37 (12.3%)	96 (32.0%)
1965–1969	375	130 (34.6)	1 (0.5)	62 (16.5)	10 (2.6)	55 (14.6)	117 (31.2)
1970–1974	375	107 (28.6)	17 (4.5)	59 (15.8)	14 (3.7)	53 (14.1)	125 (33.3)
1975–1979	485	108 (22.3)	15 (3.1)	121 (24.9)	25 (5.2)	32 (6.6)	184 (37.9)
1980–1984	500	65 (13.0)	8 (1.6)	137 (27.4)	39 (7.8)	39 (7.8)	212 (42.4)
1988/1996 2001*	260	6 (2.3)	0 (0.0)	89 (34.2)	12 (4.6)	9 (3.5)	144 (55.4)

* Last three published examinations

Table 1, Distribution of Multiple-Choice Questions, 1960–2001, presents several interesting patterns. First, the multiple-choice section has been heavily weighted with questions about politics and diplomatic/military issues. Second, there has been a steady rise in questions from social history and aspects of the social sciences. Third, the number of questions based on reading passages has shown a steady decline, especially since the 1970s. Fourth, historiography has dwindled and vanished from the multiple-choice section. Finally, both arts/humanities and symbolic representation have faded in importance on the multiple-choice section.

Several conclusions can be drawn from the table:

1. Questions about politics and diplomacy are very numerous, and a strong grounding in these topics must be the core of classroom instruction in order to master the multiple-choice section.

2. Social history topics and social science types of questions appear in increasing numbers on the test. The role of minorities, women, Native Americans, and working people must be included in your AP history course.

3. Historiography is no longer significant on the multiple-choice section. This is an area that might be de-emphasized in course study without seriously jeopardizing performance on the multiple-choice component.

4. Questions on the arts and humanities are not numerous on the test. While some preparation in these areas is worthwhile, it should not come at the expense of political, diplomatic, and social history topics.

5. While primary documents play an important role elsewhere on the test (Document-Based Questions), they are not likely to appear on the multiple-choice section. Classroom activities and teacher-made tests that ask multiple-choice questions about reading passages are not likely to prepare you for the multiple-choice component.

6. Although symbolic representations have generally declined on the test, you should receive specific instruction in interpreting cartoons, charts, and graphs. These types of items still appear on the multiple-choice section and are frequently found as sources on the Document-Based Question (DBQ) part of the test.

Strategies for the Multiple-Choice Section

The bottom line on guessing: Do not do it!

The College Board makes it clear that "It is improbable that mere guessing will improve your score significantly: it may even lower your score. . . ." To discourage guessing, there is a penalty assessed for all wrong answers on the multiple-choice section. For example:

- If you answer four multiple-choice questions correctly, you add four points to your overall raw multiple-choice score.

- If you omit four questions, you add no points to your overall raw score.

- If you guess at four questions and are wrong, you are penalized ¼ point for each wrong answer. You **LOSE** one point from your overall raw score.

Thus, wrong answers hurt your score, while omitted questions are neutral. The final determination of your multiple-choice score is calculated by taking the total right answers, subtracting one-fourth of the wrong answers, and multiplying that number by 1.125. This coefficient makes the multiple-choice section 50 percent of your final grade. (We will discuss the overall grading of the test later in the book.) You maximize your score on this section of the test by answering as many questions as possible correctly, while minimizing the number you attempt and get wrong. It is not expected that you will answer every multiple-choice question in order to score high on the test. Omitting even as many as ten questions is unlikely to jeopardize a score of four or five on the test.

While indiscriminate guessing is not a good idea, you should make educated guesses where you can on the exam. That is, when the correct response is not a certainty, try to eliminate some of the distracters and then select from the remaining choices. For example, if you can reduce the five choices to two or three, you probably will improve your multiple-choice score by attempting to answer the question.

Here are a few tips on making educated guesses:

- Read the stem of the question at least twice to determine quickly its time frame and content area. For example, try to assess the year, decade, or century of concern and whether the question is asking about politics, economics, art, civil rights, etc.

- Read all five choices before selecting the correct answer. Do not jump at the first answer that seems correct. You are looking for the BEST answer, and there may be a better answer as you read through all the choices.

- Always start by eliminating wrong choices and then selecting from the remaining possibilities.

- Eliminate choices first that are outside the chronological period. For example, if the question deals with colonial religious development, a choice about George Washington's presidency would be the first to go.

- Eliminate choices that are wrong under any and all circumstances. If, in the example just cited, you see a choice about Alexander Hamilton's support of limiting the power of government, that should go into the answer-choice trash can quickly.

- Eliminate choices that are not on the topic of the question. For example, if a question concerns religious development, you can quickly eliminate choices about nullification or Social Darwinism or other political and economic matters.

- Eliminate choices that have absolutes in them, such as *never*, *always*, and *forever*.

Once you have winnowed down the alternatives, you should be able to select from the remaining two or three options. Generally, your first choice of these is most likely to be correct. Most of the time, if you go back and change an answer about which you have some lingering doubt, you'll get it wrong. Research says to stay with your first choice.

Pacing Yourself on the Exam

It is important to pace yourself on the test. Do not get bogged down on a single question. It is imperative that you read every question on the test. If you find a question without a ready answer, mark it and move on. Even though the last twenty questions are difficult, they are not impossible. You may find many questions to which you know the answer. Make sure that you work through the entire test.

On test day, do not forget your watch. Monitor your progress carefully so that you complete the first forty-five questions within the first twenty minutes. They are the easiest items and should go quickly. Within thirty-five minutes you should read about seventy percent of the exam (questions 55 to 65). At this pace, you will finish reading all the questions at least once in forty-five minutes, and then you can go back to look again at questions that stumped you initially and proofread your answer sheet.

*E*ssay Sections

The Document-Based Question

The DBQ first appeared on the AP test in May 1973. It grew from concerns by the test committee that AP students were not thinking historically on the essay portion of the exam. Rather, students were regurgitating memorized information and parroting facts, with little real understanding. The committee decided to construct an essay question that required students to move beyond simple recall and analyze and synthesize primary sources. Students would use their knowledge and seventeen to twenty documents to address problems.

The intellectual origins of the DBQ came from the "new social studies" movement of the 1960s. This inquiry-oriented pedagogy called for students to set aside textbooks and use primary sources in their study of history. The "new history" component of this approach required students to test hypotheses, make generalizations, and de-emphasize rote factual recall. Several members of the test committee, who taught in secondary schools and had inquiry experience, brought these ideas to the test development meetings. After much discussion the DBQ was created and first appeared on the test in 1973.

The DBQ requires students to analyze sources such as documents, cartoons, tables, graphs, photographs, and posters. In addition, students employ the historian's craft of sorting, weighing, and evaluating materials as they synthesize these sources into an essay about a historical issue.

The original DBQ format was modified in 1982 because its length made it difficult for students to do more than summarize the seventeen-to-twenty documents in the time available. They did not have an opportunity to analyze and evaluate issues. In 1982, the number of documents was reduced to eight or nine, and greater reliance was placed on outside information. In its current form, the DBQ seems secure as an integral part of the AP exam.

Tackling the DBQ

The DBQ is a required essay. It counts 22.5 percent of your overall grade on the AP exam. Keep in mind that it is an essay question, and that the strategies and approaches you use with other essays apply here. Also remember that the documents are to be used as only part of the support for your thesis. **Don't forget to use outside information as well as the documents in support of your argument.**

Here are some important ideas to keep in mind as you write the DBQ. We will discuss and model many of these later in the book.

1. Read the statement carefully, noting the time frame and the guiding elements of the statement. It maybe helpful to write yourself a short summary or question about the issues at hand.

2. Write down all the facts you can think of about the time period—not just the topic of the question. **DO NOT LOOK AT THE DOCUMENTS YET.**

3. Reread the statement, look at the facts you have listed, and write a thesis statement that can be supported from these ideas.

4. Summarize the documents using the strategies suggested later in this book. As you read the documents, also make inferences about the sources. (Again, we will discuss this idea later.)

5. Look at your thesis and make a chart of the facts and documents that support your thesis and, on the other side, those that challenge the thesis.

6. Although it is not required, try to use all the documents. Probably one or two will challenge your thesis. Don't ignore them. Be prepared to write a contrary paragraph toward the end of the paper to account for these documents. This paragraph should not refute your thesis, but it should deal with the complexity of the issue. (This will show the reader that you understand that history is not always right or wrong, black or white.)

7. As you use outside information, you should underline it. This will give you a visual map of how much outside information you are including in your paper. It will also help the reader as he or she evaluates your paper. Obviously, if you do not have much underlined, you need to dig a little deeper.

8. Integrate the documents into the text of the essay. Use the documents and your outside information to support your thesis. Generally, documents belong in the middle or at the end of a sentence. **Don't start a sentence with "Document A says . . ."**

9. Do not copy large sections of the documents into your essay. If you wish to use the whole idea of the document, allude to it and then put "(Doc. A)" after your paraphrase. If you are using only a phrase from a document, put it in with quotation marks around it. The reader will recognize the document from which you are quoting.

10. The documents should be blended with outside information. **Do not just summarize the documents and call it a DBQ answer.**

11. A general outline of a DBQ response is:
    a. Introductory paragraph
    b. Background paragraph: Here you set the stage and load up on outside information.
    c. Two to five paragraphs of support
    d. Possible contrary paragraph to account for wayward documents
    e. Conclusion

DBQ Topics, 1982–2003

Tables 2 and 3 show the distribution of DBQs since the shorter format was introduced in 1982.

Table 2. Recent DBQ Topics

1982	John Brown's raid and the changing relationship between the sections, 1859–1863
1983	Farmers' problems, 1880–1900
1984	Hoover, a conservative; FDR, a liberal
1985	The Articles of Confederation and their effectiveness, 1781–1789
1986	Tensions in the 1920s
1987	The Constitution and the 1850s
1988	Decision to use the A-Bomb, 1939–1947
1989	Booker T. Washington vs. W. E. B. DuBois, 1877–1915
1990	The Jacksonians as guardians of the Constitution and liberty, etc., in the 1820s and 1830s
1991	The rejection of the Treaty of Versailles
1992	Environment and the development of the West, 1840s–1890s
1993	Compare and contrast the Chesapeake and New England colonies, 1607–1700
1994	Late nineteenth-century expansion: a continuation and a departure
1995	Changing goals, strategies, and support of the Civil Rights Movement in the 1960s
1996	Constitutional and social development between 1860 and 1877—a revolution or not?
1997	Economic and social development and women's position in society, 1890–1925

(Continued on next page)

Table 2. (continued)

1998	Jeffersonian Republicans as strict constructionists, 1801–1817
1999	The extent to which the colonists developed an identity and unity, 1750–1775
2000	The extent to which organized labor improved the position of workers, 1875–1900
2001	Cold War fears and Eisenhower's relative success in dealing with them, 1948–1961
2002	Reform movements and expansion of democratic ideals, 1825–1850
2003	The New Deal's effectiveness and the changing role of government, 1929–1941

Free-Response Essays

Format of the Section

After completing the DBQ, you must write two shorter essays. There is a choice between two sets of essays, with the student selecting one question from the first set and one from a second pair. Generally, the first two essays come from the colonial period through the Civil War and Reconstruction. The second set concern events after 1877 through the 1970s. The time frame of the DBQ impacts on the choices in the free-response section, however. For example, a DBQ on the last quarter of the nineteenth century would eliminate that era as a possible free-response question in section two and a student could find two questions exclusively from the twentieth century.

Once students select their questions, they write an analytical response. The two essays count 27.5 percent of the overall final grade. It is recommended that you spend between thirty and thirty-five minutes on each essay. The questions will ask you to evaluate developments, explain causes, and analyze results of historical events. Most of the time, the questions deal with a twenty- to thirty-year period, and you must assess some element of change during that time. Occasionally, you will be asked to compare and contrast events. For example, recently a question asked students for a comparison of American foreign policy after World War I and World War II. The essays require strong content information, and students are expected to cite specific data to support their thesis.

The colonial period has been a very popular topic in the first set of essays. This gives additional support for students' having a strong grounding in the years 1607 to 1763. Since 1994, when this new essay format was estab-

Table 3. DBQs by Chronological Time Periods

1607–1763
- Chesapeake/ New England colonies

1763–1800
- Articles of Confederation
- Colonies/identity/unity

1800–1828
- Jeffersonians as strict constructionists

1828–1848
- Jacksonians as guardians of democracy
- Reform and democratic ideals

1848–1877
- John Brown's raid
- Constitution in the 1850s
- Reconstruction as a revolution

1880–1900
- Farmers' problems
- Washington v. DuBois
- Environment and the West
- Expansion and the 1890s
- Status of Women
- Organized labor

1900–1930
- Tensions of the 1920s
- Rejection of the Treaty of Versailles

1930–1950
- FDR v. Hoover
- Use of the A-Bomb
- New Deal's effectiveness and impact

1950–1970
- Changes in the Civil Rights Movement (1960s)
- Cold War fears and Eisenhower

lished, there has been a colonial-era question on the test six of the nine years.

At the other end of the course, since 1994, essays exclusively about post-1970 America have been rare. Only in 1999 did one of the choices ask students to evaluate Asian containment to 1975. In the other eight years, there were either no questions post-1945, or they involved events of the 1950s and 1960s.

You need to be mindful that the suggested time for the two essays is thirty to thirty-five minutes per question. It is critical that time be budgeted properly to allow sufficient attention to write these two questions. The

DBQ is the first essay written, and you are not required to stop working on it and start the free-response essays. It is your responsibility to make sure the entire two hours and ten minutes allotted for section two is not consumed by the DBQ. Remember, the two free-response essays count for 27.5 percent of the final grade on the AP exam.

Types of Free-Response Essays, 1963–2001

The free-response section has undergone a number of transformations since 1963. That was the last year students were asked to write three essays from a choice of eleven. In 1964, they selected three out of twelve, and from 1965 to 1972, there were ten choices, and students wrote on three. In 1973, which was the first year of the DBQ, the number of choices fell to nine, with students choosing one. In 1976, the number of free-response choices went to five, with students choosing one free response and writing the DBQ. That format remained in place until 1994, when the current configuration was introduced. From 1956 to 1982, the essay section accounted for 75 percent of a student's grade, and since the early 1980s, it has been 50 percent of the final grade.

To analyze the free-response section of the test, I developed a categorization system that produced a matrix of essay questions in five-year periods for forty years. The seven categories of questions were:

1. Intellectual and cultural issues: questions addressing how literature, art, architecture, and religion influenced United States history

2. Minority issues: questions addressing the role of African Americans, women, and Native Americans in the development of the United States

3. Political issues: questions addressing the evolution of political parties, legislative action, Supreme Court rulings, presidential administrations, and reform movements

4. Military and diplomatic issues: questions addressing American involvement in armed conflicts, as well as relations with other nations

5. Historiographic issues: questions addressing the history of history and schools of historical interpretation

6. Economic and business issues: questions addressing employment, monetary policy, labor relations, and industrial and agricultural developments

7. Immigration issues: questions addressing trends in immigration and how immigration influenced American history

Looking at the free-response questions over the forty-year period reveals some interesting patterns and trends.

Table 4. Free-Response Essay Topics by Five-Year Periods

Years	Intellectual/ Cultural	Minority	Political	Military/ Diplomatic	Historiographic	Economic/ Business	Immigration
1963–1967	4 (7.6%)	1 (1.9%)	20 (37.7%)	11 (20.7%)	3 (5.7%)	11 (20.7%)	3 (5.7%)
1968–1972	5 (10.0)	6 (12.0)	18 (36.0)	8 (16.0)	3 (6.0)	10 (20.0)	0 (0.0)
1973–1977	5 (13.5)	6 (16.2)	14 (37.8)	5 (13.5)	0 (0.0)	6 (16.3)	1 (2.7)
1978–1982	2 (8.0)	2 (8.0)	11 (44.0)	5 (20.0)	0 (0.0)	5 (20.0)	0 (0.0)
1983–1987	5 (20.0)	4 (16.0)	7 (28.0)	4 (16.0)	0 (0.0)	4 (16.0)	1 (4.0)
1988–1992	1 (4.0)	3 (12.0)	11 (44.0)	5 (20.0)	0 (0.0)	5 (20.0)	0 (0.0)
1993–1997	1 (4.7)	3 (14.3)	9 (42.8)	4 (19.1)	0 (0.0)	4 (19.1)	0 (0.0)
1998–2002	2 (10.0)	5 (25.0)	5 (25.0)	4 (20.0)	0 (0.0)	3 (15.0)	1 (5.0)

Table 4 suggests several conclusions:

1. Traditional types of questions remain very important on the free-response essay section. The combination of political, diplomatic, and military questions as a "traditional" historical category accounts for 53.6 percent of the free-response essays since the new format was introduced in 1994. While the percentage is down slightly from the past, these types of questions remain the core of this section.

2. Minority questions, which include the new social history of the last thirty years, have continued to grow in significance. In the last ten years, these questions account for almost 20 percent of the free-response choices. These topics continue to play an important role in the AP curriculum.

3. Economic and business questions have maintained their importance as free-response choices as well. The steady numbers in this category reflect the increasing need for consideration of banking, monetary, and labor issues in AP classroom instruction.

4. Intellectual/cultural topics have maintained a small presence in this part of the exam, but they are not growing in importance. Religion continues to be an important topic, especially for the colonial era. Since 1994, there have been three colonial religious questions on the first set of essays.

5. Historiography has disappeared as topic for the free response.

6. Immigration also has faded from the free-response section.

The patterns on the free-response section reinforce the ones we saw in the multiple-choice area. Once again, to be well prepared for the exam, you must be grounded in the political, diplomatic, and social development of the United States. In the crowded AP curriculum, less attention can be given to the arts, historiography, and intellectual development as time constraints intrude during the academic year.

Table 5. AP United States Worksheet for Determining Grades

Multiple-Choice Section

_____	$- 1/4 \times$	_____	$\times 1.125 =$	_____
Number Correct (0–80)		Number Wrong		Multiple-Choice Score (0–90)

Essay Section

_____	$\times 4.5 =$	_____
DBQ Score (0–9)		
_____	$\times 2.75 =$	_____
1st Free-Response Score (0–9)		
_____	$\times 2.75 =$	_____
2nd Free-Response Score (0–9)		

_____
Total Score on Essays (0–90)

Total Score for Essays and Multiple Choice

_____
(0–180)

How is the Exam Graded?

The examination is graded in two phases. Immediately after the May testing, the multiple-choice answer sheets are machine graded by Educational Testing Service in New Jersey. The number of correct responses out of eighty questions minus ¼ of the wrong answers is tallied, and that number is multiplied by a coefficient of 1.125. Thus, a perfect score would be ninety (80 × 1.125) on the multiple choice section, which accounts for 50 percent of the 180 total points a student can accumulate on the test. (See Table 5 for the exact formula.)

The essay portion of the test is shipped by Educational Testing Service to a college campus in Texas, where nearly six hundred high school and college history teachers gather in early June to evaluate the answers. The graders are divided into tables of six or seven readers, with a table leader assigned to each group to ensure productivity and accuracy during the grading. After becoming familiar with the scoring rubric for one of the four free-response essay prompts, the readers begin grading. They work on only one question for the first two to three days of the reading and score the papers on a zero-to-nine scale. Each grader is assigned an identification number to make sure that a reader grades only one of a student's three essays (two free responses and the DBQ). The second free-response essay and the DBQ are graded at a different table and by different readers. This eliminates the possibility that a student's entire essay grade will be determined by one reader. The table leader periodically rereads selected graded papers at the table to ensure the readers are using the rubric properly and assigning fair and appropriate grades.

After several days with the free-response essay, the readers turn to the Document-Based Question. Again readers become familiar with a scoring rubric specifically constructed for the DBQ and use a nine-point scale to evaluate it. The two free-response essays and the DBQ scores are weighted so that they total ninety points, the same value as the multiple-choice section. (See Table 5.) When all the essays are graded, they are combined with the multiple-choice score to yield a possible overall score of 180 points.

All the student scores are listed in a range from 0–180. From this list, the Chief Faculty Consultant (a.k.a. the Chief Reader) and Educational Testing Service staff establish the specific number of points a student must accumulate in order to score a 5, 4, 3, 2, and 1 on the AP test. For testple, in most years a student who has a total score above 114 received a five on the test, and students with scores above 92 received fours. These threshold levels vary slightly from year to year, however. The scores are reported to students and their colleges in early July.

Chapter 1

COLONIAL PERIOD

1607–1763

Focus Questions

★ How did the settlement of the English colonies give rise to unique economic, political, and social conditions that defined an emerging American identity?

★ How did the need for labor in the colonies give rise to chattel African slavery?

★ How was religion both a unifying and a dividing force in the English colonies?

★ How did the interaction between European and Native American peoples transform both groups and cultures?

★ How did the colonies develop "democratic" principles such as representative government, written charters, and lists of basic rights between 1607 and 1763?

Summary

At the beginning of the seventeenth century, England was in turmoil. A population explosion and economic upheaval left many people rootless and impoverished. Religious struggles between the **Anglican Church** and other religious groups created a spiritual malaise as well. The newly opened areas of the Western Hemisphere beckoned to many people as a refuge from the difficulties at home. After several failed attempts, a permanent colony was established at Jamestown, Virginia, in the spring of 1607.

Colonial Development

Over the next 125 years, three distinct colonial areas developed along the Atlantic coast: New England, the Middle Colonies, and the Southern Colonies. Each possessed different religious, economic, and social characteristics. In New England, the **Congregationalists (Puritans)** dominated. They came to North America to create "a city upon a hill"—a holy commonwealth. They stressed hard work and obedience to God's will as defined by the church. Despite their idealism, the Puritans created a **theocracy** that became increasingly narrow and intolerant. Defined by a harsh climate and environment, farming was difficult. To supplement their livelihood, the New Englanders fished and traded. Over time, the religious ideals of salvation through work coalesced into the Protestant work ethic.

The Middle Colonies of New York, New Jersey, and Pennsylvania were much more tolerant religiously than their northern neighbors. Settled by the Dutch Reformed Church and the **Society of Friends (Quakers)**, this area provided freedom of worship to all Christians. The region, blessed with abundant and rich land and a temperate climate, quickly prospered. By 1770, it had the highest standard of living on the Atlantic coast as wheat became the great staple crop of the region, for sale both at home and abroad.

Life was very different in the Southern Colonies. Here, the Anglican Church gained a foothold, although it lacked the political and economic influences of its counterpart in England. Economically, the Southern Colonies developed the cash crops of tobacco, rice, and indigo. Requiring an extensive labor supply and large tracts of land, these crops structured a society constantly in search of labor and land. Specifically, the great quest became finding sufficient numbers of field workers.

Starting with the **headright system** of land distribution and **indentured servants**, these colonies eventually settled on African slaves to solve their labor needs.

Native Americans

In all the colonies, English relations with Native Americans followed a sad and consistent pattern. At first, the two groups warily interacted with each other. In many cases, Native Americans supplied food and agricultural know-how that allowed the colonists to survive and get established. Sooner or later, however, the colonists' appetite for land and their lack of respect for Native American cultures brought trouble. Beginning with the Powhatans' uprising in 1622 and followed by the Pequot Wars of the 1630s and King Philip's War in the 1670s, armed conflict broke Native American power. By the eve of the American Revolution, epidemics and wars had driven Native Americans from their land and away from the British settlements.

Pocahontas. The illustration above shows Pocahontas, the daughter of Powhatan, with John Smith.

Mercantilism and Dissent

Mercantilism was the bedrock of British colonial control. The goal was to make the mother country economically self-sufficient by restricting colonial trade to the home islands. The **Navigation Acts**, first passed in the 1660s, were intended to achieve this control. Mercantilism held that the colonies should provide raw materials, markets, and hard currency. It discouraged colonial manufacturing by restricting production of such items as iron, woolens, and hats. Yet, the system had glaring holes in it as the colonists smuggled in violation of the acts and produced iron in such quantities that by 1770, they manufactured more iron than England and Wales.

Dissent and conflict between the colonists began almost from day one. The Puritans, with their restrictive religious beliefs, had trouble with **Roger Williams** and **Anne Hutchinson**, who challenged church doctrines and were banished in the 1630s. In Virginia, **Nathaniel Bacon (Bacon's Rebellion)** created trouble over Indian policy. Bacon and his band rose up, temporarily ousted the royal governor, and burned Jamestown in 1676. The rebellion not only called attention to insensitive British policies, but also cast doubts on Virginia's labor system as well. Many of the rebels were landless former indentured servants, who roamed throughout the countryside. As it put down the rebellion, Virginia began to reconsider indentured servitude and to look at permanent African slavery instead.

Women in the Colonies

Women were greatly valued but poorly treated in colonial America. They were in demand because they could "grow labor" for a settlement, but they faced many hardships. Society expected women to be submissive to their husbands, watchful of their children, and attentive to their religion. They had a much higher mortality rate than men because of the dangers of childbirth. (On average, a woman had a child every two years.) For all this, a woman received no political rights and was given only one-third of her husband's estate to live on after his death. (This was surrendered upon remarriage.)

Despite their differences, by 1770 the colonies had developed a nascent American identity. The focus and form of this new feeling was still not clear, but as Britain sought to end its **salutary neglect** of the colonies, its manifestation became more concrete and explosive.

HIGH*lights* of the Period

★ **Act of Toleration** — an act passed in Maryland 1649 that granted freedom of worship to all Christians; although it was enacted to protect the Catholic minority in Maryland, it was a benchmark of religious freedom in all the colonies. It did not extend to non-Christians, however.

★ **Anne Hutchinson** — charismatic colonist in Massachusetts Bay who questioned whether one could achieve salvation solely by good works; she led the Antinomian controversy by challenging the clergy and laws of the colony. She was banished from Massachusetts in 1638 and was killed by Indians in 1643.

★ **Anglican Church** — Church of England started by King Henry VIII in 1533; the monarch was head of the church, which was strongest in North America in the Southern Colonies. By 1776, it was the second-largest church in America behind the Congregationalists.

★ **Bacon's Rebellion** — attack by frontiersmen led by Nathaniel Bacon against the Native Americans in the Virginia backcountry; when the governor opposed Bacon's action, Bacon attacked Jamestown, burned it, and briefly deposed the governor before the rebellion fizzled. This revolt is often viewed as the first strike against insensitive British policy, as a clash between East and West, and as evidence of the dangers of the indentured-servant system.

★ **Board of Trade and Plantations** — chief body in England for governing the colonies; the group gathered information, reviewed appointments in America, and advised the monarch on colonial policy.

★ **Congregationalists (Puritans)** — believed the Anglican Church retained too many Catholic ideas and sought to purify the Church of England; the Puritans believed in predestination (man saved or damned at birth) and also held that God was watchful and granted salvation only to those who adhered to His goodness as interpreted by the church. The Puritans were strong in New England and very intolerant of other religious groups.

★ **Dominion of New England** — attempt to streamline colonial rule by combining all the New England colonies under the control of one governor in 1688; it was dissolved after the Glorious Revolution in England when its sponsors were deposed.

★ **Edmund Andros** — autocratic and unpopular governor of the Dominion of New England; he was toppled from power and was caught while trying to make his escape dressed as a woman.

★ **First Great Awakening** — religious revival in the colonies in 1730s and 1740s; George Whitefield and Jonathan Edwards preached a message of atonement for sins by admitting them to God. The movement attempted to combat the growing secularism and rationalism of mid-eighteenth century America.

HIGH*lights* of the Period

★ **Halfway Covenant** — Puritan response to the dilemma of what to do with the children born to nonchurch members as fewer and fewer Puritans sought full membership (visible sainthood) in the church; leaders allowed such children to be baptized, but they could not take communion, nor could nonchurch males vote in government/church affairs.

★ **Headright system** — means of attracting settlers to colonial America; the system gave land to a family head and to anyone he sponsored coming to the colony, including indentured servants. The amount of land varied from fifty to two hundred acres per person.

★ **House of Burgesses** — first popularly-elected legislative assembly in America; it met in Jamestown in 1619.

★ **Indentured servants** — mainstay of the labor needs in many colonies, especially in the Chesapeake regions in the seventeenth century; indentured servants were "rented slaves" who served four to seven years and then were freed to make their way in the world. Most of the servants were from the ranks of the poor, political dissenters, and criminals in England.

★ **Jonathan Edwards** — Congregational minister of the 1740s who was a leading voice of the Great Awakening; his *Sinners in the Hands of an Angry God* attacked ideas of easy salvation and reminded the colonists of the absolute sovereignty of God.

★ **John Smith** — saved Jamestown through firm leadership in 1607 and 1608; he imposed work and order in the settlement and later published several books promoting colonization of North America.

★ **John Winthrop** — leader of the Puritans who settled in Massachusetts Bay in the 1630s; he called for Puritans to create "a city upon a hill" and guided the colony through many crises, including the banishments of Roger Williams and Anne Hutchinson.

★ **Mayflower Compact** — written agreement in 1620 to create a body politic among the male settlers in Plymouth; it was the forerunner to charters and constitutions that were eventually adopted in all the colonies.

★ **Mercantilism** — economic doctrine that called for the mother country to dominate and regulate its colonies; the system fixed trade patterns, maintained high tariffs, and discouraged manufacturing in the colonies.

★ **Navigation Acts** — series of English laws to enforce the mercantile system; the laws established control over colonial trade, excluded all but British ships in commerce, and enumerated goods that had to be shipped to England or to other English colonies. The acts also restricted colonial manufacturing.

★ **Roger Williams** — Puritan who challenged the church to separate itself from the government and to give greater recognition of the rights of Native Americans; he was banished in 1635 and founded Rhode Island. (Critics called it Rogue Island.)

★ **Salem witchhunt** — period of hysteria in 1692, when a group of teenaged girls accused neighbors of bewitching them; in ten months, nineteen people were executed and hundreds imprisoned. The hysteria subsided when the girls accused the more prominent individuals in the colony, including the governor's wife.

★ **Salutary neglect** — policy that British followed from 1607 to 1763, by which they interfered very little with the colonies; through this lack of control, the colonies thrived and prospered. It was an attempt to end this policy that helped create the friction that led to the American Revolution.

★ **Society of Friends (Quakers)** — church founded by George Fox which believed in "The Inner Light "—a direct, individualistic experience with God; the church was strongly opposed to the Anglican Church in England and the Congregationalist Church in America. In 1681, William Penn established Pennsylvania as a haven for Quakers persecuted in England and in the colonies.

★ **Stono Rebellion** — slave rebellion in South Carolina in September 1739; twenty to eighty slaves burned seven plantations, killed twenty whites, and tried to escape to Florida. The rebellion was crushed. All the slaves were killed and decapitated, and their heads were put on display as a deterrent to future uprisings.

★ **Theocracy** — government organized and administered by the church; in Massachusetts Bay colony, only church members could vote in town meetings. The government levied taxes on both church members and nonmembers and required attendance for all at religious services.

★ **William Penn** — Quaker founder of Pennsylvania; he intended it to be a Quaker haven, but all religions were tolerated. The colony had very good relations with Native Americans at first.

HIGH*lights* of the Period

Ideas to Ponder

After reviewing the chapter's summary, highlights, and your primary text,
discuss the following with members of your study group.

1   In the early seventeenth century, what conditions in England "pushed" people towards the North American colonies?

2   What hardship did the early colonists in British North America face? How did these challenges shape the character of the people?

3   Why was there a labor shortage in the colonies? How did the English try to solve it?

4   What economic activities developed in the various regions? Compare and contrast economic life in New England, mid-Atlantic, and Chesapeake colonies.

5   Why were relations with Native Americans often so troubled and violent? Was the clash inevitable? Why or why not?

6   How did religious beliefs affect the development of the colonies from 1607 to 1763?

7   What patterns of political development emerged in the colonies? How were these similar to and different from English political life?

8   What signs of discontent emerged in the colonies in the seventeenth century? How did these conflicts affect the social and economic system of the British colonies?

9   Why did the slave system evolve in the middle of the seventeenth century?

10 Why did the Chesapeake colonies develop differently from the Carolinas and Georgia?

11 What was mercantilism? Why did it fall so lightly upon the colonists' daily lives?

12 How did the development of colonial assemblies in the eighteenth century set the stage for a "crisis of empire" in the 1770s?

13 What function did cities play in colonial development and life?

14 Why do you think no new colonies were settled after 1734 in British North America?

15 If you were a British official in the colonies in 1760, how would you describe colonial attitudes to the government in England?

16 How were colonial problems in 1760 different when compared to 1660's problems?

Essay Skill

Identifying Critical Words in an Essay Question

One of the most basic skills in essay writing is determining what the question is asking. As a first step, you should always look for the important components of the prompt. When examining an essay question, you should ask three questions:

1. What is the time period of the question?
2. What am I to do with the question?
3. What content is appropriate in answering the question?

Every essay question will have these three elements in it. The time frame will either be stated clearly or alluded to; you will be given a task to perform; and the content area or areas will be apparent.

Below are some common phrases and words that are likely to appear in free-response questions.

What to Do

1. **Evaluate/assess the validity:** This is just a fancy way to ask, "Is this statement accurate or inaccurate about a historical problem?" The student is to weigh the pros and cons of the issues and decide the relative accuracy of the statement. Most AP questions use this phrasing.

2. **Analyze the extent to which:** This asks a student to make an argument that divides and separates the events and ideas of a problem in order to weigh whether a statement accurately describes a historical period. It is very similar to the process of assessing the validity of a statement.

3. **Discuss:** Consider and argue the pros and cons of an issue. The student should present all sides of the debate and make some evaluation of the issue.

4. **Compare:** Look for similarities between events, causes, persons, or ideas.

5. **Contrast:** Look for differences between events, causes, persons, or ideas.

Content Areas

These are the most common content areas that essay questions ask students to draw from as they support their argument.

1. **Political:** dealing with governmental issues, voting, parties, legislative action, and partisan affairs

2. **Diplomatic:** dealing with relations between the United States and other countries

3. **Economic:** dealing with financial issues, income, money, business activities, production, and distribution of goods and services

4. **Social:** dealing with people living together and their relationships with other people in recreational, educational, and communal settings

5. **Cultural:** dealing with works of art and literature and their expressions of the interests, skills, and dispositions of a time period

6. **Intellectual:** dealing with ideas, thoughts, understandings, and reasoning

Essay Skill

Practicing the Skill

The following statement has been broken into its three components. After reviewing it, you should discuss it among your classmates to make sure you understand the process of identifying key parts of an essay.

> "Although the thirteen American colonies were founded at different times by people with different motives and with different forms of colonial charters and political organizations, the seeds of democracy grew in America."

Assess the validity of this statement.

Time period: 1607–1734 (Why is this the period to write about?)

What to do: decide whether this statement is accurate about colonial development

Content: political activities in the colonial period

Look at the statement below and fill out the accompanying exercise. This can be discussed by the entire class or within your study group, depending on how you are using the book. A set of suggested answers is found on page 219 of the Suggested Responses section. At some point you will want to compare what you wrote with the answers in the back of the book.

> "In the seventeenth century, the cultivation of tobacco made a profound impact on the social and economic development of the Chesapeake colonies."

Assess the validity of this statement.

Time period: _____

What to do: _____

_____

_____

_____

Content: _____

_____

_____

_____

Document SKILL

Determining What Documents Mean

One of the critical skills necessary for success in the AP history course, and ultimately on the examination, is the ability to read and understand primary documents. Each chapter of this book will develop this skill. The early chapters will build basic understandings of how to analyze a primary source. Later in the book, you will be asked to combine documents with other primary sources to argue a thesis in a document-based essay.

When you see a primary document, you should analyze it in a consistent and systematic manner. You should always ask the four *Ws*.

1. *When* was it written? (time or setting)
2. *Who* wrote it? (author)
3. *What* is it saying? (Limit yourself to no more than three major ideas; otherwise, you will just be recopying the document.)
4. *Where* is the message directed? (audience)

These four questions should be the first things you address whenever you examine a document in your AP history class.

Practicing the Skill

Look at the sample document below. After reading this letter, discuss the answers to the four *Ws* that are suggested.

My friends, there is one great God and power that has made the world and all things. This great God has written his law in our hearts by which we are taught to love, help, and to do good to one another. Now this great God has been pleased to make me concerned in your part of the world. The king of the country where I live has given unto me a great province, but I desire to enjoy it with your love and consent, that we may always live together as neighbors and friends. . . . I have great love and regard towards you and I desire to gain your love and friendship by a kind, and peaceable life . . .

—William Penn to the Delaware Indian Chiefs, 1681

---

1. *When:* 1681, when Pennsylvania was founded.

2. *Who:* William Penn, proprietor of colony and a devout Quaker.

3. *What:*

   a. God brought the Quakers to Pennsylvania.

   b. The Quakers want to follow the teachings of God.

   c. Penn wants cooperation and peace with the Native Americans.

4. *Where:* The audiences are the Delaware Indians and the Quaker settlers.

   Below you will find two more primary documents. You should identify the four *Ws* for each and discuss them with your class. You can also go to the Suggested Responses section on page 219 and compare your answers with the suggested answers, and discuss any discrepancies.

★ Document A

> *We the inhabitants and residents of Windsor, Hartford and Wethersfield. . . . well knowing where a people are gathered together the word of God requires that to maintain the peace and union of such a people there should be an orderly and decent government established according to God . . .*
>
> *1. It is ordered, sentenced and decreed that there shall be yearly two general assemblies or courts . . .*
> *4. It is ordered that no person be chosen governor above once in two years, and that the governor be always a member of some approved congregation.*
>
> —Fundamental Orders of Connecticut, January 14, 1639

When: _____

Who: _____

What: _____

_____

Where: _____

Document SKILL

★ Document B

> Now, dear brother, I will obey your command and give you a short description of the part of the world in which I now live. South Carolina is a vast region near the sea. Most of the settled part is flat . . . South Carolina is filled with fine navigable rivers and great forests of fine timber. The soil in general is fertile. There are few European or American fruits or grains that cannot be grown here . . .
>
> The people in general are hospitable and honest. The better sort of people are polite and gentle. The poorest sort are the laziest people in the world. Otherwise they would never be poor and wretched in a land as rich as this.
>
> —Eliza Lucas, *Journal and Letters*, 1742

When: _____

Who: _____

What: _____

_____

Where: _____

Chapter 2
REVOLUTIONARY PERIOD
1763–1783

Focus Questions

★ How did the Seven Years War bring on a crisis of empire between the colonies and the crown?

★ How did British policies from 1764 to 1775 appear to violate colonial economic and political rights?

★ How did the colonial mindset provide the backdrop for the Revolution?

★ How did British military strategy develop and fail during the Revolution?

★ Why can the Revolution be considered the first war of national liberation?

★ How did world politics affect the course and outcome of the Revolution?

★ How did the Revolution affect the lives of women and African Americans?

Summary

At the conclusion of the Seven Years War, Great Britain dominated North America. In the Treaty of Paris (1763), France surrendered all its holdings and the Spanish were forced to the western side of the Mississippi River. In addition, the American colonists seemed content in the British imperial system. Mercantilism rested lightly on them as they enjoyed a strong measure of home rule. George III and Parliament controlled external matters, but the colonial assemblies made many local decisions.

Statutory Neglect Ends

All that changed in 1763; the war had doubled Britain's national debt. It had started in America, and British leaders believed the colonies should pay the cost of their defense. Further, the Ottawa chief Pontiac went on a rampage and killed two thousand settlers. An inexpensive new Indian policy emerged with the Proclamation of 1763, which forbade colonial settlement on the western side of the Appalachian Mountains. The Americans ignored the restriction, however, because they believed it violated their rights to travel and property. This was the first overt breach between the colonies and their mother country.

The American mindset changed even more as Parliament modified salutary neglect after 1763. For many years, English writers such as John Trenchard and Thomas Gordon warned that the Crown and Parliament were becoming too powerful and were encroaching on the liberty of the people. These ideas were an extension of the writings of John Locke, who had warned of the dangers of an unrestrained government in the seventeenth century. The colonists increasingly accepted the Whig view of politics that placed Parliament in a conspiracy of oppression and tyranny. As Parliament took a more active role in colonial affairs, the colonists grew to believe their rights as Englishmen were under attack and must be defended.

Significant trouble began in 1764 over money and taxes. Parliament passed the Sugar Act, which regulated trade and raised revenue. The next year, a bombshell exploded—the Stamp Act. This law placed a tax on over fifty items, and the colonists reacted strongly. Some colonial leaders, such as John Dickinson, acknowledged Parliament's authority to regulate trade but challenged its right to tax only for revenue purposes. Samuel Adams, a more radical leader, denied that Parliament had any rights over the colonies at all.

Colonial Resistance

In response to the Stamp Act, the colonists organized. Nine of the colonies sent representatives to a Stamp Act Congress, which petitioned the king and organized a boycott of British goods to pressure Parliament to repeal the tax. The Sons of Liberty formed to intimidate British officials, enforce boycotts, and destroy the property of people who supported the crown. Parliament repealed the act in 1766, after British merchants felt the financial hardship the boycott inflicted. The Stamp Act was a significant step towards separation. Revolutionary rhetoric emerged ("no taxation without representation," etc.), and radicals such as Sons of Liberty were emboldened. Moreover, the face-saving Declaratory Act (1766) could not cover up that Parliament's will had been tested and faltered.

The British quest to raise money in the colonies without provoking colonial resistance continued but failed. The Townshend Acts (1767) taxed various imported items such as paper, paint, and tea. When the colonists protested and boycotted, Parliament repealed the taxes on all items except tea in 1770. However, the lawlessness and unrest these laws provoked prompted Britain to move troops into some colonial cities after 1768. This resulted in a confrontation and the death of five colonials at the Boston Massacre in March 1770.

In 1773, the final crisis arrived with the Boston Tea Party. Hoping to provoke the crown, the Sons of Liberty destroyed 342 chests of tea at the Boston Harbor. Parliament played into the radicals' hands by retaliating with the Coercive Acts in 1774. This series of laws punished the entire colony of Massachusetts and unified the other colonies in defense of New England. During the next two years, the First and Second Continental Congresses met in Philadelphia, where they petitioned the king, called for boycotts of British goods, organized an army, and finally issued the Declaration of Independence.

The War for Independence

The British hoped to crush the rebellion with their 32,000-man army and the world's strongest navy. They also counted on colonial Loyalists to help subdue the rebels. Making up 20 percent of the colonial population, this group had enormous military potential. The British plan was to divide the colonies along the Hudson River Valley and cut off troublesome New England. This strategy resulted in spectacular failure at the Battle of Saratoga in October 1777, where 6,000 British troops were trapped and surrendered to American forces.

Colonial military success hinged on two factors. First was George Washington's ability to maintain his army until Great Britain grew weary and agreed to independence. In addition, the Americans needed foreign help. This was achieved after Saratoga when France signed a treaty with the colonies in 1778. This alliance doomed Britain's hope of keeping possession of the colonies.

By 1781, the British had not crushed Washington's army despite inflicting major defeats on him at New York City in 1776 and around Philadelphia in 1777. The British underestimated the colonials and were stretched too thin around the world after 1778. The English people became restless, and when another British army surrendered at Yorktown, Virginia, in 1781, independence seemed assured.

Results of the Revolution

The Treaty of Paris settled the American Revolution and marked another truce in the long struggle between England and France. The Americans achieved their goals: total independence, the right to settle most of the land west of the Appalachian Mountains and east of the Mississippi, and fishing rights off Newfoundland. All this was accomplished despite French and Spanish scheming to keep America pinned east of the Appalachian Mountains. American diplomats led by John Jay succeeded in playing England and France off each other and gaining this diplomatic triumph.

While the Revolution marked a major political upheaval—the transition from monarchy to confederation—it had a muted social impact. African Americans played a small role in the conflict, with about 5,000 serving the colonial cause in return for their freedom. Despite Lord Dunmore's similar attempt to recruit slaves for the British, only about 2,000 answered the call. Most significantly, the Revolution did not end slavery. Although all states north of the Mason-Dixon line began gradual emancipation between 1777 and 1804, the South made no wholesale changes. By the 1790s, revolutionary idealism was spent, and southern slavery seemed permanent.

Women also experienced little change in their lives after the Revolution. From 1763 to 1783, they supported boycotts, made homespun clothing, and nursed the troops. In 1783, however, they could not vote or hold office, nor did they have their sphere of activity expanded beyond the home. Overall, women and African Americans found little new in their day-to-day lives as a result of independence.

HIGH*lights* of the Period

* **Battle of Saratoga** — a turning point of the Revolution in October 1777, when an army of 6,000 British soldiers surrendered in New York; the battle resulted from a British attempt to divide the colonies through the Hudson River Valley. The American victory convinced the French to ally with the colonies and assured the ultimate success of independence.

* **Battle of Yorktown** — a siege that ended in October 1781 when Washington trapped 8,000 British soldiers on a peninsula in Virginia after a British campaign in the southern colonies; this defeat caused the British to cease large-scale fighting in America and to start negotiations, which eventually led to the colonies' independence.

* **Ben Franklin** — America's leading diplomat of the time who served as a statesman and advisor throughout the Revolutionary era. He was active in all the prerevolutionary congresses and helped to secure the French alliance of 1778 and the Treaty of Paris, which formally ended the Revolution in 1783.

* **Boston Massacre** — confrontation between British soldiers and Boston citizens in March 1770. The troops shot and killed five colonials. American radicals used the event to roil relations between England and the colonies over the next five years.

* **Coercive Acts (1774)** — British actions to punish Massachusetts for the Boston Tea Party; they included closing the port of Boston, revoking Massachusetts's charter, trying all British colonial officials accused of misdeeds outside the colony, and housing British troops in private dwellings. In the colonies, these laws were known as the Intolerable Acts, and they brought on the First Continental Congress in 1774.

* **Declaratory Act (1766)** — passed as the British Parliament repealed the Stamp Act; a face-saving action, it asserted Parliament's sovereignty over colonial taxation and legislative policies.

* **George III** — king of England during the American Revolution. Until 1776, the colonists believed he supported their attempt to keep their rights. In reality, he was a strong advocate for harsh policies toward them.

* **George Washington** — commander of the colonial army; while not a military genius, his integrity and judgment kept the army together. Ultimately, he was indispensable to the colonial cause.

* **John Dickinson** — conservative leader who wrote *Letters from a Farmer in Pennsylvania*; he advocated for colonial rights but urged conciliation with England and opposed the Declaration of Independence. Later, he helped write the Articles of Confederation.

HIGH*lights*
of the Period

★ **John Jay** — lead diplomat in negotiating the Treaty of Paris (1783); he secretly dealt with the British representatives at Paris and gained all of America's goals for independence despite the deviousness and meddling of France and Spain.

★ **John Locke** — English philosopher who wrote that governments have a duty to protect people's life, liberty, and property; many colonial leaders read his ideas and incorporated them into their political rhetoric and thinking.

★ **Loyalists (Tories)** — colonists who remained loyal to England; they often were older, better educated people who were members of the Anglican Church. The British hoped to use them as a pacification force but failed to organize them properly.

★ **Patrick Henry** — an early advocate of independence who was a strong opponent of the Stamp Act and great defender of individual rights; in 1775, he declared: "Give me liberty, or give me death."

★ **Pontiac's Rebellion (1763)** — Indian uprising in the Ohio Valley region that killed 2,000 settlers; as a result, the British sought peace with the Indians by prohibiting colonial settlement west of the Appalachian Mountains (the Proclamation of 1763). The Americans saw this ban as an unlawful restriction of their rights and generally ignored it.

★ **Salutary neglect** — British policy before 1763 of generally leaving the colonies alone to conduct their own internal affairs; the abandonment of this policy after 1763 was a major factor leading to revolution and independence.

★ **Samuel Adams** — agitator and leader of the Sons of Liberty, who supported independence as soon as the British veered from salutary neglect; he was the primary leader of the Boston Tea Party and later a delegate to the Continental Congress.

★ **Seven Years War** — fought between England and France, 1756–1763; known as the French and Indian War in the colonies, it started in 1754, over control of the Ohio River Valley and resulted in France's withdrawal from North America. It was the impetus for Parliament's taxing policy that led to the American Revolution.

★ **Sons of Liberty** — street gangs that formed during the Stamp Act crisis to enforce the boycotts and prevent the distribution and sale of the tax stamps; they were the vanguard of the Revolution as they intimidated British officials with violence.

★ **Stamp Act (1765)** — a tax on over fifty items such as pamphlets, newspapers, playing cards, and dice; it set off a strong protest among the colonists, who claimed it was an internal tax designed only to raise revenue and therefore unlawful for Parliament to levy.

★ **Stamp Act Congress (1765)** — met in New York City to protest the Stamp Act; nine of the thirteen colonies petitioned the king and organized a boycott that eventually helped to force the repeal of the tax. This meeting and action was a major step to colonial unity and resistance of British authority.

★ **Sugar Act (1764)** — designed to raise revenue by stiffening the Molasses Act (1733), establishing new customs regulations, and trying smugglers in British vice-admiralty courts; this was the first attempt to tax the colonies in order to raise revenue rather than regulate trade. It actually *lowered* the tax on imported sugar in hopes of discouraging smugglers and thereby increasing collection of the tax.

★ **Thomas Jefferson** — lead author of the Declaration of Independence; in it, he explained the colonists' philosophy of government and the reasons for independence. He wrote that governments that did not protect unalienable rights should be changed.

★ **Thomas Paine** — writer of *Common Sense*, an electrifying pamphlet of January 1776 calling for a break with England; written with great passion and force, it swept the colonies and provided a clear rationale for colonial independence.

★ **Townshend Acts (1767)** — levied taxes on imported items such as paper, glass, and tea; these taxes were designed to address colonial resistance to "internal taxation" like the Stamp Act, which had no connection to trade and was intended only to raise revenue. However, the colonials viewed the Townshend Acts as revenue-raising measures and refused to pay these taxes as well.

★ **Virtual representation** — idea offered by Britain to colonists' demands for representation in Parliament and to establish lawful authority to tax them; the explanation was that Parliament was a collective representation of all Englishmen regardless of where they lived. According to this argument, a group's interest was represented in London by virtue of it being English. Colonial leaders rejected this position.

HIGHlights of the Period

Ideas to Ponder

After reviewing the chapter's summary, highlights, and your primary text, discuss the following with members of your study group.

1   How did the British victory in the Seven Years War help bring on the American Revolution?

2   How did the colonial view of the nature of the British Empire evolve from 1763 to 1776?

3   In what ways did the Whig view of politics make the Revolution inevitable?

4   Which single action between 1763 and 1776 was most damaging to British-colonial relations? Defend your choice.

5   Despite the British legislative retreat between 1770 and 1776, how did events overtake British attempts to pacify the colonies?

6   Which three individuals were most responsible for the rupture between Britain and the colonies? Defend your answer.

7   Why did Britain believe the military phase of the revolt would be brief?

8   How did the British fail to use the Loyalists effectively during the American Revolution?

9   Militarily, why did the British fail to win the Revolution?

10   How could one argue that the Americans did not win their independence but rather that the British lost the colonies?

11   Why did France help the colonies? How did this motivation cause friction in 1783 between France and the fledgling United States?

12   What conflicting interests appeared among the nations in settling the Revolution in 1783?

13   In what ways was the Revolution revolutionary? In what ways was it not?

14   What impact did the Loyalists' exodus after the Revolution have in England and America?

Essay Skill

Focus on the Question: What Is It Asking?

Along with the skills discussed in Chapter 1, you should develop a strategy for focusing on the specific issues to be addressed when preparing to write an essay. In most cases on the AP test, the free-response essay prompts are questions about a historical era. On occasion, however, there will be a quote or statement to be evaluated for its validity. If the historical problem is a statement, quickly jot down a series of questions that breaks the statement into its fundamental components. For example:

> "The American Revolution was the culmination of unavoidable mistakes and misunderstandings in England and America from 1763 to 1776."

To address this prompt effectively, you would first ask:

- Was the Revolution unavoidable?
- What were the major mistakes and misunderstandings?
- Were both sides equally responsible for them?

Posing such questions will help you to focus on the specific terms and/or issues that must be addressed to score high on the essay.

If, on the other hand, the prompt is a *question*, you should pose clarifying questions that will help you structure your answer.

For example:

> "How did the American Revolution transform European politics from 1775 to 1783?"

If this were the question to be addressed, you might first ask:

- What European countries were involved?
- What interest did each country pursue?
- How did the Revolution impact any existing European rivalries?
- How did the colonies take advantage of these developments?

Essay Skill

Practicing the Skill

Look at the following statement and question, and develop a series of clarifying questions about each. A set of suggested answers is found in Suggested Responses, page 219.

1. British policy from 1763 to 1776 was "a history of repeated injuries and usurpations" designed to establish "an absolute tyranny" over the colonies.

   Ask:

   a. _____

   b. _____

   c. _____

   d. _____

2. How was the colonial social and economic structure affected by the Revolution's ideology?

   Ask:

   a. _____

   b. _____

   c. _____

   d. _____

Document SKILL

Determining Credibility: Whom Do You Believe?

When looking at sources in general and specifically on the DBQ portion of the AP test, you must be able to assess their credibility quickly. That is, which document provides the most accurate information concerning the event or phenomenon? When you confront conflicting points of view, you must decide which author left the most reliable account. In other words, you must weigh the evidence.

Below are some questions that will help assign credibility to a speaker and a source.

1. Is the source a primary or secondary one? A primary document is a first-hand account of an event. Examples of primary sources are letters, speeches, court rulings, and newspaper articles. A secondary source is written by someone who acquired the information second-hand and at a later date. He or she was not actually present at the event. An example of a secondary source is your history textbook. Primary sources are usually given greater weight than secondary sources but not always.

2. Was the document produced at the time the event occurred? Some primary sources such as newspaper articles, journals, and diaries are eyewitness accounts but may have been written many years after the fact. Always look for the date of the source.

3. What do you know about the writer? Did the author have a vested interest in the event that would color his or her perspective? For example, were they describing a battle in which they participated? Did they own slaves? Did they command the ship that torpedoed the passenger liner? You would generally place greater credence in a neutral observer.

4. Was the person in a position to know what happened? Were they actually present at the battlefront or on the bow of the ship? Were they in the Senate when Charles Sumner was actually attacked? Could they give an accurate first-hand account?

On the DBQ, students must look for the date, writer's agenda, and opportunity immediately. Since the DBQ is composed exclusively of primary sources, it is important to assess these components quickly to establish credibility. For example, both William Lloyd Garrison and George Fitzhugh were first-hand observers of slavery, but they held diametrically opposing views and represented totally different constituencies. Also, dates are important because their attitudes changed over the antebellum period. All these factors must be considered when deciding which man most accurately described the institution of slavery.

Practicing the Skill

Below are two sets of documents about the battle of Lexington and Concord on April 19, 1775, and about the causes of the American Revolution. Read both sets of documents and select one document from each set that you believe gives the most accurate information about the events. Also, write a short rationale why you selected the documents you did. At some point, you may wish to look in the Suggested Responses section, page 220, for suggested answers.

Set 1: Who fired first?

★ Document A

> I, Thomas Fessenden, of lawful age, testify and declare, that being in a pasture near the meeting house at said Lexington, on Wednesday, last, at about half an hour before sunrise, . . . I saw three officers on horseback advance to the front of said Regulars, when one of them being within six rods of the said Militia, cried out, "Disperse, you rebels, immediately;" on which he brandished his sword over his head three times; meanwhile, the second officer, who was about two rods behind him, fired a pistol pointed at the Militia, and the Regulars kept huzzaing till he had finished brandishing his sword.
>
> —Thomas Fessenden, a colonial onlooker at Lexington, April 23, 1775

★ Document B

> However the best of my recollection about 4 oClock in the Morning being the 19th of April 5 front Compys [sic] was ordered to Load which we did, about half an hour after we found that precaution had been necessary, . . . it was Lexington when we saw one of their Compys [sic] drawn up in regular order Major Pitcairn of the Marines second in command call'd [sic] to them to disperse, but their not seeming willing he desired us to mind our space which we did when they gave us a fire then run off to get behind a wall.
>
> —Ensign Jeremy Lister, British officer, writing in 1832

Best source is _____

_____

_____

_____

Document SKILL

Set 2: What caused the Revolution?

★ Document C

> In the winter of 1774–75 the British government learned that America had become a powder keg. Blame for this situation must be attributed in far larger measure to the inadequacies of George III and British politicians than to the activities of the radical leadership in America. . . . Had the new policy been firmly and steadily pushed in the Stamp Act crisis, it is barely possible that American resistance might have been peacefully overcome. But wiser by far than a consistent course of coercion would have been the abandoning of the effort to turn back the colonial clock. An American policy to be based upon recognition of the maturity of the colonies and of their value to the mother country, together with an attitude of goodwill, might have postponed indefinitely the era of American independence. . . .
>
> —John R. Alden, *The American Revolution, 1775–1783*
> (written in 1954)

★ Document D

> The parliament unquestionably possesses a legal authority to regulate the trade of Great Britain, and all her colonies. Such an authority is essential to the relation between a mother country and her colonies. . . . This power is lodged in the parliament; and we are as much dependent on Great Britain, as a perfectly free people can be on another.
>
> I have looked over every statute relating to these colonies, from their first settlement to this time; and I find every one of them founded on this principle, till the Stamp Act administration. All before, are calculated to regulate trade. . . . Thus the King by his judges in his courts of justice, imposes fines which all together amount to a very considerable sum, . . . But this is merely a consequence arising from restrictions the British parliament till the period above mentioned, think of imposing duties in America fore THE PURPOSE OF RAISING A REVENUE . . . that is, to raise money upon us without our consent.
>
> —John Dickinson, *Letters from a Farmer in Pennsylvania*, 1767

Best source is _____

_____

_____

_____

Chapter 3

THE NEW NATION
1783–1801

Focus Questions

★ How were the Articles of Confederation an outgrowth of the American Revolution?

★ Why did the Articles of Confederation fail to create an effective, long-term government in America?

★ How did developments at home and abroad create a call to strengthen the Articles of Confederation?

★ How did the Constitution represent a conservative counter-revolution to the Articles of Confederation?

★ How did the Washington administration develop Federalist solutions to the nation's economic and political problems?

★ How did the war between England and France involve the United States in another European conflict?

Summary

A s they snapped their political bonds with England, the colonials constructed a new government to replace the monarchy. The product of this effort, the Articles of Confederation, was written in 1777 and ratified in 1781, after long wrangling over western land claims.

The new government was "a firm league of friendship" that maintained individual state equality and sovereignty. Each state had one vote in Congress regardless of its size or population. In theory, the unicameral legislature could conduct foreign affairs, settle disputes between the states, and regulate commerce. Yet, in reality, the central government had very little authority, with true power remaining at the state level. There was no executive officer, and the government possessed neither the power of the purse nor of the sword. Its armed forces were minimal, and the government did not have direct taxing power. In addition, the Articles were inflexible. They required all thirteen states to approve major governmental change. Overall, the government created by the Articles lacked the powers necessary to protect the domestic tranquility or to conduct foreign relations.

Problems with the Articles

The inadequacies of the Articles became apparent shortly after the Revolution ended. A severe depression hit America and the per capita GNP declined over 50 percent in the 1780s. The country was awash in paper money, with all the states and the central government issuing currency to pay their debts. This lack of a stable monetary system retarded interstate commerce. Moreover, the central government was unable to negotiate agreements on international trade policy. Europe took advantage of America's divisions to close its markets and flood the United States with European goods.

In foreign relations, Britain refused to evacuate forts around the Great Lakes, Spain closed the Mississippi River, and the Barbary Pirates made the Mediterranean Sea a war zone for American shipping. All this added to America's economic woes and degraded its image abroad.

Most alarming to many, the government seemed unable to maintain order and protect the property of its citizens at home. A series of domestic disturbances in the mid 1780s culminated with **Shays's Rebellion** in 1786–1787. When the central government was unable to put down Shays and his rebels, many leaders became convinced the Articles must be radically changed.

Successes of the Articles

The Confederation government was not a complete failure, however. The Congress created a systematic land policy for the national domain west of the Appalachian Mountains. With the Land Ordinance of 1785 and the **Northwest Ordinance of 1787**, a process to organize and admit new territories to full statehood was established and the nation's future growth assured. In addition, the Northwest Ordinance provided steps to limit the spread of slavery. Finally, the Articles outlined on paper the general powers a central government should possess.

Changing the Articles

By the mid 1780s, national-minded leaders such as **James Madison** and **Alexander Hamilton** became convinced the Articles of Confederation must be replaced with a stronger central government. Starting at the **Annapolis Convention** in 1786, the nationalists began a campaign to revise the Articles of Confederation. With Shays's Rebellion reverberating through the land, all the states except Rhode Island agreed to meet, and in May 1787, fifty-five delegates convened in Philadelphia to revise the Articles.

The delegates were national-minded as they quickly discarded the Articles and established a stronger central government. Both the **Virginia Plan**, favored by the large states, and the **New Jersey Plan**, favored by the small states, greatly enhanced the powers of Congress. The disagreement between the two proposals was not whether Congress should have more powers but whether the big states or the small states would control its agenda. These lawyers, landholders, and slave owners wanted a government that could preserve the union, protect property, provide sound money, and promote liberty. They opposed universal suffrage and believed that owning property as a requirement for voting was a bulwark against anarchy.

The areas of greatest debate were over congressional representation, slavery, and the presidency. All were resolved by compromise. Congress would have two houses—one favoring large states and one favoring small states; slavery would not be touched; the slave trade would continue for twenty years; and the president would serve a four-year term and be eligible for reelection.

Putting the Constitution in Place

Ratification of the Constitution divided the nation into factions. The **Federalists**, who supported the document, lived mainly around mercantile centers and owned substantial property. The **Anti-Federalists**, who opposed the Constitution, feared the powers of the new government and were less commercial-minded. While the Constitution was approved, the Anti-Federalists did manage to get a Bill of Rights added to protect the people's liberty.

First president George Washington confronted an immediate financial crisis. The combined national debt was $75 million, and the people had a long aversion to taxation. Washington tapped Alexander Hamilton to address the nation's financial problems. In a series of controversial moves, Hamilton proposed a tariff, excise taxes, and a National Bank.

Thomas Jefferson organized opposition to Hamilton's plan. Specifically, he objected to the National Bank. As a **strict constructionist** Jefferson believed the new Constitution did not give Congress the powers to establish a bank. Hamilton, a **loose constructionist** argued the Constitution's "necessary and proper" clause provided the authority for the bank's creation.

This dispute, along with disagreements over levying the excise taxes, crushing the **Whiskey Rebellion**, and funding the national debt, gave rise to the nation's political party system. Jefferson's **Democratic Republican Party** supported limiting the powers of the central government. Hamilton's **Federalist Party** believed the government must have significant taxing and governmental authority.

Foreign Problems

A war between France and Britain in the 1790s further divided the nation. Jefferson argued that the United States should support France; however, Hamilton believed America needed Britain's commercial support. Washington decided to remain neutral, and both nations retaliated by seizing American ships. He further angered the French and the Democratic Republicans by sending John Jay to England in 1794 to resolve problems over British forts in the Great Lakes region and shipping difficulties. The French, outraged over **Jay's Treaty**, stepped up their interference with U.S shipping. Before leaving office, Washington issued a **Farewell Address**, in which he advised the nation to maintain its commercial ties to Europe, to avoid entangling military alliances, and to reject divisive political parties at home.

John Adams inherited Washington's foreign problems. As the undeclared naval war with France intensified, Adams attempted a diplomatic solution. The French, however, humiliated the American delegation in the **XYZ Affair**, and the two nations went to brink of war. Adams dampened the war fever with a preparedness campaign, another diplomatic mission, and a series of repressive domestic measures highlighted by the **Alien and Sedition Acts** While Adams avoided war and abrogated the American-French alliance of 1778, his actions cost him reelection in 1800.

HIGH*lights* of the Period

★ **Alexander Hamilton** — strong nationalist, first secretary of the treasury; he supported a strong central government and was founder of the Federalist Party.

★ **Alien and Sedition Acts** — series of acts designed to suppress perceived French agents working against American neutrality; the acts gave the president power to deport "dangerous" aliens, lengthen the residency requirement for citizenship, and restrict freedoms of speech and press.

★ **Annapolis Convention** — meeting held at Annapolis, Maryland, in 1786 to discuss interstate commerce; only five states sent delegates, but Alexander Hamilton used the forum to issue a call for the states to meet the next spring to revise the Articles of Confederation. The Annapolis Convention was a stepping-stone to creation of the Constitution.

★ **Anti-Federalists** — persons who opposed ratification of the U.S. Constitution by the states; in general, they feared the concentration of power the Constitution would place in the national government.

★ **Democratic Republican Party** — political party led by Thomas Jefferson; it feared centralized political power, supported states' rights, opposed Hamilton's financial plan, and supported ties to France. It was heavily influenced by agrarian interests in the southern states.

★ **Farewell Address** — presidential message in which Washington warned the nation to avoid both entangling foreign alliances and domestic "factions" (political parties); the ideas of the address became the basis of isolationist arguments for the next 150 years.

★ **Federalist Papers** — eighty-five essays written by Alexander Hamilton, James Madison, and John Jay and published in newspapers to convince New York to ratify the Constitution; taken together, they are seen as a treatise on the foundations of the Constitution.

★ **Federalist Party** — political party led by Alexander Hamilton; it favored a strong central government, commercial interests, Hamilton's financial plan, and close ties to England. Its membership was strongest among the merchant class and property owners.

★ **Federalists** — persons who favored ratification of the U.S. Constitution by the states; they are not to be confused with the later Federalist Party.

★ **Great Compromise** — broke the impasse at the Constitutional Convention over congressional representation. Congress would consist of two houses—seats in the lower assigned according to each state's population and states having equal representation in the upper chamber.

★ **James Madison** — strong nationalist who organized the Annapolis Convention, authored the Virginia Plan for the Constitution, and drafted the constitutional amendments that became the Bill of Rights; he was also a founding member of the Democratic Republican Party.

★ **Jay's Treaty (1794)** — agreement that provided England would evacuate a series of forts in U.S. territory along the Great Lakes; in return, the United States agreed to pay pre-Revolutionary War debts owed to Britain. The British also partially opened the West Indies to American shipping. The treaty was barely ratified in the face of strong Republican opposition.

★ **Loose constructionist** — person who believes that the "elastic clause" of the Constitution (Article 1, Section 8, paragraph 18) gives the central government wide latitude of action; loose constructionists hold that even powers not explicitly set forth in the Constitution may be exercised if it is "necessary and proper" to carry out powers that are specifically stated.

★ **New Jersey Plan** — offered by William Paterson to counter the Virginia Plan; it favored a one-house of Congress with equal representation for each state. It maintained much of the Articles of Confederation but strengthened the government's power to tax and regulate commerce.

★ **Northwest Ordinance (1787)** — the major success of Congress under the Articles of Confederation that organized the Northwest Territory for future statehood; the law provided territorial status for a region when its population reached 5,000. At 60,000, the territory could petition for statehood with the same rights as existing states. It set into law the procedure for expanding the nation that eventually led to the admission of many other new states. Also, by outlawing slavery in the Northwest Territory, it represented the first action by the national government against that institution.

★ **Pinckney's Treaty (1795)** — agreement with Spain that opened the Mississippi River to American navigation and granted Americans the right of deposit in New Orleans; Spain agreed to the treaty because it feared that Jay's Treaty included an Anglo-American alliance.

★ **Shays's Rebellion** — an uprising in western Massachusetts between August 1786 and February 1787 that closed the courts and threatened revolution in the state; the central government's inability to suppress the revolt reinforced the belief that the Articles of Confederation needed to be strengthened or abandoned.

★ **Strict constructionist** — person who interprets the Constitution very narrowly; a strict constructionist believes that a power not explicitly stated in the Constitution could not be exercised by government. Historically, strict constructionists have hoped to restrict authority of the central government and preserve states' rights.

★ **Thomas Jefferson** — first secretary of state, who led opposition to the Hamilton/Washington plan to centralize power at the expense of the states; after founding the Democratic Republican Party to oppose these plans, Jefferson was elected vice president in 1796 and president in 1800.

* **Three-Fifths Compromise** — agreement at the Constitutional Convention that broke the impasse over taxation and representation in the House of Representatives; the delegates agreed to count slaves as three-fifths of a person for both. This formula had been used in 1783 to make financial assessments among the states under the Articles.

* **Virginia and Kentucky Resolutions** — reaction against the Sedition Act; written by Madison for Virginia and Jefferson for Kentucky, they stated that when the national government exceeded its powers under the Constitution, the states had the right to nullify the law. Essentially, the resolutions held that the Constitution was a compact among the states and they were its final arbiter.

* **Virginia Plan** — Edmund Randolph's and James Madison's proposal for a new government that would give Congress increased taxing and legislative power; it called for two houses of Congress—an elected lower house and an upper house appointed by the lower house. Because seats in Congress would be apportioned according to the states' populations, this plan was favored by the large states.

* **Whiskey Rebellion** — uprising in western Pennsylvania in 1794 over an excise tax levied on whiskey; farmers saw the tax as an unjust and illegal levy, like the Stamp Act. President Washington crushed the rebellion with overwhelming force and thereby demonstrated the power of the new government to maintain order and carry out the law.

* **XYZ Affair** — diplomatic effort by President John Adams to soothe the French, who were upset over Jay's Treaty and American neutrality in their conflict with Britain; three American delegates to France were told they must offer a bribe before any negotiations could begin. They refused, and the humiliation heightened tensions between the two countries and set off war hysteria in the United States.

HIGH*lights* of the Period

Ideas to Ponder

After reviewing the chapter's summary, highlights, and your primary text,
discuss the following with members of your study group.

1   How did the Articles of Confederation reflect America's political experiences of the previous twenty years?

2   Who were the supporters of the Articles of Confederation throughout the 1780s? Why did they support them?

3   What groups opposed the Articles? Why?

4   Was the Constitution a betrayal of the American Revolution? Why or why not?

5   Why did the Federalists triumph over the Anti-Federalists in the ratification struggle?

6   What factors were most important in creating political factions (parties) in the 1790s?

7   Why did the Federalist Party go into decline after 1795?

8   How did the Federalists look to the future economically but to the past politically?

9   How did Hamilton's financial plan have both an economic and a political agenda?

10 As the 1790s unfolded, how did George Washington show himself to be a Federalist?

11 How did the United States follow its self-interest in the French and English struggle of the 1790s?

12 In what ways did John Adams help ensure a Republican victory in 1800?

Essay Skill

Which Question to Write About?

A subtle but important challenge on the AP exam is selecting a question or facet of a question about which to write. In Parts A and B of the free-response section, there is always a choice of questions. Many times, there are several topics within these questions from which students must select to support their position. Thus, choice abounds in the free-response section. Moreover, with only thirty-five minutes available to write each essay, you must make these choices quickly.

One direct strategy in choosing questions or parts of a question is to make lists. Look at the choices and write down all the relevant information about each question as quickly as possible. Make sure, however, that the ideas and facts are within the time frame under investigation. For example, if the question is about slavery in the eighteenth century, don't put down information about the abolitionists or the Missouri Compromise. Once you have made these lists, you should determine which list is longer and more specific and write an answer to that question.

Use the same strategy when working with questions that offer choices from several facets of a topic. Look at each aspect of the question, list what you know about it, and select those categories with the longest and most specific information to support your argument.

Study the two examples below and see how this strategy can be employed.

Part A

Choose ONE statement from this part:

1. "The political parties of the 1790s grew from unresolved issues of sovereignty and economics in the 1780s."

2. "The Articles of Confederation developed an effective Indian policy in the 1780s."

Assess the validity of ONE of the statements:

Essay 1	**Essay 2**
• Commercial vs. agrarian groups	• Indian betrayal (Treaty of Paris)
• Shays's Rebellion	• Indians killed many settlers
• Paper money vs. hard money	• British forts/Indian unrest
• Barbary pirates	• No army to combat Indians
• Federalists v. Anti-Federalists	• Signed several treaties
• Federalists v. Republicans	
• Hamilton's financial plan	
• War between England and France	
• Depression in the 1780s	
• States' rights	
• Direct taxation	
• Whiskey Rebellion	

Essay Skill

It is clear from the two lists that this student knows more about essay 1 than essay 2, as that list is longer and more specific. This student has only vague ideas of how the Confederation government dealt with Indians. He/she will write a stronger essay by choosing the first question.

Part B

Look at the following statement, which gives students choices within the question.

> "The Articles of Confederation provided inadequate solutions to the nation's problems in the 1780s."

Assess the validity of this statement considering TWO of the following:

Foreign policy
Domestic trade policy
Monetary policy

Foreign Policy

- Problems with forts (Brits)
- Owed money to Europe
- Alliance with France
- Barbary pirates
- Spain closed the Mississippi R.
- England stirring up Indians
- West Indies closed

Domestic Trade Policy

- Lack of state cooperation
- Mt. Vernon Conference
- Annapolis Convention
- No common exchange
- Tariff barriers between states
- No central trade authority
- Foreign goods flooding America

Monetary policy

- Could not tax
- Too much paper money
- Inflation
- No backing for paper money

Looking at the lists, it is clear that if the student uses foreign relations and domestic trade policies, he/she will write a stronger essay than if he/she uses monetary policy. While this student has some broad ideas about financial conditions, he/she has a greater understanding of foreign relations and trade policy.

Essay Skill

Practicing the Skill

Part A

Below is a set of prompts. Make a list of relevant facts and ideas about each one and then decide the question you would select to write your strongest essay answer. After completing the lists, discuss your choices among your classmates or within your study group members.

1. "The most glaring weakness of the Constitution was its failure to protect individual rights."

2. "American foreign policy under George Washington was a defensive reaction to events and threats from abroad."

Assess the validity of ONE of these two statements:

Essay 1

_____

_____

_____

_____

_____

_____

Essay 2

_____

_____

_____

_____

_____

_____

Best essay choice is: _____

Essay Skill

Part B

Examine the following essay prompt and list the relevant facts for each facet of the issue. After looking at the various lists, decide the two areas to use in assessing the statement.

"The governmental philosophy of the Washington Administration was revealed by its exercise of power."

Assess the validity of this statement by considering TWO of the following:

The Whiskey Rebellion
The establishment of the National Bank
Jay's Treaty

Whiskey Rebellion

_____

_____

_____

_____

_____

_____

_____

National Bank

_____

_____

_____

_____

_____

_____

_____

_____

Essay Skill

Jay's Treaty

_____

_____

_____

_____

_____

_____

_____

_____

_____

_____

Best two categories are: _____

Document SKILL

Making Inferences from Documents

Earlier in the book, the focus was on finding the meaning of documents. You used the four Ws method for analyzing sources, a system that identified specific information found in a document. A next step is to add a fifth W to the process—the "why" behind the text. To do this, you must make inferences about the material by establishing connections between what is stated and what is left unstated in a source. An inference is an educated guess based on information provided. To formulate an inference, you must go beyond the information given and suggest ideas about an author's possible motives and values. These hypotheses are grounded in the text but are not explicitly stated there. You must look for implications in the document and place them in a larger context.

This is an important skill on the AP exam because it allows students to use documents in a sophisticated and complex manner. An inference demonstrates in-depth thinking about a source. Rather than simply reporting its content, you propose applications, analysis, and evaluations of the document that demonstrate a deeper understanding of a historical problem.

Examine the following document and review the possible inferences that could be made about it. Notice that while the ideas are based on the source, they are not explicitly stated within it.

---

1. *Congress shall appoint a governor, a secretary and three judges for the Northwest Territory. These officials shall adopt suitable laws from the original states. When the territory has 5,000 free male inhabitants of full age they shall be allowed to elect representatives. . . .*

2. *The inhabitants shall be entitled to the benefits of trial by jury and other judicial proceedings according to the common law.*

3. *Religion, morality and knowledge being necessary to good government and happiness of mankind, schools . . . shall forever be encouraged.*

5. *There shall be neither slavery, nor involuntary servitude in the said territories, otherwise than in the punishment of crimes whereof the party shall have been duly convicted.*

—Northwest Ordinance, 1787

Inferences

   a. The nation was expanding.

   b. Americans wanted written rules of government.

   c. Statements of rights had political importance.

   d. Women did not count politically.

   e. Education was important.

   f. Concerns about slavery existed.

Document SKILL

Practicing the Skill

Below is a document about the Alien and Sedition Acts. After you read it, make a list of inferences that are suggested by the text. At some point, you may wish to look in the Suggested Responses section, page 220, for possible inferences from this source.

The Alien Law has been bitterly criticized as a direct attack upon our liberties. In fact, it affects only foreigners who are plotting against us, and has nothing to do with American citizens. It gives authority to the President to order out of the country all aliens he judges dangerous to the peace and safety of the United States, or whom he suspects of treason or secret plots against the government. . . .

The Sedition Act has likewise been wrongly criticized as an attack, upon freedom of speech and of the press. On the contrary, it allows punishment only for disturbers of order "who write, print, utter or publish any false, scandalous and malicious writings against the government of the United States, or either house of the Congress . . . or the President . . ."

What honest person can justly be alarmed at such a law? Who can wish that unlimited permission be given to publish dangerous lies . . . ? Because we have the right to speak and publish our opinions, it does not necessarily follow that we may use it to utter lies about our neighbor or government. After all, freedom of action does not give us the right to knock down the first person we meet and excuse ourselves from punishment by pleading that we are free persons . . .

—from *The Life of Timothy Pickering*, 1873

Inferences

a. _____

b. _____

c. _____

d. _____

e. _____

f. _____

g. _____

h. _____

Chapter 4

THE JEFFERSONIAN ERA
1801–1825

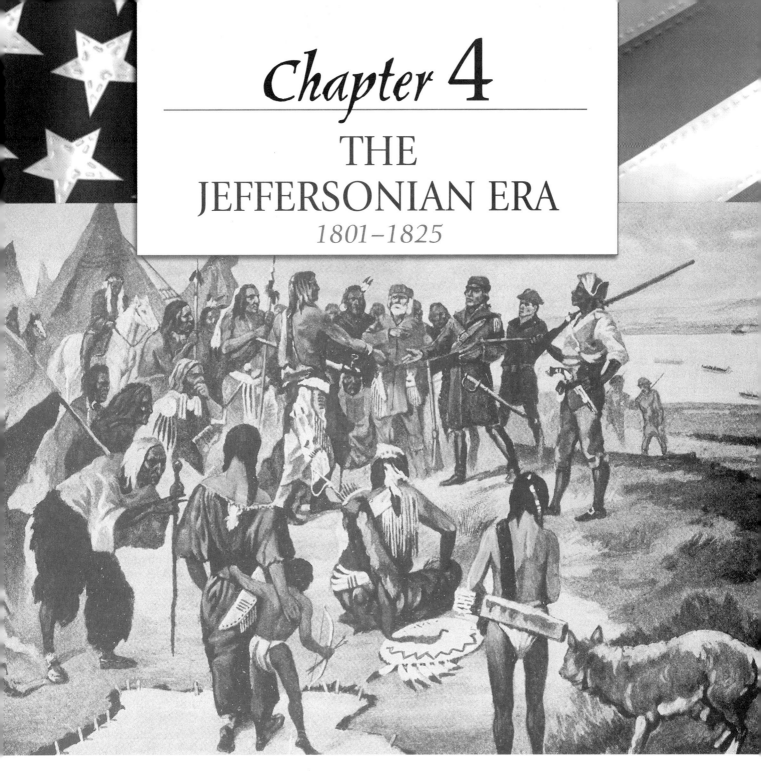

Focus Questions

★ How did Thomas Jefferson and the Democratic Republicans strengthen American democracy?

★ How did America's attempts at neutrality entangle the nation in European conflicts?

★ Why did the United States resort to war in 1812 to solve its problems with England?

★ How did the War of 1812 change America politically and economically?

★ How was the postwar era marked by the rise and fall of nationalism?

★ How did the War of 1812 help launch the Market Revolution?

Summary

Thomas Jefferson's election over John Adams was the first transition from one political party to another. Unlike the Federalists, the Democratic Republicans supported a limited, frugal government. Jefferson's primary goals were reductions in the central government, the national debt, the excise tax, and the military. He also tried to reign in the Federalist-dominated judiciary. He encouraged the repeal of the Judiciary Act of 1801, denounced the Supreme Court's decision in **Marbury v. Madison**, and supported the impeachment of two Federalist judges. Despite the triumph of **John Marshall** in strengthening the Supreme Court, Jefferson fought to restrain its influence. The overall thrust of his governance was reducing the power of the central government and increasing the agrarian, states' rights influence of his constituents.

Jefferson's Successes and Failures

Among Jefferson's greatest achievements was his extension of the "empire of liberty" in 1803 with the purchase of Louisiana. This 828,000-square-mile deal was not only a great bargain at $15 million, it also secured navigation on the Mississippi River, doubled the size of the nation, and eliminated France as a potentially dangerous neighbor. Despite his strict-constructionist views, Jefferson simply could not pass up such an opportunity.

He failed, however, to protect the national interest when war resumed between Great Britain and France in 1803, and both nations again interfered with American commerce. In addition, Britain began the **impressment** of American sailors into its navy. This practice reached a crisis in 1807 during the **Chesapeake-Leopard Affair** when British forces killed or wounded over twenty U.S. Navy sailors and impressed several others. To dampen war fever, Jefferson asked Congress to pass the **Embargo Act**, which withheld trade from the world until America's rights as a neutral nation were recognized. The embargo backfired, however, because it throttled American trade and pitted the commercial Northeast against the agrarian South. Jefferson retreated to the less restrictive **Non-Intercourse Act** as he left office, but impressment continued, with six thousand Americans seized between 1808 and 1811.

The War of 1812

The maritime problems carried over to the presidency of James Madison, as the British continued to seize ships, impress sailors, and encourage Indian resistance in the Old Northwest. Despite Madison's modification of the embargo with **Macon's Bill No. 2** and the victory over Native Americans at the Battle of Tippecanoe, war pressures mounted. Finally in June 1812, Madison asked for a declaration of war against Britain. The **War Hawks** in his party were delighted, but the Federalists had grave doubts. Rejecting the argument that an armed force would advance America's maritime rights, the Federalists opposed the war in Congress. For many New Englanders, this was "Mr. Madison's War" and not their fight.

War of 1812 British army burning the White House during the War of 1812.

The War of 1812 was a military disappointment for the United States. Despite some American success on the Great Lakes and several more victories over Native Americans, the British army and navy outclassed U.S. forces. Poorly prepared, equipped, and led, the American military failed to invade Canada and suffered the grievous humiliation of seeing Washington, D.C., burned in August 1814. Opposition in New England prevented a truly national effort in the conflict. Only defensive victories in 1814 and 1815 at Baltimore, Plattsburg, and **New Orleans** maintained American morale and prevented major American concessions at the peace conference in Ghent, Belgium, in 1815.

The war ended with the **Treaty of Ghent** restoring the status quo. Neither side achieved its objectives, and each accepted the draw. The war did produce unintended consequences, however. Saddled with its wartime behavior, the Federalist Party collapsed. The Federalists' seeming lack of patriotism and the **Hartford Convention** sealed the party's political fate. The conflict also ignited political and economic nationalism, with Congress proposing a new National Bank, protective tariffs, and internal improvements. With the demise of the opposing political party, the "Era of Good Feelings" was at hand.

The Era of Good Feelings

The early postwar years were a time of peace, political tranquility, and economic consensus. Without effective partisan opposition, President Monroe and the Democratic Republicans (by now known merely as "Republicans") dominated the political agenda. The nation embarked on a nationalistic celebration marked by the chartering of the **Second National Bank** and partial implementation of the **American System** of internal improvements. John Marshall and the Supreme Court contributed to the nationalistic spirit with a series of decisions that buttressed the power of the national government over the states and created a favorable business environment. In cases such as **McCulloch v. Maryland, Dartmouth College v. Woodward,** and **Gibbon v. Ogden,** nationalistic, mercantile principles were promoted and upheld.

The United States also strengthened its position in foreign relations. America warned Europe against future colonization in the western hemisphere with the **Monroe Doctrine.** The country repaired its relationship with Britain, as the two nations reached agreements on Great Lakes disarmament and on parts of the Canadian boundary. In 1819, the United States and Spain agreed to the **Adams-Onís Treaty,** by which America purchased Florida, defined the western boundary of the Louisiana Purchase, and gained a tenuous claim to the Pacific Northwest.

The Good Feelings End

The nationalism and unity did not last, however, as the **Panic of 1819** and Missouri's statehood divided the nation. The panic hit western farmers particularly hard, and many blamed the newly chartered Second National Bank for their hardships. Resentment over the Bank's political and economic power divided mercantile easterners and agrarian westerners. More ominously, slavery reemerged as a political issue in 1819 when the Missouri territory sought admission to the Union as a slave state. Although **Henry Clay** cobbled together the **Missouri Compromise** and the crisis subsided, neither northerners nor the southerners were completely satisfied with Clay's solution. By the early 1820s, the Era of Good Feelings was a rapidly fading memory.

HIGH*lights* of the Period

* **Adams-Onís Treaty (1819)** — also known as the Florida Purchase Treaty and the Transcontinental Treaty; under its terms, the United States paid Spain $5 million for Florida, Spain recognized America's claims to the Oregon Country, and the United States surrendered its claim to northern Mexico (Texas).

* **American System** — set of proposals by Henry Clay that called for a national bank, protective tariffs, and internal improvements; their goal was American economic self-sufficiency.

* **Andrew Jackson** — U.S. general who defeated the Native Americans at Horseshoe Bend and commanded the victory over the British at New Orleans; he became a national hero as a result of his record in the War of 1812 and later rode that fame to the presidency.

* **Battle of New Orleans** — a major battle of the War of 1812 that actually took place after the war ended; American forces inflicted a massive defeat on the British, protected the city, and propelled Andrew Jackson to national prominence.

* **Chesapeake-Leopard Affair** — incident in 1807 that brought on a war crisis when the British warship *Leopard* attacked the American warship *Chesapeake*; the British demanded to board the American ship to search for deserters from the Royal Navy. When the U.S. commander refused, the British attacked, killing or wounding 20 American sailors. Four alleged deserters were then removed from the *Chesapeake* and impressed. Many angry and humiliated Americans called for war.

* **Dartmouth College v. Woodward (1819)** — case in which the Supreme Court prevented New Hampshire from changing Dartmouth's charter to make it a public institution; the Court held that the contract clause of the Constitution extended to charters and that contracts could not be invalidated by state law. The case was one of a series of Court decisions that limited states' power and promoted business interests.

* **Embargo Act (1807)** — law passed by Congress stopping all U.S. exports until British and French interference with U.S. merchant ships stopped; the policy had little effect except to cause widespread economic hardship in America. It was repealed in 1809.

* **Fletcher v. Peck (1810)** — Supreme Court case that established the Court's power to invalidate state laws contrary to the Constitution; in this case, the Court prevented Georgia from rescinding a land grant even though it was fraudulently made.

★ **Gibbon v. Ogden (1824)** — landmark case in which the Supreme Court struck down a New York law that granted a monopoly to certain steamboats operating between New York and New Jersey; the ruling expanded the powers the Constitution gave Congress to regulate interstate commerce. It was another of the cases during this period whereby the Supreme Court expanded federal power and limited states' rights.

★ **Hartford Convention** — meeting of New England state leaders in 1814; among other things, the delegates called for restrictions on embargoes and limits on presidential tenure. The end of the war brought an end to the gathering, but it was later branded as unpatriotic and helped bring on the collapse of the Federalist Party.

★ **Henry Clay** — a leading American statesman from 1810 to 1852; he served as a member of Congress, Speaker of the House, senator, and secretary of state and made three unsuccessful presidential bids. He was known as the Great Compromiser for his role in the compromises of 1820, 1833, and 1850.

★ **Impressment** — the forceful drafting of American sailors into the British navy; between 1790 and 1812, over ten thousand Americans were impressed, the British claiming that they were deserters from the Royal navy. This was the principle cause of the War of 1812.

★ **John Marshall** — Chief Justice of the United States Supreme Court, 1801–1835; arguably America's most influential Chief Justice, he authored Court decisions that incorporated Hamilton's Federalist ideas into the Constitution. He also established the principle of judicial review, which gave the Court equality with the other branches of government.

★ **Louisiana Purchase** — an 828,000-square-mile region purchased from France in 1803 for $15 million; the acquisition doubled the size of the United States and gave it control of the Mississippi River and New Orleans. Jefferson uncharacteristically relied on implied powers in the Constitution (loose construction) for the authority to make the purchase.

★ **Macon's Bill No. 2 (1810)** — modified embargo that replaced the Non-Intercourse Act of 1809; this measure reopened trade with both Britain and France but held that if either agreed to respect America's neutrality in their conflict, the United States would end trade with the other.

★ **Marbury v. Madison (1803)** — court case that established the principle of judicial review, which allowed the Supreme Court to determine if federal laws were constitutional. In this case, the Court struck down part of the Judiciary Act of 1789, which the justices believed gave the Court power that exceeded the Constitution's intent.

★ **McCulloch v. Maryland (1819)** — Supreme Court case in which the Court established the supremacy of federal law over state law; in this case, the Court set aside a Maryland law that attempted to control the actions of the Baltimore branch of the Second National Bank by taxing it. By preventing Maryland from regulating the Bank, the ruling strengthened federal supremacy, weakened states' rights, and promoted commercial interests.

HIGH*lights*
of the Period

* **Missouri Compromise (1820)** — settlement of a dispute over the spread of slavery that was authored by Henry Clay; the agreement had three parts: (1) Missouri became the twelfth slave state; (2) to maintain the balance between free states and slave states in Congress, Maine became the twelfth free state; (3) the Louisiana territory was divided at 36° 30', with the northern part closed to slavery and the southern area allowing slavery. This compromise resolved the first real debate over the future of slavery to arise since the Constitution was ratified.

* **Monroe Doctrine (1823)** — issued to counter a perceived threat from European powers to the newly-independent nations of Latin America; it proclaimed: (1) no new colonization in the western hemisphere; (2) existing colonies would not be interfered with; and (3) the United States would not interfere in European affairs. It became the cornerstone of U.S. Latin American policy for the next century.

President James Monroe

* **Non-Intercourse Act (1809)** — replaced the embargo policy by allowing American trade with all countries *except* Britain and France; like the Embargo Act, this attempt to use American trade as an instrument of foreign policy failed. British and French interference with U.S. shipping continued and the Non-Intercourse Act was repealed in 1810.

* **Panic of 1819** — severe depression that followed the economic boom of the post-War of 1812 years; the Second National Bank, trying to dampen land speculation and inflation, called loans, raised interest rates, and received the blame for the panic. All this helped divide the commercial interests of the East from the agrarian interests of an expanding West.

* **Second Bank of the United States** — national bank organized in 1816; closely modeled after the first Bank of the United States, it held federal tax receipts and regulated the amount of money circulating in the economy. The Bank proved to be very unpopular among western land speculators and farmers, especially after the Panic of 1819.

* **Treaty of Ghent (1815)** — agreement that ended the War of 1812 but was silent on the causes of the war; all captured territory was returned and unresolved issues such as ownership of the Great Lakes were left to future negotiation.

* **War Hawks** — young Congressmen in the 12th Congress from the South and West who demanded war with Britain; led by Henry Clay and John Calhoun, they hoped to annex Canada, defend U.S. maritime rights, and end troubles with Native Americans in the Trans-Appalachian West.

HIGH*lights*
of the Period

Ideas to Ponder

After reviewing the chapter's summary, highlights, and your primary text,
discuss the following with members of your study group.

1   How did Jeffersonian Republicans try to follow the ideals of 1776 when they came to power?

2   In what ways did President Jefferson modify his political philosophy to address opportunities and problems?

3   How did the Louisiana Purchase change America's future?

4   How did the United States attempt to avoid war with Europe from 1800 to 1812?

5   Given America's policy of neutrality from 1793 to 1812, was war inevitable?

6   What factors hindered America's military preparedness before the War of 1812?

7   Could one argue the War of 1812 was a senseless waste of resources and men? Why or why not?

8   In what ways did the War of 1812 benefit America?

9   How did the division in the country hurt the war effort?

10   How was the "Era of Good Feelings" a misnomer?

11   In what ways was John Marshall America's most influential Chief Justice?

12   How did sectionalism enter American politics between 1819 and 1821?

13   How can one make the case that John Quincy Adams deserves the title of America's greatest secretary of state?

14   In what ways were the seeds of the Market Revolution of the 1830s planted after the War of 1812?

15   Which U.S. leader made the greatest contribution to American nationalism from 1801 to 1824? Defend your choice.

Essay Skill

Putting Your Answer into a Graphic Organizer

Once you decide which essay question to write about and identify the main problem to be addressed, you will find it useful to organize your thoughts quickly. A graphic organizer is one means to help plan and visualize an answer in an effective and efficient manner.

There are many types of graphic organizers, but for history questions, a network tree can be an effective and quick means to plan your answer. This device defines the problem and suggests the broad themes and support materials useful to planning your answer.

Examine the network tree for the essay question below:

"Between 1801 and 1825, the United States achieved more of its foreign policy goals at the bargaining table than on the battlefield."

Assess the validity of this statement.

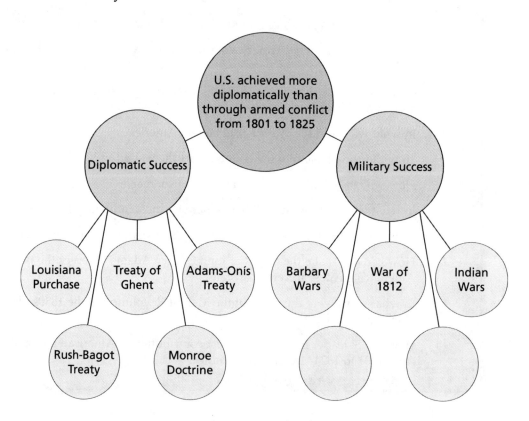

From this sample network tree, it is clear that this student plans to agree with the statement. He/she will account for some military achievements, but the preponderance of the argument and evidence will support the idea that the Louisiana Purchase, Treaty of Ghent, Adams-Onís Treaty, Rush-Bagot Treaty, and Monroe Doctrine had a more profound impact on America's place in the world from 1801 to 1825 than its martial efforts.

The tree can be "rooted" further into the question by adding details to each subtopic. This takes time, however, which is at a premium on the free-response essay section. The advantage of the network tree is that it gives a quick visual path to follow as you prepare to answer the question.

Practicing the Skill

Study the following essay prompt and fill in the network tree below that would plan and organize an answer to it. A suggested network tree for the question is in the Suggested Responses section, page 221.

Evaluate the role of TWO of the following individuals in promoting American nationalism from 1801 to 1825.

Thomas Jefferson
John Marshall
John Quincy Adams

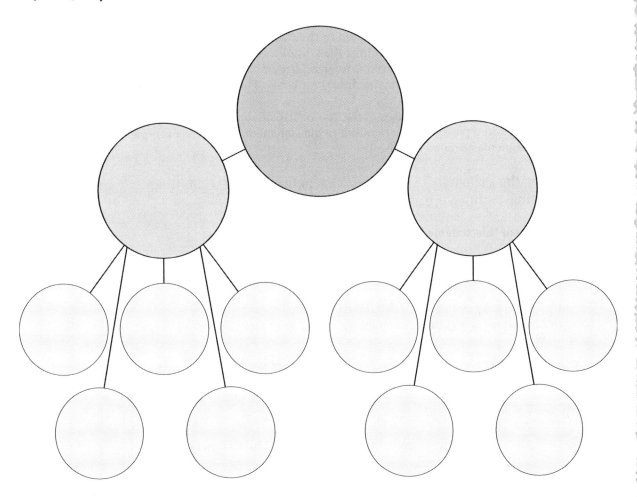

Document SKILL

Using Documents to Support an Argument

The use of documents to support a point of view is vital on the AP exam. This is the heart of the DBQ exercise. In addition to outside information (facts not mentioned in the documents), students must use primary sources to support their ideas. In most cases, a student should not use a document at the beginning of a sentence and should avoid beginning any citation with "Document A says . . ." The document should be placed within the sentence or at the end of the sentence or paragraph to support a generalization or broad idea.

Documents can be quoted in one of two fashions. If you are using an idea from part of a document, it should be cited with parentheses around it. If, on the other hand, you plan to use the general idea expressed in the document, you can paraphrase the content and then indicate at the end of the sentence that the entire idea came from (Doc. A), for example. Under no circumstances should you spend time copying large parts of documents into your essay. This is a waste of valuable time on the examination.

Below are a statement about the causes of the War of 1812 and a document that could be cited to support a position in responding to the statement. Study the example to see how the documents are cited and used.

"In fighting the British in 1812, Americans believed that more than their maritime rights were at stake."

Assess the validity of this statement.

For my part I am not prepared to say that this country shall submit to have her commerce interdicted or regulated by any foreign nation. Sir, I prefer war to submission.

Over and above these unjust pretensions of the British Government, for many years past they have been in the practice of impressing our seamen, from merchant vessels; this unjust and lawless invasion of personal liberty calls loudly for the interposition of this Government.

—Felix Grundy, *Annals of Congress*, 12th Congress, 1811

By quoting Felix Grundy, a student demonstrates that America not only saw its economic well-being threatened but also wanted to protect its honor and pride.

One possible way for using the whole idea of the passage to show this would be to write:

> In 1812, War Hawks such as Felix Grundy had enough of British interference with United States shipping. These actions not only caused economic hardship, but wounded America's pride as well. Many in the Congress were advocating war to solve the problem. (Doc. A)

A second way to use the document to explain America's motivation for war is to quote selectively from the passage. A student using this method might write:

> In 1812, Congress made clear that America would not allow its "commerce interdicted or regulated by any foreign nation." This action not only hurt America economically but was also an "unjust and lawless invasions of personal liberty" and made some Americans "prefer war to submission."

Always remember that documents are there to prove your point. They are pieces of information to be used along with outside information.

Practicing the Skill

Using the passage below, defend the idea that

> "The Monroe Doctrine was designed to protect not only the Western Hemisphere but American nationalism as well."

The object of Canning appears to have been to obtain some public pledge from the government of the United States, ostensibly against the forcible interference of the Holy Alliance between Spain and South America; but really or especially against the acquisition to the United States themselves of any part of the Spanish American possessions. . . . By joining with her, therefore, in her proposed declaration, we give her a substantial and perhaps inconvenient pledge against ourselves and really obtain nothing in return. . . .

—John Quincy Adams, *Memoirs*, Philadelphia, 1875

Document **SKILL**

Write a short answer (two or three sentences) using the whole idea of the document to support the ideas about the Monroe Doctrine.

_____

_____

_____

_____

_____

_____

_____

_____

_____

Write a short answer using several quotes from Document B to prove your point.

_____

_____

_____

_____

_____

_____

_____

_____

_____

Chapter 5

THE AGE OF JACKSON
1828–1848

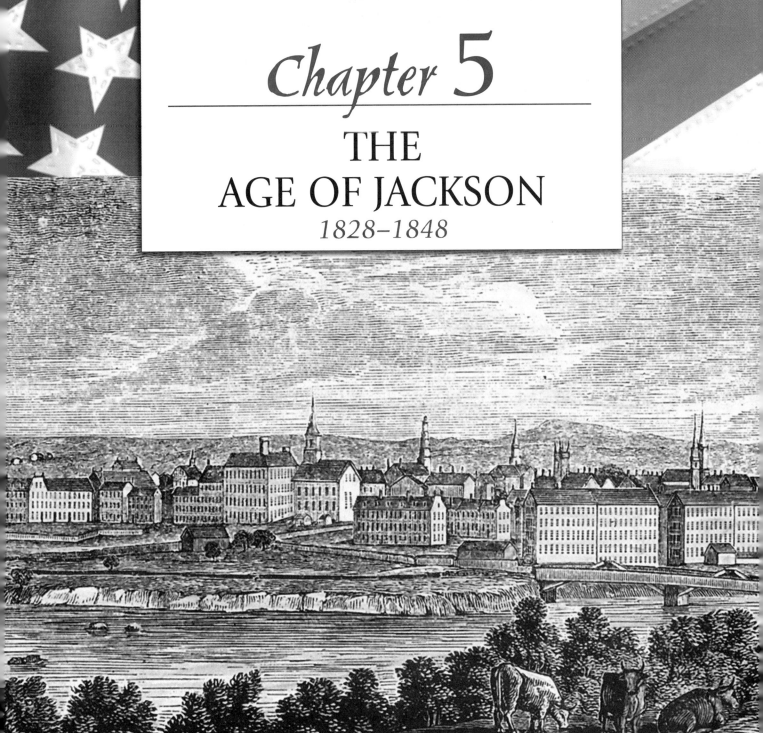

Focus Questions

★ How did democratic ideals evolve during the Jacksonian era?

★ How did Andrew Jackson change the focus and role of the presidency?

★ How were states' rights issues defined in the Jacksonian era?

★ How did economic disagreements develop around the Market Revolution?

★ How were certain groups excluded in the reforms of the Jacksonian era?

★ How did the second party system develop during the 1830s?

Summary

The presidential election of 1824 brought an end to the postwar political tranquility. With five regional candidates running, no one received an electoral majority. In a decision by the House of Representatives, John Quincy Adams was elected president after gaining support from Henry Clay, a rival candidate. Andrew Jackson, who had won a plurality of the popular vote, claimed a "corrupt bargain" between Clay and Adams had denied him the presidency. Adams spent four difficult years in the White House, living with the corruption charge and trying to implement his program of economic nationalism.

Jacksonian Democracy

Andrew Jackson won a presidential rematch with John Quincy Adams in 1828. His inauguration in 1829 marked the beginning of Jacksonian democracy which, in part, represented a return to the principles of Jefferson. Jacksonians glorified individualism, declared war on privilege, vowed to restrain the federal government, and promoted states' rights—all this with an eye to the interests of southern and western farmers.

In the sprit of egalitarianism, most states abandoned their property requirements for voting and the percentage of eligible voters that participated in elections skyrocketed. Jackson spoke for southern, agrarian interests whose political voices had been muted in the 1820s. While Jacksonians claimed to protect democracy from the forces of corruption and privilege, their vision was rather narrow by present-day standards. Women, blacks, and Native Americans were not part of Jackson's coalition, and his policies actually worked against their political and economic interests.

Jackson's attack on the forces of political and economic privilege centered on the battle to recharter the National Bank in 1832. The Second Bank was an effective economic institution that provided a depository for federal funds, promoted a sound currency, and regulated "wild cat" banks around the nation. On the other hand, the Bank was unpopular in the West where it was viewed as a tool of the eastern mercantile elite. Jackson vetoed the recharter bill on the grounds that the Bank benefited only the rich and was an unconstitutional federal intrusion into the affairs of the states. He also realized that Henry Clay and **Nicholas Biddle** proposed the recharter as the centerpiece of a plan to deny him another term.

Henry Clay

Challenges to Jackson

After vetoing the Bank, Jackson removed all government funds and placed them into "**pet banks,**" that is, state banks with **Democratic Party** connections. These banks helped finance a real estate boom that resulted in a five-fold increase in the sale of land. In order to dampen the resulting inflation, Jackson approved the **Specie Circular** in 1836, which cooled prices but also helped cause the **Panic of 1837.**

The tariff of 1828 also created a major crisis during Jackson's presidency. Although a defender of states' rights and low tariffs, Jackson would not accept South Carolina's defiance of federal tariff law in 1832 and 1833. The crisis had been brewing since 1828, when the **Tariff of Abominations** was enacted and South Carolina issued *Exposition and Protest.* The tariff rose to an all-time high, and South Carolina declared a right to nullify the tax, which it deemed to be unconstitutional. **John C. Calhoun,** the leader of the **nullification** movement, drew heavily on Madison's and Jefferson's Virginia and Kentucky Resolutions of the 1790s and on the compact theory of government.

Andrew Jackson challenged South Carolina's refusal to collect the tariff. He asked Congress to authorize a Force Bill to coerce the nullifiers. Unable to win over other southern states to the cause, Calhoun sought a compromise. In 1833, Henry Clay provided a bill that gradually lowered the tariff in exchange for repeal of Jackson's Force Bill.

Jackson accepted the compromise and credit for preserving the Union. He realized, however, that the real issue was not the tariff but the South's growing fear of federal power in regulating its way of life. He predicted that future conflicts would emerge.

Indian Removal

Andrew Jackson continued a policy of Indian removal that began in the presidency of Thomas Jefferson. Jackson wanted to eliminate the tribes living east of the Mississippi River, especially in Georgia, Alabama, and Florida. He made Indian removal his top priority in his first message to Congress. In 1830, he signed the **Indian Removal Act**, which eventually resulted in the exchange of one hundred million acres of Indian lands east of the Mississippi in return for thirty-two million acres in Oklahoma and $68 million in cash payments. Through a series of treaties, 45,000 Native Americans were transported west, with the most tragic exodus occurring in 1838 during the **Trail of Tears.**

The Whigs and Panic of 1837

Jackson's use of presidential power and especially his numerous vetoes prompted the rise of a second party system. The opposition to Jackson took the name **Whigs**, in reference to those in England who had opposed the tyranny of the British crown. Whigs believed in economic expansion through an activist government, with a program that included recharter of the National Bank and support for the American System's protective tariffs and internal improvements.

Jackson retired in 1837, and Martin Van Buren, his hand-picked successor, moved into the White House. The **Panic of 1837** struck almost immediately and destroyed Van Buren's presidency. By 1840, with the economy still flattened, the nation selected it first Whig president, William Henry Harrison. Tragically, Harrison died only one month after his inauguration, and Vice President John Tyler took over. As a life-long Democrat, Tyler was an ersatz Whig. "**His Accidency**" rebuffed Henry Clay, vetoed the National Bank bill, and refused to raise the tariff. By the end of Tyler's term, his entire Cabinet had resigned, and the House of Representatives explored his impeachment.

HIGH*lights*
of the Period

★ **Corrupt Bargain** — agreement between presidential candidates Henry Clay and John Quincy Adams during the disputed election of 1824; Clay threw his support to Adams in the House of Representatives, which decided the election, and in return, Adams appointed Clay secretary of state. Andrew Jackson, who had a plurality (but not a majority) of the popular and electoral votes, believed he had been cheated out of the presidency.

★ **Daniel Webster** — noted orator, constitutional lawyer, senator, secretary of state, and major spokesman for nationalism and the union in the 1830s, 1840s, and 1850s.

★ **Democratic Party** — the modern-day, major political party whose antecedents can be traced to the Democratic Republican Party of the 1790s and early 1800s; it was born after the disputed election of 1824, in which the candidates—all Democratic Republicans—divided on issues and by sections. Supporters of Andrew Jackson, outraged by the election's outcome, organized around Jackson to prepare for the election of 1828. After that election, this organization became known as the Democratic Party.

★ *Exposition and Protest* — document secretly written by Vice President John Calhoun in support of nullification; calling on compact theory, he argued the tariff of 1828 was unconstitutional and that South Carolina could lawfully refuse to collect it.

★ **"His Accidency"** — nickname given to John Tyler in 1841 by his opponents when he assumed the presidency upon the death of William Henry Harrison; the first vice president to succeed to the presidency, his nickname reflected his conflict with the Whig party leaders over rechartering the National Bank, raising the tariff, and supporting internal improvements at government expense.

★ **Indian Removal Act (1830)** — gave the president authority to negotiate treaties with southeastern tribes and to trade their land in the east for territory in the west; it also provided money for land transfer and relocation of the tribes.

★ **John C. Calhoun** — vice president under both John Quincy Adams and Andrew Jackson; he wrote *Exposition and Protest* and led the nullification fight in 1832 and 1833. As senator and vice president, he was the leading voice for southern states' rights from 1828 to 1850.

★ **John Quincy Adams** — son of President John Adams and secretary of state who helped purchase Florida and formulate the Monroe Doctrine and president who supported an activist government and economic nationalism; after Jackson defeated his bid for a second term in 1828, he continued to serve America as a member of Congress.

★ **Market Revolution** — the process that took place in nineteenth-century America in which an economy dominated by small farms and workshops was transformed into an economy in which farmers and manufacturers produced for a distant cash market; it was also characterized by the emergence of a permanent "working class." These changes had significant consequences for American social institutions, religious practices, political ideology, and cultural patterns.

★ **Martin Van Buren** — senator, vice president, and president of the United States; the Panic of 1837 ruined his presidency, and he was voted out of office in 1840. He later supported the Free Soil Party.

★ **Nullification** — theory that the states created the Constitution as a compact among them and that they were the final judge of constitutionality of federal law; the doctrine held that states could refuse to obey or enforce federal laws with which they disagreed. The theory was first presented in the Virginia and Kentucky Resolutions (1798) and reappeared in *Exposition and Protest* (1828).

★ **Panic of 1837** — a major depression that lasted from 1837 to 1844; crop failures, European financial troubles, and the Specie Circular all contributed to the crash, which helped ruin the presidency of Martin Van Buren.

★ **Pet banks** — financial institutions friendly to Andrew Jackson's administration that received federal funds when he vetoed the Second National Bank's recharter in 1832 and removed all government deposits from it.

★ **Specie Circular (1836)** — a federal government action to dampen inflation brought on by land speculation following the closure of the Second National Bank; Jackson issued an order requiring payment for public lands only in gold or silver. This action contracted credit, caused overextended banks to fail, and precipitated the Panic of 1837.

★ **Spoils system** — practice of appointing people to government positions as a reward for their loyalty and political support; Jackson was accused of abusing this power, yet he only removed about 20 percent of office holders during his tenure.

★ **Tariff of Abominations** — name given to a high tariff passed in 1828; after years of steadily rising duties, this tariff raised rates on certain goods to an all-time high, leading to the nullification crisis of 1832.

★ **Trail of Tears (1838)** — the removal of some 18,000 Cherokees, evicted from lands in southeastern United States and marched to Indian Territory (Oklahoma); nearly 25 percent of the people perished from disease and exhaustion during the trip.

★ **Whigs** — political party formed in 1832 in opposition to Andrew Jackson; led by Henry Clay, it opposed executive usurpation (a strong president) and advocated rechartering the National Bank, distributing western lands, raising the tariff, and funding internal improvements. It broke apart over the slavery issue in the early 1850s.

HIGH*lights* of the Period

Ideas to Ponder

After reviewing the chapter's summary, highlights, and your primary text, discuss the following with members of your study group.

1   How did the election of 1824 bring an end to the Era of Good Feelings?

2   How did the election of Andrew Jackson represent the rise of the common man?

3   In what ways did the Jacksonians have a narrow view of democracy?

4   How did the spoils system support the ideas of Jacksonian democracy?

5   Why did Jackson want to remove Native Americans from the southeastern states?

6   How did Jackson refine the meaning of states' rights during his presidency?

7   What events helped alienate John C. Calhoun from Andrew Jackson?

8   In what way was the Webster-Hayne debate about a larger issue than land policy?

9   How did the struggle over the Second National Bank symbolize the ideals of Jacksonian democracy?

10 How were women and African Americans left out of the democratization of the 1830s?

11 How did the Whig Party project a clearer view of America's economic future than the Democrats?

12 How was Martin Van Buren's relationship with Andrew Jackson both a blessing and a curse?

13 How did John Tyler disappoint both the Democrats and the Whigs?

14 What lasting outcomes on American politics did John Tyler have?

Essay Skill

Organizing Your Answer: Writing an Outline

Another method to organize an essay answer is to construct an outline. This is a general plan of the main ideas to be used in answering a question. An outline provides a detailed overview of an essay answer and arranges the supportive materials in a coherent and logical fashion. It is an excellent means to assess the depth of your knowledge about a particular topic. It also aids in organizing facts by connecting them to each other. In addition, by constructing an outline, a student clearly manifests the level of detail and complexity he/she possesses concerning the question.

When outlining, you must subdivide the topics into supporting pieces of information. Without these divisions, the outline becomes a mere list of random facts. In other words, if you have an "A" in your outline, you must also have at least a "B." And if you have a "1" you must have at least a "2" in the form. This process of dividing the information into discrete pieces of data allows you to organize the answer into an increasingly complex response.

Below is a sample outline for the following essay prompt.

"The Jacksonians viewed themselves as defenders of democracy and promoters of economic opportunity."

Assess the validity of this statement.

A. Defender of democracy
   1. Rise of the common man
      a. reduction in property requirements to vote
      b. in 1824, 27 percent participated; 1828, 56 percent; rose to high 70 percent by 1840
   2. Voice of the people clearly heard
      a. reaction to the corrupt bargain
      b. no deal in 1828
   3. Less government the best government
      a. states' rights in Indian affairs
      b. blocked many internal improvements (Maysville Road)
   4. Upheld Constitution
      a. nullification controversy
      b. Bank violated Constitution
B. Promoter of economic opportunity
   1. Bank battle—fighting monopoly
   2. Charles River Bridge
   3. created "pet banks" to make money available for more people
C. Limitations of Jacksonian Democracy
   1. excluded women
      a. no suffrage
      b. coverture and economic inequality continued
   2. Slavery
      a. no attempt to end it
      b. Jackson's interest represented interest of southern slaveholders
      c. supported states' rights

3. Indian removal
   a. reasons
   b. Indian Removal Act 1830
   c. Trail of Tears (1838)
4. Opposition to abolitionists
   a. Jackson's speeches against them
   b. post office opened suspicious mail from North

    Working from this outline, this student can write a richly detailed defense of the Jacksonians as promoters of political and economic opportunity. Each of the headings defines a paragraph in the body of the paper and how each paragraph will be developed. Also from the outline, it is clear that a concession or contrary paragraph on the limits of Jacksonian Democracy is planned in the answer.

Practicing the Skill

Analyze the essay prompt:

> "The beliefs and policies of the Whig Party contained the seeds of its political failure."

Assess the validity of the statement from 1832–1845.

Construct an outline plan below that would answer this prompt.
(Look in the Suggested Responses section, page 222, for a sample outline.)

A. _____

   1. _____

      a. _____

      b. _____

      c. _____

   2. _____

      a. _____

      b. _____

      c. _____

B. _____

   1. _____

      a. _____

      b. _____

      c. _____

Essay Skill

2. _____

    a. _____

    b. _____

    c. _____

3. _____

    a. _____

    b. _____

    c. _____

C. _____

  1. _____

    a. _____

    b. _____

    c. _____

  2. _____

    a. _____

    b. _____

    c. _____

  3. _____

    a. _____

    b. _____

    c. _____

Document SKILL

Dealing with Documents That Contradict Each Other

In history and on the AP examination, students are often confronted with conflicting points of view in the documents with which they work. On the DBQ, in particular, there are sources that do not support the statement a student must address and may, in fact, contradict the statement's position completely. These conflicting documents should not be ignored because they interfere with the point of view a student is promoting in answering the question.

As mentioned earlier, contradictory sources need to be addressed on the DBQ. This process may require a student to qualify his/her thesis somewhat, but he/she should never refute it. The documents may be used alongside other documents in sentences or, if they represent a major contrary position, may require a paragraph near the end of the DBQ that accounts for their challenge to the thesis. This paragraph should make concessions to the thesis but not overturn it. By including these documents, a student acknowledges the complexity of the issues that he/she is addressing.

Examine the statement below about the Market Revolution that unfolded during the Age of Jackson. Also look at the two documents related to its social and economic impact. Below you will find a sample paragraph that could, in part, answer the statement. As you see, while the two documents have contrary views on the impact of commercialization on America, they can be woven together to support a topic sentence. As suggested, in a larger essay, the contrasting documents could occupy an entire paragraph.

> "The Market Revolution strengthened the economic and social fabric of the United States as it unfolded."

Assess the validity of this statement.

★ (Sample) Document A

> *But among them all there were fewer than perhaps in any other community in the world who live without any ostensible avocation. The richest capitalists still take a part in the business proceedings of the day; and men who have professedly retired and have no counting-house or mercantile establishment still retain so much of the relish for profitable occupations that they mingle freely with the merchants, and are constantly found to be the buyers and sellers of stock, in funds, or shares in companies, canals, railroads, banks, et cetera. The result of all this is to produce the busiest community that any man could desire to live in.*
>
> —J. S. Buckingham, *America, Historical, Statistic and Descriptive*

Document SKILL

★ **(Sample) Document B**

> *Cutting the wages was not the only grievance, nor the only cause of this strike. Up till now the corporation had paid 25 cents a week toward the board of each worker. Now it intended to have the girls pay the sum. This, in addition to the cut in wages, would make a difference of at least one dollar each week. It was estimated that as many as 1,500 girls went on strike and walked as a group through the streets. They had neither flag nor music; instead, they sang songs, a favorite one being:*
>
> *"Oh, isn't it a pity, such a pretty girl as I—should be sent to the factory to pine away and die?"*
>
> —Harriet Hanson Robinson,
> *Loom and Spindle: Life Among the Early Mill Girls*, 1898

★ **Sample Paragraph**

> While the Market Revolution of the 1830s produced great wealth and progress in the nation, its impact was uneven and unfair. The commercial developments made New York capitalists rich and powerful as they mingled "freely with merchants, and [were] constantly found to be the buyers and sellers of stocks. . . ." On the other hand, the women of Lowell faced great hardships when their wages were reduced to the point where they wondered if they "should be sent to the factory to pine away and die."

As you can see, the two documents present different pictures of the impact of the Market Revolution in America. It was possible, however, to use both documents in the same paragraph by structuring the topic sentence to suggest that while progress occurred it was not spread evenly over the society.

Practicing the Skill

Look at the statement below and the two documents that accompany it. Write a paragraph that uses both of the documents and addresses the issues raised by the statement:

> "John C. Calhoun is often viewed as the voice of discord and sectionalism."

To what extent is this assessment accurate for the career of John C. Calhoun from 1817 to 1833?

Document SKILL

★ Document A

> *Let it not be said that internal improvements may be wholly left to the enterprise of the states and individuals. I know that much may justly be expected to be done by them; but, in a country so new and so extensive as ours, there is room enough for all the general and state governments and individuals in which to exert their resources. But many of the improvements contemplated are on too great a scale for the resources of the states or individuals. . . .They require the resources and the general superintendence of this government to effect and complete them. . . .*
>
> —John Calhoun, *Works*, February 1817

★ Document B

> *"The Senate and House of South Carolina. . . . solemnly Protest against the system of protecting duties . . .*
>
>   5th. *Because, from the Federalists . . . it is clear the power to regulate commerce was considered by the Convention as only incidentally connected with the encouragement of agriculture and manufactures . . .*
>
>   6th. *Because, whilst the power to protect manufactures is nowhere expressly granted to Congress, nor can be considered as necessary and proper to carry into effect any specified power, it seems to be expressly reserved to the states, by the 10th section of the 1st article of the Constitution."*
>
> —South Carolina's Exposition and Protest, December 19, 1828

Write your paragraph on a separate sheet of paper. Once you have written your paragraph, compare it and discuss it with other members of your class or study group to see how to include documents that do not support a point of view and may, in fact, contradict it. At some point you should look in the Suggested Responses section, page 223, to see some possible ideas that could be included in the paragraph.

Chapter 6

THE AGE OF REFORM
1830–1850

Focus Questions

★ How did the rise of evangelical Protestantism promote the reform movements of the 1830s and 1840s?

★ How did various personalities and philosophies divide the abolitionist movement in the 1830s and 1840s?

★ How did the reform movement make America a gentler society in the 1830s and 1840s?

★ How did the "cult of domesticity" both promote and restrain the women's movement in the 1840s and 1850s?

★ How did the political reforms of the Age of Jackson clash with the social reforms of the era?

Summary

℞ esponding to the transformation of American society after the War of 1812, reformers in the 1820s and 1830s began reconsidering the conventional thinking of their times. With the rise of the Market Revolution and the increase of urbanization and immigration in the 1820s, many Americans experienced uncertainty and anxiety as they confronted a rapidly changing society. ℘

Sources of Reform

The **Second Great Awakening** addressed many of these feelings. Led by evangelical spokesmen such as **Charles Finney**, the movement preached spiritual rebirth, individual self-improvement, and perfectionism. Traveling in the "**burned-over district**" of western New York and throughout New England, these itinerant evangelists ignited a spirit of change with their ideas that moral rectitude could lead to salvation. This message provided part of the philosophical foundation for the reforms of the 1830s.

Along with the religious fervor of the times, the writings of the Transcendentalist writers such as Ralph Waldo Emerson and Henry David Thoreau also fueled the spirit of reform. These authors and poets believed that truth was found beyond experience. They called on individuals to follow their conscience, to think for themselves, and to trust in their intuition.

Ironically, the Jacksonians, who rhetorically championed egalitarianism and political equity, opposed the reformers of the 1830s. Jackson and his followers were states' right advocates dedicated to reducing the reach of the central government. Reformers, on the other hand, wanted the central government to take an active role in confronting society's ills, especially the plague of slavery.

Ralph Waldo Emerson

Penal Reform and Utopian Societies

One aspect of the reforms of the 1830s and 1840s was improvement in the penitentiary and asylum systems. There was a growing desire to change the focus of prisons in America. States like New York and Pennsylvania moved away from incarceration as punishment and toward rehabilitation of prisoners. **Dorothea Dix** supported these efforts as she lobbied the states to remove mental patients from the prisons and house them in special hospitals and facilities where they could be treated rather than punished. Through her dedicated efforts, 28 of the 33 states had created public institutions for the mentally ill by 1860.

Another attempt to redeem the flawed society of the Jacksonian Era was the formation of alternative communities that featured communal living, collective ownership of property, and in some cases, unusual sexual practices. These utopian societies grew up in places such as Oneida, New York; New Harmony, Indiana; and **Brook Farm**, Massachusetts. Most of these radical experiments were short-lived, as the members found it difficult to share property, deal with celibacy, overcome the hostilities of local citizens, and maintain stable leadership. Only Oneida survived more than a few years.

Temperance and Women's Rights

The abuses of alcohol generated one of the strongest reform movements of the 1820s and 1830s. Drinking was a serious social problem that destroyed families, bred crime, and fostered disease. Temperance organizations quickly developed after reformers founded the **American Society for the Promotion of Temperance** in 1826. By the 1830s, there were over 5,000 state and local temperance groups. In 1851, the **Maine Law** made

Maine the first state in the Union to prohibit the sale and consumption of alcohol statewide. The temperance movement was strongly anti-immigrant in its message. It connected drinking and its abuses with foreigners, especially Irish Catholic and German immigrants. Temperance provided the Protestant middle class with a means to attack out-of-favor groups such as laborers, immigrants, and Catholics.

Although in the shadow of the abolitionist crusade, the women's movement flickered to life in this time as well. Led by **Elizabeth Cady Stanton** and **Lucretia Mott**, the first women's rights convention met in Seneca Falls, New York, in July 1848. This meeting inaugurated the quest for equal rights by passing the **Declaration of Sentiments**. Later joined by **Susan B. Anthony**, Stanton waged a futile campaign for women's suffrage throughout the nineteenth century. Hampered by subordination to the abolitionist movement, adherence to the "**cult of domesticity**," and divisions over black men's voting rights, women would not achieve the right to vote until 1920.

Abolition

Of all the reforms of the 1830s and 1840s, none had more energy or intensity than the abolitionist movement. This crusade dominated the era. While there had been earlier attempts to abolish slavery with the forma-tion of the **American Colonization Society**, the movement began in earnest in 1831, when **William Lloyd Garrison** started his newspaper, *The Liberator*. In 1833, Garrison and his allies founded the influential **American Anti-Slavery Society**.

Garrison remained at the center of the abolitionist endeavor for the next thirty years. He recruited former slaves such as **Frederick Douglass** as agents, opposed compensation for the slaveholders, opposed political action by a government he believed hopelessly under the inluence of the corrupt slaveholding interests, and championed an equal role for women in the movement. Garrison's uncompromising and extreme views caused division among the reformers. By 1840, a rival group of abolitionists broke with his positions. Led by **Lewis and Arthur Tappan**, the **American and Foreign Anti-Slavery Society** was formed. It supported political action, embraced the Constitution, allied with churches, endorsed compensation for slaveholders, and opposed women's full participation in meetings. This struggle between Garrison and his critics dominated the abolitionist movement in the 1840s and 1850s.

Often reformers were involved in more than one type of reform. Many women who crusaded for gender equality received their training in the abolitionist movement. And other abolitionists supported a variety of reforms including temperance and penal reform. The goal of all these individuals was expansion of democracy and fulfillment of the ideals of the Declaration of Independence.

HIGH*lights*
of the Period

★ **Abby Kelley** — effective public speaker in the American Anti-Slavery Society; her election to an all-male committee caused the final break between William Garrison and his abolitionist critics in 1840 that split the organization.

★ **American Anti-Slavery Society** — organization of reformers who embraced moral persuasion to end slavery; founded in 1833, it opposed gradual emancipation, rejected compensation to slaveholders, supported many types of reform, and welcomed women as full and active members.

★ **American Colonization Society** — organization founded in 1817 that advocated sending freed slaves to a colony in Africa; it established the colony of Liberia in 1827 and encouraged free African Americans to emigrate there as well.

★ **American and Foreign Anti-Slavery Society** — organization founded in 1840 and led by the Tappan brothers that opposed the radical ideas of William Lloyd Garrison, especially his attacks on the churches and the Constitution; it followed a more moderate approach and supported the political activities of the Liberty Party.

★ **American Society for the Promotion of Temperance** — first national temperance organization, founded in 1826, which sent agents to preach total abstinence from alcohol; the society pressed individuals to sign pledges of sobriety and states to prohibit the use of alcohol.

★ **Brook Farm** — utopian society established by transcendentalist George Ripley near Boston in 1841; members shared equally in farm work and leisure discussions of literature and art. Author Nathaniel Hawthorne and others became disenchanted with the experiment, and it collapsed after a fire in 1847.

★ **Burned-over district** — area of New York State along the Erie Canal that was constantly aflame with revivalism and reform; as wave after wave of fervor broke over the region, groups such as the Mormons, Shakers, and Millerites found support among the residents.

★ **Charles Finney** — a leading evangelist of the Second Great Awakening; he preached that each person had capacity for spiritual rebirth and salvation, and that through individual effort one could be saved. His concept of "utility of benevolence" proposed the reformation of society as well as of individuals.

★ **Compensated Emancipation** — approach to ending slavery that called for slaveholders to be paid for the loss of their "property" as slaves were freed; such proposals were based on the belief that slaveholders would be less resistant to abolition if the economic blow were softened by compensation. A variety of such programs were proposed, some with the support of government leaders, up to and even during the Civil War. Some compensated emancipation existed on a very small scale, as some anti-slavery organizations purchased slaves and then set them free.

Nathaniel Hawthorne

★ **Cult of domesticity** — the belief that as the fairer sex, women occupied a unique and specific social position and that they were to provide religious and moral instruction in the home but avoid the rough world of politics and business in the larger sphere of society.

★ **Declaration of Sentiments** — series of resolutions issued at the end of the Seneca Falls Convention in 1848; modeled after the Declaration of Independence, the list of grievances called for economic and social equality for women, along with a demand for the right to vote.

★ **Dorothea Dix** — schoolteacher turned reformer; she was a pioneer for humane treatment of the mentally ill. She lobbied state legislatures to create separate hospitals for the insane and to remove them from the depravity of the penal system.

★ **Elizabeth Cady Stanton** — pioneer in the women's movement; she organized the Seneca Falls Convention in 1848 and fought for women's suffrage throughout the 1800s.

★ **Frederick Douglass** — former slave who became an effective abolitionist with an authenticity to his speeches unmatched by other antislavery voices; initially a follower of William Lloyd Garrison, he broke away and started his own abolitionist newspaper, *The North Star*. From the 1840s to his death in 1895, he was the leading black spokesman in America.

★ **Gradual Emancipation** — approach to ending slavery that called for the phasing out of slavery over a period of time; many gradual emancipation proposals were built around the granting of freedom to children of slaves who were born after a specified date, usually when they attained a specified age; in this way, as existing slaves aged and died, slavery would gradually die too. Many of the northern states, which abolished slavery following the American Revolution, adopted this method of ending the institution.

★ **Horace Mann** — reformer who led a crusade to improve public education in America; as secretary of the Massachusetts Board of Education, he established a minimum school term, formalized teacher training, and moved curriculum away from religious training toward more secular subjects.

★ **James Birney** — former slaveholder who at one time was a member of the American Colonization Society, the American Anti-Slavery Society, and the American and Foreign Anti-Slavery Society; in 1840 and 1844, he ran for president on the Liberty Party ticket.

★ **Lewis and Arthur Tappan** — founders of the American and Foreign Anti-Slavery Society; as successful businessmen, they funded many antislavery activities in the 1830s and 1840s. They also supported the Liberty Party in the 1840s.

★ **Liberty Party** — political party formed in 1840 that supported a program to end the slave trade and slavery in the territories and the District of Columbia; James Birney ran as the party candidate in 1840 and 1844. In 1848, it merged into the Free Soil Party.

★ **Lucretia Mott** — Quaker activist in both the abolitionist and women's movements; with Elizabeth Cady Stanton, she was a principal organizer of the Seneca Falls Convention in 1848.

★ **Maine Law (1851)** — first statewide attempt to restrict the consumption of alcohol; the law prohibited the manufacture and sale of alcohol except for medical reasons.

★ **Sarah and Angelina Grimke** — Quaker sisters from South Carolina who came north and became active in the abolitionist movement; Angelina married Theodore Weld, a leading abolitionist, and Sarah wrote and lectured on a variety of reforms including women's rights and abolition.

★ **Second Great Awakening** — period of religious revivals between 1790 and 1840 that preached the sinfulness of man yet emphasized salvation through moral action; it sent a message to turn away from sin and provided philosophical underpinnings of the reforms of the 1830s.

★ **Susan B. Anthony** — friend and partner of Elizabeth Cady Stanton in the struggle for women's rights; meeting in 1851, Anthony and Stanton founded the National Woman Suffrage Association after the Civil War. The Nineteenth Amendment, which extended the right to vote to women in 1920, is sometimes called the "Anthony" amendment.

★ **Transcendentalists** — writers who believed in the search for reality and truth through spiritual intuition; they held that man was capable of discovering truth without reference to established authority. This belief justified the reformers' challenges to the conventional thinking of their time.

★ **William Lloyd Garrison** — most prominent abolitionist leader of the antebellum period; he published the antislavery newspaper *The Liberator* and founded the American Anti-Slavery Society.

HIGH*lights*
of the Period

Ideas to Ponder

After reviewing the chapter's summary, highlights, and your primary text,
discuss the following with members of your study group.

1   How did economic and social changes after the War of 1812 fuel the reforms of the 1830s?

2   How did religious developments promote the reforms of the 1830s?

3   How did the Market Revolution give rise to the developments of utopian societies in the 1830s and 1840s?

4   Why did the Jacksonians oppose many of the reforms of the 1830s?

5   Why was the "burned-over district" so involved in the reforms of the period?

6   Why did William Lloyd Garrison adopt such a radical approach to ending slavery?

7   Was Garrison a positive or negative force in ending slavery in America?

8   Why did the American and Foreign Anti-Slavery Society form?

9   What role did African Americans play in the abolitionist movement?

10 How did the formation of the Liberty Party change the nature of the abolitionist debate?

11 Did the American Colonization Society hurt the abolitionist crusade? Explain why or why not.

12 What was the attitude of most Americans toward the abolitionist movement?

13 Why did many Americans blame the abolitionists for the Civil War? Was this fair?

14 In what ways were the temperance reformers both progressive and repressive in their ideology and tactics?

15 Why were women unable to make significant improvement in their position in society before the Civil War?

16 In what ways could women identify with the plight of African-American slaves?

17 Why did the Whig Party support many of the social and economic reforms of the 1830s and 1840s?

Essay Skill

Writing a Strong Thesis Statement

A thesis statement is a critical part of writing an effective AP essay. In fact, when you examine the rubrics, or grading standards, used to evaluate AP essays later in this book, you will see that the first thing a reader is instructed to look for in any essay is a strong thesis statement. This thesis should appear early in the first paragraph of the essay, ideally as the first sentence. Some students underline the thesis statement to make certain their paper clearly focuses on their argument and to ensure that anyone evaluating their paper can easily see what position they are taking in answering the question.

In defining a thesis statement, keep in mind that it is:

1. a controlling idea around which your paper is built
2. a one-sentence answer to the historical question being asked
3. a concise statement of your essay's argument
4. a point of view adopted about a historical problem
5. a proposition to be defended or argued

The basic elements of a strong thesis include a statement that:

1. deals with all aspects of the topic suggested by the question
2. takes a clear position on the issue
3. provides an organizational framework from which to structure your essay
4. addresses the core issues defined by the question (i.e., is on target)

Look at the following statement and the three thesis statements offered as possible beginnings in answering the prompt.

> **"The utopian societies of the 1830s and 1840s formed in response to the social and economic upheavals that affected America after the War of 1812."**

Assess the validity of this statement.

Possible thesis statements:

1. There were many changes in America after the War of 1812 that gave rise to utopian societies.

2. The emerging Market Revolution, increasing urbanization, and immigration after the War of 1812 promoted the rise of utopian societies.

3. The rise of Jacksonian democracy, the common man, and the abolitionist movement made many people seek alternative life styles in the 1830s.

Essay Skill

Discussion of the Statements

The best thesis statement is statement 2. It deals with economic and social issues; it takes a clear position that these factors caused utopian societies to form; it provides an organizational framework to the structure of the essay (i.e., Market Revolution, growth of cities, impact of immigration); and it deals with the topics suggested by the question.

Statement 1 is too general. It does not identify the changes that affected America, give a structure for the essay, or address the core issues of economic and social issues. It does take a weak position on the question, however.

Statement 3 is a weak thesis statement because it is off topic. There is a danger that it will take the paper in the wrong direction. Following it, a writer is likely to drift into politics and abolition. It may address utopian societies—but only in a secondary way. On the positive side, it does take a position and provides an organizational framework. In fact, it is actually a good thesis for a different question!

Practicing the Skill

Evaluate the following three thesis statements and decide which is the strongest start for discussing the statement below.

"Although the end of slavery was an agreed upon goal, the abolitionists were divided over the best means to achieve it."

1. William Garrison wanted to use moral persuasion to end slavery and other abolitionists wanted to form political parties to achieve an end to slavery.

2. The abolitionists wanted to end slavery but did not know exactly how to do it.

3. While the abolitionists wanted to end slavery, they disagreed over the political, social, and economic means to do it.

Choice No._____ Why did you select this thesis statement?

_____

_____

After making your choice, discuss it with your classmates or your study group members. After your discussion, consult page 223 in the Suggested Responses section for an explanation of the best thesis statement.

Essay Skill

Write a thesis statement for the following prompt and then compare your statement with those of your classmates or a member of your study group.

"The abolitionist movement was both a catalyst and a hindrance for the women's rights movement."

Assess the validity of this statement.

_____

_____

_____

Document SKILL

Analyzing Charts

Another important skill on the AP test, especially on the DBQ essay section, is analyzing charts. Not all of the eight or nine sources on the DBQ are written text. Along with documents, photographs, and cartoons, charts are often used as potential support materials for a student's argument on the DBQ. Charts have been a popular source on the exam. For example, on three of the last five DBQs, there has been a chart to analyze.

Although it is not possible to spend a great deal of time on any one source during the DBQ preparation period (recommended 15 minutes), students should have a consistent plan for analyzing charts. Below are two versions of a chart analysis model—one for the early part of the school year and another, shorter "AP test" version that can be used later in the term. It is likely that at the beginning of the year, when you and your study group are familiarizing yourselves with the process of chart analysis, the longer form will be useful. As the year progresses and you become more comfortable working with charts, you can move to the shorter version.

Look at the chart below and complete the two versions of the worksheet. Compare your answers with your classmates or with the members of your study group. After your discussion, turn to page 223 in the Suggested Responses section for suggested answers to the exercises.

Chart. Women's Population, Age, and Child-Bearing, 1810–1860

Year	White Female Population (in thousands)	Number of Children Under Age of 5 Born to Women Age 20–44 (per 1,000 white women)	Women 65 and Older (in thousands)
1810	2,874	1,358	N.A.
1820	3,866	1,295	N.A.
1830	5,171	1,145	209
1840	6,940	1,085	281
1850	9,526	892	408
1860	13,111	905	585

Source: *Historical Statistics of the United States, Colonial Times to 1970*

Document SKILL

Chart Analysis Worksheet

1. What time period is being examined? _____

2. What item/items/topics are being described? _____

   _____

3. What trends do you see in the chart? _____

   _____

4. Is each trend consistent, or does it vary back and forth? _____

   _____

5. Why do you think the trend occurred, or why did it vary back and forth? (Make a

   guess/hypothesis about the patterns.) _____

   _____

6. Is there a relationship or connection between the items shown? (Does one item go up

   or down in relation to another item?) _____

   _____

7. Who would benefit from the trend? (Why?) _____

   _____

8. Who would be hurt? (Why?) _____

   _____

9. What generalization can you make from the chart? _____

   _____

(Shorter Version) 3TRG Chart Analysis Worksheet*

1. Time? _____

2. Topics? _____

3. Trends? _____

4. Relationship/connection? _____

5. Generalization _____

*3TRG (Time, Topic, Trends, Relationship, Generalization)

Chapter 7

EXPANSION AND ITS CONSEQUENCES
1840–1854

Focus Questions

★ How did the ideas of Manifest Destiny emerge from nationalistic beliefs about America's past and its future?

★ How did the Texas-Mexican conflict of the 1830s encourage America's drive westward to the Pacific Ocean?

★ How did the Mexican War promote sectional division rather than national unity?

★ How was the Compromise of 1850 more a triumph of sectional self-interest than a true national compromise?

★ How did the Kansas-Nebraska Act realign the American political system?

Summary

In the early 1840s, America increasingly viewed territorial expansion as a means to restore its confidence and prosperity lost during the Panic of 1837. The editor **John L. O'Sullivan** added a divine quality to this quest when he wrote America should expand "by the right of our manifest destiny to overspread . . . [the] continent. . . ." Expansionist ideas also reflected America's successful experiment with democracy, as leaders called on the nation to expand "the area of liberty" to include lands controlled by Mexico and by Native Americans. In addition, for slaveholding southerners and their allies, expansion meant more land for slavery and increased influence in Congress.

Texas War for Independence

The focus of expansion became Texas and its surrounding territories. Newly independent Mexico (1821) had a massive, undeveloped empire that included the Texas territory. Hoping to improve its economy and to create a buffer against the United States, Mexico opened Texas to immigration. Thousands of Americans, led by **Stephen Austin**, flocked to Texas to accept Mexican land grants. Agreeing to become Mexican citizens and to abide by Mexican law, over 30,000 Americans occupied Texas by 1835. These new immigrants failed to live up to their bargain, however, as they began to "Americanize" Texas. General **Antonio Lopez de Santa Anna** tried to subdue the rebellious Texans. After the massacre of Texans at the **Alamo** and the Battle of San Jacinto, **Sam Houston** and his fellow rebels achieved independence from Mexico in 1836 and formed the Lone Star Republic. Meanwhile, the Texans also sought annexation by the United States. Fearing war with Mexico (which still claimed Texas), dealing

James K. Polk

with the Panic of 1837, and divided over the addition of new slave territory, Congress repeatedly rejected Texas-statehood bids from 1836 to 1845.

In early 1845, lame-duck President John Tyler convinced Congress to pass a joint resolution that admitted the Lone Star Republic to the Union. Texas, although now officially a state, still presented problems. The new president, **James K. Polk**, wanted Mexican agreement to Texas annexation and to the Rio Grande as the border between the United States and Mexico. He also hoped to buy California for land-hungry America.

The Oregon Question

As the controversy between Mexico and the United States heated up, Polk confronted a dispute with Great Britain over the Oregon country. The two nations had jointly occupied the region since 1818. In the 1840s, thousands of Americans got "Oregon fever" and settled in the region. Increasingly, American leaders called for sole ownership of the region, with the northern boundary at 54 degrees, 40 minutes latitude. Polk threatened war if the British refused America's demands. Although the British would not accept the boundary, neither side truly wanted to fight over Oregon, and a compromise was reached. In June 1846, shortly after war began with Mexico, the Senate approved a treaty that gave the United States sole ownership of the Oregon country—with the northern boundary farther south, at 49 degrees. Polk reluctantly agreed to the compromise.

The War with Mexico

To resolve the troubles with Mexico, Polk pursued a two-pronged policy. He sent **John Slidell** to negotiate an agreement to resolve the Texas annexation and boundary problem. Slidell also hoped to buy California for $20–25 million. At the same time, the president ordered General **Zachary Taylor** and 3,500 American troops to the disputed border area. When Slidell's mission failed, Taylor moved his troops from the Nueces River, which Mexico claimed as the border, south to the Rio Grande river. Mexico viewed this as an aggressive act, and in April 1846, Mexican and American troops clashed. On May 13, 1846, Congress declared war on Mexico.

Over the next two years, Zachary Taylor and **Winfield Scott** led American troops to victory after victory against the poorly prepared Mexican army. By 1848, most of Mexico was under American control. In addition, Stephen Kearny successfully seized parts of California and established American claims to the region. Although the war was a military success, the conflict gave Polk and the Democrats political headaches. Military successes promoted the presidential aspirations of Taylor and Scott, both of whom were Whigs. Also, by 1848, the Whigs were raising charges that Polk had deliberately maneuvered the country into war by provoking the border incident in the spring of 1846.

Under mounting political pressure, Polk accepted the **Treaty of Guadalupe Hidalgo** in 1848, which finally resolved the issue of Texas and gave the United States control of the **Mexican Cession**. It did not, however, quell the political turmoil. Instead, the new territories proved to be a "dose of poison" for American unity. Polk's opponents charged him with provoking the war to satisfy a "**slave power**" in the South. During the war, Polk's political enemies introduced the **Wilmot Proviso**, which attempted to block the spread of slavery into any new lands that might be acquired from the war. Although never approved, the proviso roiled congressional debate for the next several years.

The Compromise of 1850

The immediate crisis generated by the war was California's statehood bid in 1849. The South opposed the admission of another free state and feared the exclusion of slavery from all of the Mexican Cession. Henry Clay, sensing an opportunity to settle several sectional issues around the admission of California, proposed the **Compromise of 1850**. This four-part legislative package included California statehood, an end to the slave trade in the District of Columbia, a stronger fugitive slave law, and **popular sovereignty** for the remaining territories of the Mexican Cession. When Clay was unable to get congressional approval for the compromise, **Stephen Douglas** stepped in and drove the compromise through Congress as four separate bills. While the compromise postponed sectional conflict, it seemed an "artful evasion" to many observers. It restored an uneasy peace but provided no guidelines for settling future disputes over slavery in the territories.

Slavery and Politics

The debate over slavery's spread also divided the political parties. The Democrats split between those who saw slaveholding as a constitutional right that should expand without restriction and the supporters of popular sovereignty, who wanted the decision about slavery left in the hands of the voters in the specific territories. The Whigs, already weakened by internal divisions, could not find a middle ground on slavery and disappeared after the election of 1852. Third parties such as the **Free Soil Party** and the **Know-Nothing Party** tried to fill the void, but neither caught on with the electorate.

When Stephen Douglas introduced the **Kansas-Nebraska Bill** in 1854, the nation's fragile political alignment collapsed. Douglas's bill divided the Nebraska territory into two territories and called for a vote among the settlers to decide the future of slavery there. This de facto repeal of the Missouri Compromise created a firestorm of protest and within months of its passage, the **Republican Party** formed, dedicated to combating the growing influence of the "slave power."

HIGH*lights* of the Period

★ **Alamo** — mission and fort that was the site of a siege and battle during the Texas Revolution, which resulted in the massacre of all its defenders; the event helped galvanize the Texas rebels and eventually led to their victory at the Battle of San Jacinto and independence from Mexico.

★ **Antonio Lopez de Santa Anna** — political opportunist and general who served as president of Mexico eleven different times and commanded the Mexican army during the Texas Revolution in the 1830s and the war with the United States in the 1840s.

★ **Compromise of 1850** — proposal by Henry Clay to settle the debate over slavery in territories gained from the Mexican War; it was shepherded though Congress by Stephen Douglas. Its elements included admitting California as a free state, ending the buying and selling of slaves in the District of Columbia (DC), a more stringent Fugitive Slave Law, postponed decisions about slavery in the New Mexico and Utah Territories, and settlement of the Texas-New Mexico boundary and debt issues.

★ **Franklin Pierce** — northern Democratic president with southern principles, 1853–1857, who signed the Kansas-Nebraska Act and sought sectional harmony above all else.

★ **Free Soil Party** — formed from the remnants of the Liberty Party in 1848; adopting a slogan of "free soil, free speech, free labor, and free men," it opposed the spread of slavery into territories and supported homesteads, cheap postage, and internal improvements. It ran Martin Van Buren (1848) and John Hale (1852) for president and was absorbed into the Republican Party by 1856.

★ **Gadsden Purchase (1853)** — U.S. acquisition of land south of the Gila River from Mexico for $10 million; the land was needed for a possible transcontinental railroad line through the southern United States. However, the route was never used.

★ **James K. Polk** — Democratic president from 1845 to 1849; nicknamed "Young Hickory" because of his close political and personal ties to Andrew Jackson, he pursued an aggressive foreign policy that led to the Mexican War, settlement of the Oregon issue, and the acquisition of the Mexican Cession.

★ **John L. O'Sullivan** — influential editor of the *Democratic Review* who coined the phrase "manifest destiny" in 1845.

★ **Kansas-Nebraska Act (1854)** — Stephen Douglas's bill to open western territories, promote a transcontinental railroad, and boost his presidential ambitions; it divided the Nebraska territory into two territories and used popular sovereignty to decide slavery in the region. Among Douglas's goals in making this proposal was to populate Kansas in order to make more attractive a proposed route for a transcontinental railroad that ended in Chicago, in his home state of Illinois.

★ **Know-Nothing Party** — influential third party of the 1840s; it opposed immigrants, especially Catholics, and supported temperance, a waiting period for citizenship, and literacy tests. Officially the American Party, its more commonly used nickname came from its members' secrecy and refusal to tell strangers anything about the group. When questioned, they would only reply, "I know nothing."

★ **Lewis Cass** — Democratic senator who proposed popular sovereignty to settle the slavery question in the territories; he lost the presidential election in 1848 against Zachary Taylor but continued to advocate his solution to the slavery issue throughout the 1850s.

★ **Manifest Destiny** — set of ideas used to justify American expansion in the 1840s; weaving together the rhetoric of economic necessity, racial superiority, and national security, the concept implied an inevitability of U.S. continental expansion.

★ **Mexican Cession** — region comprising California and all or parts of the states of the present-day American Southwest that Mexico turned over to the United States after the Mexican War.

★ **Nashville Convention** — meeting of representatives of nine southern states in the summer of 1850 to monitor the negotiations over the Compromise of 1850; it called for extension of the Missouri Compromise line to the Pacific Ocean and a stronger Fugitive Slave law. The convention accepted the Compromise but laid the groundwork for a southern confederacy in 1860–1861.

★ **Ostend Manifesto (1854)** — a statement by American envoys abroad to pressure Spain into selling Cuba to the United States; the declaration suggested that if Spain would not sell Cuba, the United States would be justified in seizing it. It was quickly repudiated by the U.S. government but it added to the belief that a "slave power" existed and was active in Washington.

★ **Popular sovereignty** — political process promoted by Lewis Cass, Stephen Douglas, and other northern Democrats whereby, when a territory organized, its residents would vote to decide the future of slavery there; the idea of empowering voters to decide important questions was not new to the 1840s and 1850s or to the slavery issue, however.

★ **Republican Party** — political party formed in 1854 in response to the Kansas-Nebraska Act; it combined remnants of Whig, Free Soil, and Know-Nothing Parties as well as disgruntled Democrats. Although not abolitionist, it sought to block the spread of slavery in the territories. It also favored tariffs, homesteads, and a transcontinental railroad.

★ **Sam Houston** — leader of the Texas revolutionaries, 1835–1836, first president of the Republic of Texas, and later a U.S. Senator from the state of Texas; he was a close political and personal ally of Andrew Jackson.

* **"slave power"** — the belief that a slave-holding oligarchy existed to maintain slavery in the South and to spread it throughout the United States, including into the free states; this belief held that a southern cabal championed a closed, aristocratic way of life that attacked northern capitalism and liberty.

* **Stephen Austin** — leader of American immigration to Texas in the 1820s; he negotiated land grants with Mexico and tried to moderate growing Texan rebelliousness in the 1830s. After Texas became an independent nation, he served as its secretary of state.

* **Stephen Douglas** — a leading Democratic senator in the 1850s; nicknamed the "Little Giant" for his small size and great political power, he steered the Compromise of 1850 and the Kansas-Nebraska Act through Congress. Although increasingly alienated from the southern wing of his party, he ran against his political rival Abraham Lincoln for president in 1860 and lost.

* **Treaty of Guadalupe Hidalgo (1848)** — agreement that ended the Mexican War; under its terms Mexico gave up all claims to Texas north of the Rio Grande and ceded California and the Utah and New Mexico territories to the United States. The United States paid Mexico fifteen million dollars for the land, but the land cession amounted to nearly half that nation's territory.

* **Wilmot Proviso** — measure introduced in Congress in 1846 to prohibit slavery in all territory that might be gained by the Mexican War; southerners blocked its passage in the Senate. Afterward, it became the congressional rallying platform for the antislavery forces in the late 1840s and early 1850s.

* **Winfield Scott** — arguably the finest military figure in America from the War of 1812 to the Civil War; he distinguished himself in the Mexican War, ran unsuccessfully for president (1852), and briefly commanded the Union armies at the beginning of the Civil War.

* **Zachary Taylor** — military hero of Mexican War and the last Whig elected president (1848); his sudden death in July 1850 allowed supporters of the Compromise of 1850 to get the measures through Congress.

HIGH*lights* of the Period

Ideas to Ponder

After reviewing the chapter's summary, highlights, and your primary text,
discuss the following with members of your study group.

1   How did the ideas of Manifest Destiny dominate the presidential election of 1844?

2   How did U.S. miscalculations over Oregon almost cause war with Great Britain in 1846?

3   How did the Texas Revolution lead to the Mexican War?

4   How did President Polk use "the carrot and the stick" approach towards Mexico to settle the disputes over Texas in 1846?

5   Why did many Americans believe that the United States caused the Mexican War, even though the Mexicans fired the first shots?

6   What political problems did President Polk face during the Mexican War?

7   Was the Wilmot Proviso the first political shot of the Civil War? Explain.

8   Why did the Treaty of Guadalupe Hidalgo fail to satisfy either the Democratic president or the Whig Congress?

9   Why was the Compromise of 1850 only a short-term solution to the sectional conflicts of the 1850s?

10   How did the belief in a "slave power" influence political developments in the 1850s?

11   How did implementing popular sovereignty prove more difficult than its supporters anticipated?

12   How was the land acquired from Mexico "a dose of poison" to American unity?

13   How did the Kansas-Nebraska Act change the political landscape in the mid 1850s?

14   How did the Ostend Manifesto reinforce the belief in a "slave power"?

15   How did the formation of the Republican Party provide a political home for disgruntled groups and philosophies in the mid 1850s?

Essay Skill

Writing a Positive or Negative Thesis Statement

Earlier in the book, we defined a thesis statement, identified its main elements, and suggested its best placement in an essay answer. In this section, we address possible ways a thesis statement can be expressed to answer an essay prompt. A thesis statement is a one-sentence answer to a historical problem suggested by an essay question/statement. You may agree, disagree, or do a little of both when evaluating the validity of the prompt. As long as you can defend your position, it is permissible to challenge the ideas expressed by the question/statement. **It is, however, imperative that you be able to support your contrary position with facts.**

In many cases, you will agree with the ideas expressed in the prompt and write a positive thesis statement that supports the question/statement. For example, a prompt that suggests expansion into Texas and Oregon greatly influenced the outcome of the presidential election of 1844 is an accurate summary of the issues of the campaign. It would be answered with a positive thesis statement that affirms the validity of the prompt.

On the other hand, you may confront a question/statement that is an overstatement or even an inaccuracy about a historical event or phenomenon. In this case, you may want to disagree with the ideas expressed and write a negative thesis statement that challenges the ideas of the prompt. For example, a question/statement that suggests the Mexican War promoted American unity in the 1840s cannot be defended, and your thesis statement would negate the assertions being made.

A final possibility is a question/statement that is partially correct. It may express some ideas that you can defend and others with which you disagree. Here, you would use a positive/negative thesis—that is, one which acknowledges both agreement and disagreement with the ideas expressed by the prompt. For example, an essay statement that credited the Compromise of 1850 with contributing to sectional harmony could only be accepted as partially accurate. While recognizing that the Compromise soothed tensions briefly, you would also need to point out that sectional conflict flared up again within four years. Thus, you would write a thesis that addressed both the positive and negative aspects of the prompt.

Practicing the Skill

To practice writing positive, negative, and positive/negative thesis statements, look at the following essay prompts and their respective thesis statements. Notice that each prompt was converted into a clarifying question and that the answer to that question became the thesis statement. By transforming the prompt to a question, you will be better able to decide the degree to which you agree or disagree with the ideas being expressed.

1. The Polk administration's policies toward Texas were the primary cause of the Mexican War.

Assess the validity of this statement.

> **Question:**
> Did President Polk's policies cause the Mexican War?
>
> **Positive thesis statement:**
> President Polk's aggressive and warlike policies toward Texas annexation caused armed conflict with Mexico in 1846.

The writer agrees with the ideas in the prompt and will demonstrate that Polk's policies were responsible for causing the war.

2. Popular sovereignty was an effective means to deal with the question of slavery in the territories.

Assess the validity of this statement.

Question:
How effective was popular sovereignty in dealing with slavery in the territories?

Negative thesis statement:
Rather than promoting sectional harmony, the implementation of popular sovereignty became a divisive means of dealing with the question of slavery in the territories.

The writer does not agree with the prompt's statement about the effectiveness of popular sovereignty. He/she will use evidence to show how ineffective popular sovereignty was in resolving the slavery question in the territories.

3. In the 1850s, Henry Clay's political decline hurt the nation and his place in history.

Assess the validity of this statement.

Question:
Did Henry Clay lose his political effectiveness in the 1850s?

Positive/negative thesis statement:
Although Henry Clay lost much of his political influence in the 1850s, he did author one last union-saving measure that solidified his place in history as "the Great Compromiser."

The writer sees both positive and negative ideas in the prompt. He/she plans to introduce some evidence to show Clay's diminished influence but also to acknowledge his important role in putting together the Compromise of 1850, the last of his many compromises.

Look at the following three prompts, write a clarifying question for each one, and then construct a positive thesis statement for the first prompt, a negative thesis statement for the second, and a positive/negative thesis statement for the third. Discuss your thesis statements with your classmates or your study group members. At some point, compare your answers with the suggested responses on page 224 of the Suggested Responses section.

1. From 1845 to 1855, southern actions and demands reinforced the idea that a "slave power" was at work in America.

Assess the validity of this statement.

Question:

_____

_____

Positive Thesis:

_____

_____

Essay Skill

2. President Polk's "failure of nerve" cost America its rights to the 54° 40' boundary of Oregon.

Assess the validity of this statement.

   Question:

   _____

   _____

   _____

   _____

   _____

   Negative Thesis:

   _____

   _____

   _____

   _____

   _____

3. The land acquired in 1848 hurt the United States more than it benefited the nation's development.

Assess the validity of this statement.

   Question:

   _____

   _____

   _____

   _____

   Positive/Negative Thesis:

   _____

   _____

   _____

   _____

Document SKILL

Analyzing Political Cartoons

Along with a plan to analyze documents and charts, you must have a systematic strategy for evaluating political cartoons on the AP examination. Cartoons appear often on the test. Occasionally, a cartoon will be included on the multiple-choice section. More likely, however, cartoons are used as sources on the DBQ. From 1990 to 2003, there were cartoons on twelve of the fourteen DBQs. To be successful on the test, you must be able to identify a cartoon's meaning and use the information with the Document-Based Question.

Cartoons are very difficult to analyze. When students first look at a cartoon, they are bombarded with data and some may be unable to find meaning in the drawing. Without the structure of topic sentences and paragraphs to guide them, they may go into "information overload" as they try to absorb everything presented in the cartoon all at once. They do not dissect the cartoon piece by piece and cannot see how the representation can be used as part of their DBQ response.

You must treat a cartoon as a historical source and establish a logical, step-by-step process for analyzing it, just as you would do with documents and charts. The worksheet below provides a systematic mode for reading cartoons. By using it, you can identify the key elements of the representation and ultimately develop a summary of the cartoon's information that can be used in your DBQ answer.

On the examination in May, you may not have time to use all parts of the worksheet. In September and October, as you are developing a habit of the mind for analyzing cartoons, however, you should work with the full worksheet. Later in the school year, when you have gained experience with the process, you may wish to use a shorter version of the worksheet (TACOS). This worksheet requires the identification of a cartoon's time, author, captions, objects, and summary. In this shorter form, TACOS provides a structure for cartoon analysis and is more practical for the time constraints required on the exam.

Look at the following worksheets and the cartoon on the election of 1844. Complete the worksheets and discuss your answers with your classmates or with the other members of your study group. At some point, take a look at the suggested answers for the worksheet on page 224 of the Suggested Responses section. You will also find answers for the shorter version (TACOS) used for the cartoon as well.

Political Climbing Boys Anonymous, 1844

Document SKILL

Cartoon Analysis Worksheet

1. What is the date of the cartoon?

2. What significant event(s) was or were going on for the nation at the time of the cartoon?

3. Who is the author of the cartoon? What do you know about his/her background? Is political bias apparent in the cartoon?

4. What historical figures are in the cartoon?

5. What does the caption/title mean?

6. What labels/phrases are used within the cartoon?

7. Do the labels within the cartoon support or challenge the caption?

8. What objects do you see in the cartoon? List the three most prominent. Are the objects symbols or stereotypes? Explain.

9. Summarize the point of the cartoon.

10. Who would support/oppose the message of the cartoon? Why?

Document SKILL

Shorter Version (TACOS)

1. What is the date of cartoon? _____

2. Who is the author? _____

3. What does the caption/title mean? _____

4. What objects do you see in the cartoon? List the three most prominent.

   _____

   _____

   _____

   _____

   _____

5. Summarize the point. _____

   _____

   _____

   _____

   _____

   _____

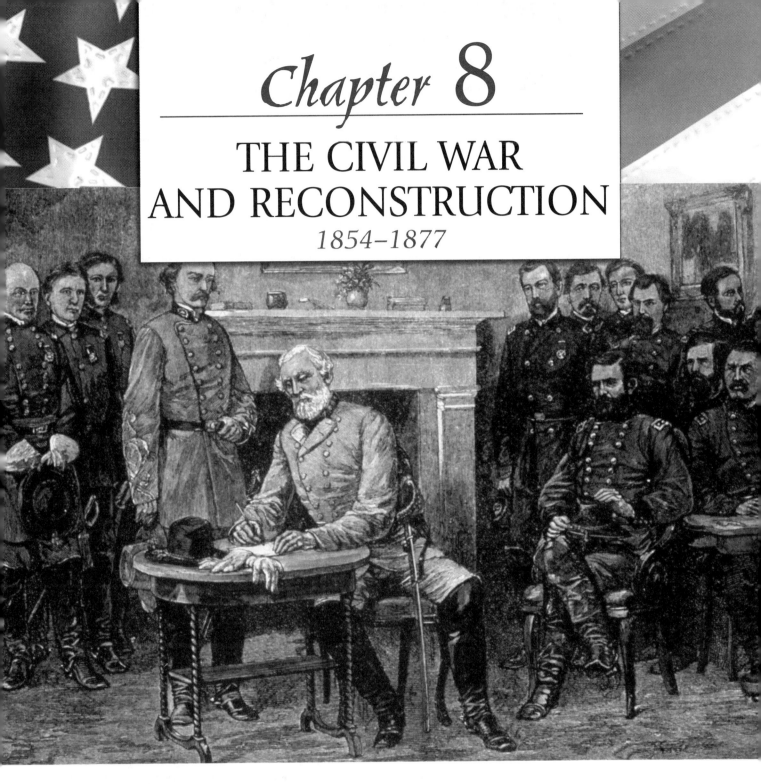

Chapter 8

THE CIVIL WAR AND RECONSTRUCTION

1854–1877

Focus Questions

★ How did Abraham Lincoln's election help bring on southern secession?

★ How did the Civil War transform the societies in both the North and the South?

★ How did slavery influence Lincoln's political and military decisions during the war?

★ How was the North able to subdue the South militarily?

★ How did Congress gain control of Reconstruction from the president?

★ Why was President Andrew Johnson impeached?

★ Why did Radical Reconstruction fail to make permanent changes in America?

Summary

Violence and political upheaval marred the second half of the 1850s. When Kansas organized in 1856, "Bleeding Kansas" resulted, as antislavery and pro-slavery paramilitary forces fought to gain political ascendancy. The violence culminated with the burning of Lawrence, Kansas, and John Brown's murder of five pro-slavery settlers. Out of the lawlessness emerged the Lecompton Constitution and Kansas's pro-slavery effort to join the Union. President James Buchanan supported the proposed state constitution, but western Democrats, led by Stephen Douglas, believed it did not have the support of most Kansans, and they defeated it in Congress. This intraparty battle postponed Kansas statehood and further damaged the Democratic Party.

Dred Scott and John Brown

In the midst of the Kansas dispute, the Supreme Court weighed into the slavery debate with the Dred Scott decision. The Court's decision effectively denied citizenship to all blacks, protected slavery's expansion into the territories, and voided the Missouri Compromise. The ruling inflamed the Republican Party, which had narrowly lost the presidency in 1856 but was now unified and energized for future political battles.

In 1859 John Brown again roiled the nation with violence. With eighteen antislavery zealots, he planned to incite a slave rebellion by seizing weapons at Harpers Ferry, Virginia. Although the plan failed and Brown was executed, his association with prominent abolitionists convinced the South it could only remain safely in the Union by controlling the White House. That control vanished in 1860 when Abraham Lincoln defeated Democrat Stephen Douglas, John Breckinridge, and third-party candidate John Bell for the presidency. Although Lincoln was not an abolitionist, his stand on slavery and its spread convinced the South that he threatened its way of life, and in December 1860 South Carolina seceded from the Union.

The Civil War

President Buchanan watched as six other states joined South Carolina and formed the Confederate States of America. Selecting Jefferson Davis as its president, the new nation seized U.S. government property throughout the South. Taking office in March 1861, President Lincoln hoped his policy of nonaggressive firmness would end the crisis, but it failed in April when the Confederates attacked Fort Sumter. After Lincoln declared a rebellion and called for 75,000 troops to crush it, four more states joined the southern cause.

The North had overwhelming supremacy in men, materiel, and money. It also had an established government, good relations with other nations, and control of the coastline. However, to end secession, the North would have to conquer the South. Southerners had only to wage a defensive war, fighting on familiar soil, defending their homes and their way of life. They also hoped "Cotton Diplomacy" would bring them foreign help.

Civil War Union troops recapturing artillery at Shiloh, Tennessee, 1862.

The North's strategy was to divide the South, isolate it diplomatically, and use overwhelming might to crush the rebellion. The South, believing in its martial spirit, expected a quick victory—that northerners would soon tire of the fight. When the war dragged on, however, Robert E. Lee twice invaded the North to apply political pressure, add Maryland to the Confederacy, and secure foreign recognition. Stopped at Antietam in 1862 and Gettysburg in 1863, Lee was forced each time to return to the South, short of his goals. By 1864, Lincoln had put his armies in the hands of Ulysses S. Grant, who relentlessly pressured Lee's army until its surrender on April 9, 1865.

The Home Front

The war transformed the governments and societies of both the Union and Confederacy. The North mobilized by instituting a draft, levying an income tax, and issuing $450 million in "greenback" currency. In addition, Lincoln expanded his powers enormously. He sent troops into battle without congressional approval, suspended *habeas corpus*, and arrested and held without charges over 13,000 people during the conflict.

Jefferson Davis, whose autocratic methods also met with opposition, presided over widespread governmental changes as well. Confederate government officials centralized authority and trampled on states' rights, the cornerstone of the Confederacy. By war's end, the government instituted a draft, enacted an income tax, regulated economic activities, and requisitioned millions of dollars of supplies. In a final act of desperation, the Confederates even proposed recruiting slaves as soldiers in return for their freedom.

Both sides faced internal dissension over the growth of governmental powers. In the North, Lincoln dealt with a deadly draft riot in 1863 and a strong Copperhead movement throughout the war. Davis encountered resistance to his wartime policies and faced riots over food shortages in 1863. After its defeat at Gettysburg, the South also experienced widespread desertions from its army.

Lincoln and Slavery

Lincoln's greatest challenge was what to do about slavery. He acted slowly because of his own racial beliefs and uncertainty about the constitutionality of any action against it. Most importantly, he feared the impact of emancipation on the Border States. These four slaveholding states remained loyal to the North and were fundamental to Lincoln's strategy for restoring the union. As pressure mounted from abolitionists and radicals in Congress, however, Lincoln decided to strike against

slavery. In September 1862, he issued a preliminary emancipation order and on January 1, 1863 he signed the Emancipation Proclamation, which freed slaves in the rebellious areas and offered black men an opportunity to fight in the Union army.

Presidential and Congressional Plans

Reconstructing the South created enormous problems for the nation after the war. Without Lincoln's political acumen behind it, his lenient ten-percent plan was quickly rejected by Congress. Andrew Johnson also could not convince Congress to seat the southerners elected under the plan and a three-year struggle between Johnson and Congress over postwar policy ensued. Rejecting the Lincoln-Johnson plan, the Radical Republicans, led by Thaddeus Stevens, called for creation of a Freedmen's Bureau, military occupation of the South, suffrage for black men, disenfranchisement of many white men, and acceptance of the Thirteenth, Fourteenth, and Fifteenth Amendments by the southern states.

Johnson fought the Radicals by vetoing 20 bills (but suffered 19 overrides), campaigning for congressional support in 1866, and replacing military commanders friendly to the Radicals. This obstructionism resulted in Johnson's impeachment in 1868. Impeached for violating the Tenure of Office Act, Johnson avoided conviction in the Senate by a single vote.

Results of Reconstruction

Reconstruction provided short-term gains for African Americans in the South. Black men gained the right to vote and held some offices, but these political gains were jeopardized by the Ku Klux Klan. These terrorists attacked blacks and their allies (scalawags, carpetbaggers), who attempted to set up southern governments that were free of control by former slaveholders. Most importantly, blacks failed to secure land ownership, and by the earlier 1870s, most were sharecropping or tenant-farming throughout the South.

Johnson's successor, Ulysses Grant, went along with the Radicals. Although Grant took military action against the KKK, he also presided over the removal of most of the occupying troops. Grant sought sectional reconciliation as the nation lost interest in the freedmen's future. Economic depression, currency problems, and political corruption crowded into the national agenda. With the Compromise of 1877, which settled the disputed presidential election of 1876, the nation closed the door on Reconstruction.

HIGH*lights* of the Period

★ **Abraham Lincoln** — president of the United States, 1861–1865; he is generally rated among America's greatest presidents for his leadership in restoring the Union. Lincoln was assassinated April 14, 1865, by John Wilkes Booth before he could implement his Reconstruction program.

★ **Andrew Johnson** — vice president who took over after Lincoln's assassination; an ex-Democrat with little sympathy for former slaves, his battles with Radical Republicans resulted in his impeachment in 1868. He avoided conviction and removal from office by one vote.

★ **Border States** — Maryland, Delaware, Kentucky, and Missouri; these slave states stayed in the Union and were crucial to Lincoln's political and military strategy. He feared alienating them with emancipation of slaves and adding them to the Confederate cause.

★ **Carpetbaggers** — northerners who went South to participate in Reconstruction governments; although they possessed a variety of motives, southerners often viewed them as opportunistic, poor whites—a carpetbag was cheap luggage—hoping to exploit the South.

★ **Charles Sumner** — senator from Massachusetts who was attacked on the floor of the Senate (1856) for antislavery speech; he required three years to recover but returned to the Senate to lead the Radical Republicans and to fight for racial equality. Sumner authored Civil Rights Act of 1875.

★ **Compromise of 1877** — agreement that ended the disputed election of 1876 between Rutherford Hayes and Samuel Tilden; under its terms, the South accepted Hayes's election. In return, the North agreed to remove the last troops from the South, support southern railroads, and accept a southerner into the Cabinet. The Compromise of 1877 is generally considered to mark the end of Reconstruction.

★ **Copperheads** — northerners (mostly Democrats) who supported the southern cause; they were strongest in Ohio, Indiana, and Illinois. Former Ohio congressman Clement L. Vallandigham was the most notorious Copperhead. Many of Lincoln's arbitrary arrests were directed against this group.

★ **Cotton Diplomacy** — a failed southern strategy to embargo cotton from England until Great Britain recognized and assisted the Confederacy; southerners hoped the economic pressure resulting from Britain's need for cotton for its textile factories would force Britain to aid the South. But direct aid was never forthcoming.

★ **Dred Scott decision (1857)** — Chief Justice Roger Taney led a pro-slavery Supreme Court to uphold the extreme southern position on slavery; his ruling held that Scott was not a citizen (nor were any African Americans), that slavery was protected by the Fifth Amendment and could expand into all territories, and that the Missouri Compromise was unconstitutional.

★ **Emancipation Proclamation** — executive order issued January 1, 1863, granting freedom to all slaves in states that were in rebellion; Lincoln issued it using his constitutional authority as commander-in-chief, as a military measure to weaken the South's ability to continue the war. It did not affect the Border States or any region under northern control on January 1. However, it was a stepping stone to the Thirteenth Amendment.

★ **Fifteenth Amendment (1870)** — granted black males the right to vote and split former abolitionists and women's rights supporters, who wanted women included as well.

★ **Fourteenth Amendment (1868)** — granted citizenship to any person born or naturalized in the United States; this amendment protects citizens from abuses by state governments, and ensures due process and equal protection of the law. It overrode the Dred Scott decision.

★ **Freedmen's Bureau** — a U.S. government-sponsored agency that provided food, established schools, and tried to redistribute land to former slaves as part of Radical Reconstruction; it was most effective in education, where it created over 4,000 schools in the South.

★ **George McClellan** — Union general who was reluctant to attack Lee because of military/political reasons; his timidity prompted Lincoln to fire him twice during the war. He ran unsuccessfully for president against Lincoln in 1864 on an antiwar platform.

★ **Harriet Beecher Stowe** — author of *Uncle Tom's Cabin*, a best selling novel about the cruelty of slavery; often called the greatest propaganda novel in United States history, the book increased tension between sections and helped bring on the Civil War.

★ **James Buchanan** — weak, vacillating president of the United States, 1857–1861; historians rate him as a failure for his ineffective response to secession and the formation of the Confederacy in 1860 and 1861.

★ **Jefferson Davis** — president of the Confederate States of America; a leading southern politician of the 1850s, he believed slavery essential to the South and held that it should expand into the territories without restriction. He served as U.S. senator from Mississippi (1847–1851, 1857–1861) and secretary of war (1853–1857) before becoming president of the Confederate States of America (1861–1865). After the war, he served two years in prison for his role in the rebellion.

★ **John Breckinridge** — vice president under James Buchanan and Democratic presidential nominee in 1860 who supported slavery and states' rights; he split the Democratic vote with Stephen Douglas and lost the election to Lincoln. He served in Confederate army and as secretary of war.

★ **John Brown** — violent abolitionist who murdered slaveholders in Kansas and Missouri (1856–1858) before his raid at Harpers Ferry (1859), hoping to incite a slave rebellion; he failed and was executed, but his martyrdom by northern abolitionists frightened the South.

* **John Fremont** — explorer, soldier, politician, and first presidential nominee of the Republican Party (1856); his erratic personal behavior and his radical views on slavery made him controversial and unelectable.

* **Ku Klux Klan** — terrorist organization active throughout the South during Reconstruction and after, dedicated to maintaining white supremacy; through violence and intimidation, it tried to stop freedmen from exercising their rights under the Fourteenth and Fifteenth Amendments.

* **Radical Republicans** — Republican faction in Congress who demanded immediate emancipation of the slaves at the war's beginning; after the war, they favored racial equality, voting rights, and land distribution for the former slaves. Lincoln and Johnson opposed their ideas as too extreme.

* **Robert E. Lee** — highly regarded Confederate general who was first offered command of the Union armies but declined; Lee was very successful until he fought against Ulysses S. Grant in 1864 and 1865. He surrendered the Army of Northern Virginia to Grant on April 9, 1865, to end major fighting in the war.

* **Scalawags** — white southerners who cooperated with and served in Reconstruction governments; generally eligible to vote, they were usually considered traitors to their states.

* **Ten-percent plan** — reconstruction plan of Lincoln and Johnson; when 10 percent of the number of voters in 1860 took an oath of allegiance, renounced secession, and approved the Thirteenth Amendment, a southern state could form a government and elect congressional representatives. The plan involved no military occupation and provided no help for freedmen. It was rejected by Radical Republicans in December 1865.

* **Tenure of Office Act (1867)** — Radical attempt to further diminish Andrew Johnson's authority by providing that the president could not remove any civilian official without Senate approval; Johnson violated the law by removing Edwin Stanton as secretary of war, and the House of Representatives impeached him over his actions.

* **Thaddeus Stevens** — uncompromising Radical Republican who wanted to revolutionize the South by giving equality to blacks; a leader in the impeachment of Andrew Johnson, he hoped for widespread land distribution to former slaves.

* **Thirteenth Amendment (1865)** — abolished slavery everywhere in the United States.

* **Ulysses S. Grant** — hard-fighting Union general whose relentless pursuit of Robert E. Lee finally brought the war to an end in April 1865; elected president in 1868, he presided over two disappointing and corrupt terms and is considered a failure as president.

★ **Wade-Davis Bill (1864)** — harsh Congressional Reconstruction bill that provided the president would appoint provisional governments for conquered states until a majority of voters took an oath of loyalty to the Union; it required the abolition of slavery by new state constitutions, the disenfranchisement of Confederate officials, and the repudiation of Confederate debt. Lincoln killed the bill with a pocket veto.

★ **William Seward** — Lincoln's secretary of state and previously his chief rival for the Republican nomination in 1860; however, his comments about the Fugitive Slave Law and "irrepressible conflict" made him too controversial for the nomination. As secretary of state, he worked to buy Alaska from Russia.

HIGH*lights* of the Period

Ideas to Ponder

After reviewing the chapter's summary, highlights, and your primary text, discuss the following with members of your study group.

1. How did "Bleeding Kansas" show the problems with popular sovereignty in settling the slavery issue in the territories?

2. How did the attack on Charles Sumner in 1856 demonstrate the violence associated with the slavery debate?

3. How did the Dred Scott decision and John Brown's raid further divide the nation?

4. Was James Buchanan a failure as president? Defend your answer.

5. Why did Lincoln make sure that the South fired the first shot of the Civil War?

6. Why were the Border States so important to Lincoln in reuniting the nation?

7. What advantages did each side have at the beginning of the war?

8. "If the North and South had exchanged presidents, the South would have achieved its independence." Do you agree or disagree with this statement? Explain.

9. How did the war destroy the political principles upon which the Confederacy was founded?

10. Select two battles as military turning points of the war. Defend your choices.

11. "Abraham Lincoln should have been impeached for his violation of civil liberties during the war." Do you agree or disagree with this statement? Explain.

12. Was Lincoln's death a greater blow to the South's future than it was to the North's? Why or why not?

13. What mistakes did Andrew Johnson make in dealing with the Radical Republicans?

14. How did the South's actions in 1865 undercut Presidential Reconstruction?

15. How did the Radical Republicans take control of Reconstruction?

16. Did Andrew Johnson deserve to be impeached? Explain why or why not.

17. Was Ulysses Grant a failure as president? Explain.

18. What motivated the "scalawags" and "carpetbaggers" during Reconstruction?

19. In what ways was Reconstruction a "tragic era" for America?

20. Was Samuel Tilden cheated out of the presidency in 1876? Explain why or why not.

Essay Skill

Creating Categories to Answer Essay Questions

Earlier in the book, you worked on analyzing essay prompts and deciding which question/statement to write about on the examination. This process asked you to identify various directive words, and list the facts you believed were most useful in answering the question/statement. A related skill is using directive words in the prompt to create categories that facts can be sorted into and used to organize and defend a thesis statement.

In creating categories to answer an essay prompt, you should look first for the obvious. That is, you should analyze the statement/question carefully and identify clues about useful categories that are apparent from the prompt. A common type of question/statement may ask students to explain the political, social, and economic developments for a historical event or phenomenon. By simply breaking down the statement/question into these elements, you will have an effective framework from which to write your answer.

Other types of prompts may call on students to deal with time frames, geographic analysis, and topical/thematic issues. For example, you could be asked to link the events of the 1850s to the events of the secessionist crisis of 1860–1861. Here, you would create two time frames—one for the events of 1850–1859 and another for 1860–1861. Another possible prompt would be one that asked students to evaluate the advantages that North and South each possessed at the beginning of the Civil War. In this instance, you would sort facts into a category for the northern advantages at the outset of the conflict and another for southern advantages. In another case, you might be asked to develop thematic categories to address the issues raised by a prompt. You might confront a statement/question about the war's impact on political rights in the North. Here, you would create categories about the suppression of speech, assembly, and trial by jury under Lincoln's administration. To summarize, when looking for categories, you should read the prompt very carefully because it contains the guide for structuring an essay answer.

Practicing the Skill

Below you will find five essay prompts about the Civil War and Reconstruction. After reading each one carefully, establish the categories that would be appropriate in constructing an answer. Discuss your categories with your classmates or with members of your study group. At some point, you should look at page 225 in the Suggested Responses section for some suggested categories.

1. "A blundering political generation from 1845 to 1860 brought on the secessionist crisis in 1860–1861."

Assess the validity of the statement.

Categories:

1. _____

2. _____

3. _____

Essay Skill

2. "Abraham Lincoln fought the Civil War to incorporate the ideals of the Declaration of Independence into the Constitution."

Assess the validity of the statement with references to Lincoln's purpose in fighting the war from 1861 to 1865.

Categories:

1. _____

2. _____

3. _____

4. _____

3. "The Radical Republican plan of reconstruction revolutionized the social, economic, and political relations of America."

Assess the validity of the statement.

Categories:

1. _____

2. _____

3. _____

4. "Southern leadership strengths during the Civil War were military rather than political."

Assess the validity of the statement.

Categories:

1. _____

2. _____

3. _____

5. To what extent did the concepts of popular sovereignty and the compact theory of government cause the Civil War?

Categories:

1. _____

2. _____

3. _____

Document SKILL

Using Charts and Documents Together

To write an effective DBQ answer, students must analyze and use all or most of the sources available on the examination. This means including not only documents, but information from charts as well. Charts are common among the eight-to-ten sources on the DBQ. Students must be able to extract information from both charts and documents and incorporate the data into their DBQ answer. In this section, you will practice taking information from these two types of sources and writing a partial answer to an essay prompt.

Below are two sources on southern Reconstruction governments—a chart of state constitutional conventions, 1867–1868, and a report by James Pike on the South Carolina legislature in 1868. In analyzing the chart, you should see that:

- Except in South Carolina, African Americans did not represent a majority in the conventions;
- "Negro domination" of the process was a myth;
- "Carpetbaggers" were a minority in every convention except Mississippi;
- Whites were in the majority in every convention except South Carolina.

In reading Pike, you should understand that he:

- looked at one state—South Carolina;
- found black domination in legislature—although the chart counters that this was rule throughout South;
- believed blacks understood debate and looked after their interests;
- saw blacks had trouble with legislative procedures;
- found underneath the "shocking burlesque" of legislative procedures, that liberty was stirring.

★ (Sample) Document A

Membership of State Conventions, 1867–68							
State	Black	%	White Native	%	Northern	%	Total Members
Alabama	18	17%	59	55%	31	28%	108
Arkansas	8	13%	35	52%	23	35%	66
Florida	18	40%	12	27%	15	33%	45
Georgia	33	19%	128	74%	9	7%	170
Louisiana	49	50%	*	*	*	*	98
Mississippi	17	17%	29	29%	54	54%	100
N. Carolina	15	11%	100	75%	18	14%	133
S. Carolina	76	61%	27	22%	21	17%	124
Virginia	25	24%	33	31%	47	45%	105
Texas	9	10%	*	*	*	*	90
* information not available							

★ (Sample) Document B

> *The blacks outnumber the whole body of whites in the House more than three to one. On the mere basis of numbers in the State the injustice of this . . . is manifest since the black population is relatively four to three of the whites. A just correction of the disproportion, on the basis of population, merely, would give fifty-four whites to seventy black members. . . .*
>
> *One of the first things that strike a casual observer in this negro assembly is the fluency of debate . . . The leading topics of discussion are well understood by the members. . . . When an appropriation bill is up to raise money to catch and punish the Kuklux [sic], they know exactly what it means. . . . The [Negro legislator] will speak half a dozen times on one question, and every time say the same things without knowing it. He answers completely to the description of a stupid speaker in Parliament. . . .*
>
> *But underneath all this shocking burlesque upon legislative proceedings, we must not forget that there is something very real to this uncouth and untutored multitude. . . . Seven years ago these men were raising corn and cotton under the whip of the overseer. Today they are raising points of order and questions of privilege. They find they can raise one as well as the other. They prefer the latter. . . . It means liberty. . . .*
>
> —James Pike, *The Prostrate South*

With these sources and outside information, a paragraph was constructed as a partial answer to the following prompt:

> "To what extent did the participation of African Americans revolutionize southern politics from 1865 to 1877?"

★ Sample Paragraph

> As a result of the Thirteenth, Fourteenth, and Fifteenth Amendments, a significant number of black men participated in the new southern governments. They were active in creating the new state constitutions mandated under Radical Reconstruction, but they did not dominate the process. (Doc. A) Furthermore, while observers such as James Pike found a "shocking burlesque upon legislative proceedings" in South Carolina, he also saw that blacks were able to understand the debate and were working toward greater liberty. (Doc. B)

Document SKILL

The paragraph, using data from the chart, Pike's report, and outside information, demonstrated the limited but complex role that African Americans played in certain phases of Reconstruction politics. The chart helps temper the impression of "Negro rule" in the South suggested by the early part of Pike's report and could be addressed elsewhere in the answer.

Practicing the Skill

Look at the table and document below, extract information from each, and write one paragraph that would be a **partial** answer to the prompt. After you have compared your answer with classmates or members of your study group look at page 225 in the Suggested Responses section for suggested ideas that might be included in your paragraph.

★ Document A

> It is a fact well known to every intelligent Southerner that we are compelled to go to the North for almost every article of utility and adornment, from matches, shoepegs, and painting up to cotton mills, steamships and statuary, that we have not foreign trade, no princely merchants, nor respectable artists. . . . Whilst the free states retain not only the larger proportion of those born within their own limits, but induce, annually, hundreds of thousands of foreigners to settle and remain amongst them . . . owning to the absence of a proper system of business amongst us, the North becomes in one way or another, the proprietor and dispenser of all our floating wealth. . . .
>
> —Hinton Helper, *The Impending Crisis*

★ Document B

Region	Persons in Manufacturing		Urban Population as % of Total Population of Region	
	1850	1860	1850	1860
Northeast States	574,307	734,134	27.2%	36.0%
North Central States	86,834	143,055	9.7%	13.8%
Southern States	59,154	68,960	7.0%	8.7%

Information from Document A:

_____

_____

_____

_____

_____

_____

_____

_____

Information from Document B:

_____

_____

_____

_____

_____

_____

_____

_____

Document SKILL

Using the information from the documents and your knowledge, write a paragraph for the prompt:

"Discuss the impact of slavery on the economic and social life of the South from 1850 to 1860."

_____

_____

_____

_____

_____

_____

_____

_____

_____

_____

_____

_____

Chapter 9

AMERICA TRANSFORMED

1865–1900

Focus Questions

★ How did the actions of the federal government open the West to settlement after the Civil War?

★ How did industrialization and urbanization change economic and social relationships in America in the last half of the nineteenth century?

★ How did industrialization transform the role of the government in American society after the Civil War?

★ How did farmers and workers try to improve their quality of life between 1865 and 1890?

★ How did the promise of equality for African Americans turn into the inequality of Jim Crow?

Summary

From the end of the Civil War to the turn of the century, Americans headed west and the population of the western states and territories exploded. The federal government encouraged this migration by practically giving away land (**Homestead Act**), building the **Transcontinental Railroad**, and subduing the Plains Indians. While some people who headed west took up mining and ranching, for million of setters farming remained the American Dream. However, these farmers faced a world far different from the agrarian conditions that existed before the war. They specialized in a cash crop, marketed their produce by railroad, bought costly planting and harvesting equipment, and borrowed heavily. By the 1890s, many farmers were demoralized and alienated by overproduction, falling prices, crushing debt, and exploitations by the railroads.

Indian Policy

The Plains Indians were seen as the greatest obstacle to westward expansion. The United States government took measures to eliminate this barrier by forcing Native Americans onto reservations. From 1865 to 1890, the two groups engaged in intermittent warfare highlighted by Custer's Last Stand, Chief Joseph's odyssey, and the battle at Wounded Knee. The government realized that the key to controlling Native Americans was destroying the buffalo, and over 15 million bison were slaughtered between 1865 and 1890. When the buffalo vanished, Indians were forced onto reservations, where, under the **Dawes Act**, tribal land ownership was abolished and a further erosion of Indian culture occurred.

Industrialization

The years after the Civil War witnessed explosive industrial growth as well. In 1869, there were 2 million factory workers; by 1899 that number more than doubled to 4.7 million. Moreover, the nation, which produced 20,000 tons of steel in 1867, was generating ten million tons a year by 1900. **John D. Rockefeller** and **Andrew Carnegie** created vast monopolies known as trusts. By 1900, just 1 percent of American corporations controlled 33 percent of all manufacturing output. With this power, these "robber barons" amassed great fortunes. For example, 1 percent of American families controlled 88 percent of the nation's assets in 1900.

These powerful businessmen subscribed to **Social Darwinism**. They explained their wealth by applying Darwin's theory of "survival of the fittest" to their business activities. Rockefeller and others said the natural order of competition rewarded them with power and wealth. They warned that labor unions and government regulations were disruptive to this ordering of human affairs and should be avoided at all cost.

Workers Organize

Industrialization produced a growing urban working class. Fueled by the arrival of 25 million immigrants from 1865 to 1915, factory and service workers grew to 51 percent of the labor force by the turn of the century. This "**new immigration**" flooded into the cities, and by 1900, some 40 percent of the U.S. population lived in an urban area. These workers toiled long hours for low pay and faced hazardous working conditions. Among their ranks were many women (17 percent of the labor force by 1900) and children (1.7 million child workers in 1900). Increasingly, workers realized their need to organize to improve their lives and future.

Unions faced many challenges, however, and by 1900, only 4 percent of workers were organized. Unions such as the **Knights of Labor** were labeled radical because they advocated abolishing the wage system. The **American Federation of Labor** was criticized as elitist because it only accepted skilled workers. In addition, the violence of the national railway strike (1877), the **Haymarket Riot** (1886), the **Homestead Strike** (1892), and the **Pullman Strike** (1894) reinforced the public perception that unions disrupted the domestic tranquility. Governments, at all levels, sided with management against labor. Officials issued injunctions to force workers back to work, arrested their leaders (**Eugene v. Debs**), and sent troops to break their strikes.

*F*armers and the Populists

From 1868 to 1896, the two political parties were evenly divided. Although the Republicans dominated the White House, the elections were closely contested. The Republicans counted on northern Protestants, prairie farmers, African Americans, and Union army veterans for support. Their platform included waving the **Bloody Shirt** and supporting high tariffs, railroad construction, the **spoils system**, and the gold standard. The Democrats, trying to recover from their association with the Civil War, elected **Grover Cleveland** to nonconsecutive terms as president during this era. They depended on the **Solid South**, immigrants, Catholics, and urban dwellers for their votes. Their platform defended states' rights, low tariffs, the gold standard, and the spoils system.

The **Credit Mobilier** and other scandals in Ulysses Grant's second term soured the nation on politicians and made honesty in government the dominant issue for a generation after the war. Finally, with the assassination of President James Garfield in 1881, Congress passed the **Pendleton Act**, which struck a blow against the spoils system. After Grant, every presidential candidate was scrutinized for his political and personal integrity. In addition, the nation debated "**free silver**," tariff reduction, and government regulations of trusts. The two parties agreed in general on what to do—or not to do—about these issues, with the exception of President Cleveland's attempt to lower the tariff in 1887.

Farmers grew increasingly disillusioned with the major parties. They suffered as food prices fell by 33 percent from 1865 to 1898. Farmers blamed their hardships on the gold standard, which both parties supported. They also saw no political will to confront the power of the railroads and bankers. This growing resentment against the political establishment gave rise to the **Granger Movement** (1870s), the Farmers' Alliance (1880s), and the **Populist Party** (1890s). The Populists called for free silver, regulation of railroads, a graduated income tax, immigration restrictions, and direct election of the United States Senate. Their candidate for president in 1892, **James Weaver**, garnered over one million votes and twenty-two electoral votes in six states.

The 1890s were a tumultuous decade, with the Populists providing the political sparks and the nation suffering through its deepest depression of the century. The economic problems gave ominous meaning to the Populists' rising power, and **Coxey's Army** frightened many people into believing the country was on the verge of social disintegration. The Democrats were discredited by the Depression of 1893, and in 1896, the western wing of the party nominated **William Jennings Bryan** on a "**free silver**" platform. Although the Populists joined the Democrats, Bryan went down to defeat under the weight of his economic ideas and the well-financed campaign of **William McKinley**.

*J*im Crow

Driven by the Compromise of 1877, the death of most Radical Republicans, and a conservative Supreme Court, the promise of equality for African Americans melted into the inequality of the South's **Jim Crow laws**. Redeemers gained control throughout the South and created the myth of "separate but equal" for race relations. In **Plessy v. Ferguson** (1896), the Supreme Court endorsed the Jim Crow system and made "separate but equal" the law of the land for the next fifty-eight years.

HIGH*lights* of the Period

★ **Andrew Carnegie** — Scottish-born industrialist who developed the U.S. steel industry; his is a rags-to-riches story as he made a fortune in business and sold his holdings in 1901 for $447 million. He spent the rest of his life giving away $350 million to worthy cultural and educational causes.

★ **Bloody Shirt** — Republican campaign tactic that blamed the Democrats for the Civil War; it was used successfully in campaigns from 1868 to 1876 to keep Democrats out of public office, especially the presidency.

★ **Coxey's Army (1894)** — unemployed workers led by Jacob Coxey who marched to Washington demanding a government road-building program and currency inflation for the needy; Coxey was arrested for stepping on grass at the Capitol and the movement collapsed.

★ **Credit Mobilier** — a major scandal in Grant's second term; a construction company, aided by members of Congress, bilked the government out of $20–40 million in building the transcontinental railroad. Members of Congress were bribed to cover up the overcharges.

★ **Dawes General Allotment Act (1887)** — abolished communal ownership on Indian reservations; each family head got 160 acres of reservation land; 80 acres for a single person; 40 acres for each dependent child. More than two-thirds of Indians' remaining lands were lost due to this law.

★ **Eugene V. Debs** — Labor leader arrested during the Pullman Strike (1894); a convert to socialism, Debs ran for president five times between 1900 and 1920. In 1920, he campaigned from prison where he was being held for opposition to American involvement in World War I.

★ **"Free silver"** — political movement to inflate currency by government issuance of $16 of silver for every $1 of gold in circulation; it was supported by farmers, who sought to counter declining crop prices and increase the money supply. It became a symbol of liberating poor farmers from the grasp of wealthy easterners.

★ **"Grandfather clause"** — laws in southern states that exempted voters from taking literacy tests or paying poll taxes if their grandfathers had voted as of January 1, 1867; it effectively gave white southerners the vote and disenfranchised African Americans.

★ **Granger Movement (National Grange of the Patrons of Husbandry) (1867)** — a farmers' organization and movement that started as a social/educational association; the Grange later organized politically to pass a series of laws to regulate railroads in various states.

★ **Grover Cleveland** — only Democrat elected to presidency from 1856 to 1912; he served two nonconsecutive terms; elected in 1884, losing in 1888, and winning again in 1892. His second term was marred by the Depression of 1893.

★ **Haymarket Riot (1886)** — violent incident at a workers' rally held in Chicago's Haymarket Square; political radicals and labor leaders called the rally to support a strike at the nearby McCormick Reaper works. When police tried to break it up, a bomb was thrown into their midst, killing 8 and wounding 67 others. The incident hurt the Knights of Labor and Governor John Altgeld, who pardoned some of the anarchist suspects.

★ **Homestead Act (1862)** — encouraged westward settlement by allowing heads of families to buy 160 acres of land for a small fee ($10–30); settlers were required to develop and remain on the land for five years. Over 400,000 families got land through this law.

★ **James B. Weaver** — former Civil War general who ran for president with the Greenback Party (1880) and the Populist Party (1892).

★ **Jim Crow laws** — series of laws passed in southern states in the 1880s and 1890s that segregated the races in many facets of life, including public conveyances, waiting areas, bathrooms, and theaters; it legalized segregation and was upheld as constitutional by *Plessy v. Ferguson*.

★ **John D. Rockefeller** — founder of Standard Oil Company; at one time his companies controlled 85–90 percent of refined oil in America. Standard Oil became the model for monopolizing an industry and creating a trust.

★ **Knights of Labor** — labor union founded in 1869 and built by Terence V. Powderly; the Knights called for one big union, replacement of the wage system with producers' cooperatives, and discouraged use of strikes. By 1886, they claimed membership of 700,000. Membership declined after the union's association with the Haymarket Riot of 1886.

★ **"New immigration"** — wave of immigration from the 1880s until the early twentieth century; millions came from southern and eastern Europe, who were poor, uneducated, Jewish, and Catholic. They settled in large cities and prompted a nativist backlash and, eventually, restrictions on immigration in the 1920s. These immigrants provided the labor force that allowed the rapid growth of American industry in the late 1800s and early 1900s.

★ **Pendleton Act (1883)** — reform passed by Congress that restricted the spoils system; passed in part in reaction to assassination of President Garfield by a disappointed office seeker in 1881, it established the U.S. Civil Service Commission to administer a merit system for hiring in government jobs.

★ *Plessy v. Ferguson* **(1896)** — Supreme Court case about Jim Crow railroad cars in Louisiana; the Court decided by 7 to 1 that legislation could not overcome racial attitudes, and that it was constitutional to have "separate but equal" facilities for blacks and whites.

★ **Populist Party (1892)** — a largely farmers' party aiming to inflate currency and to promote government action against railroads and trusts; it also called for a graduated income tax and immigration restrictions. Its platform was never enacted in the 1890s, but it became the basis of some Progressive reforms in the early twentieth century. It is also known as the Peoples Party.

★ **Samuel Gompers** — labor leader and president of American Federation of Labor, founded in 1886; Gompers believed that craft unionism would gain skilled workers better wages and working conditions. He emphasized support for capitalism and opposition to socialism.

★ **Sherman Anti-Trust Act (1890)** — first federal action against monopolies; the law gave government power to regulate combinations "in restraint of trade." Until the early 1900s, however, this power was used more often against labor unions than against trusts.

★ **Social Darwinism** — the application of Charles Darwin's theory of evolution to the business world; William Graham Sumner, a Yale professor, promoted these ideas and lobbied against any government regulation in society. Industrialists and social conservatives used these arguments to justify ruthless business tactics and widespread poverty among the working class.

★ **Stalwarts** — Republicans in the 1870s who supported Ulysses Grant and Roscoe Conkling; they accepted machine politics and the spoils system and were challenged by other Republicans called Half-Breeds, who supported civil service reform.

★ **Transcontinental railroad** — linked the nation from coast to coast in 1869; the Union Pacific Railroad built west from Omaha and the Central Pacific started east from Sacramento. The federal government supported construction with over $75 million in land grants, loans and cash.

★ **Tweed Ring** — scandal in New York City (1868–1871); William Marcy Tweed headed a corrupt Democratic political machine (Tammany Hall) that looted $100–200 million from the city. Crusading journalists and others pointed to this organization and its activities as another example of the need for social and political reform.

★ **William Jennings Bryan** — a spokesman for agrarian western values, 1896–1925, and three-time Democratic presidential candidate (1896, 1900, 1908); in 1896 his "Cross of Gold" speech and a free-silver platform gained support from Democrats and Populists, but he lost the election.

★ **William McKinley** — Republican president, 1897–1901, who represented the conservative Eastern establishment; he stood for expansion, high tariffs, and the gold standard. He led the nation during the Spanish-American War (1898) and was assassinated in 1901 by a radical political anarchist.

HIGH*lights* of the Period

Ideas to Ponder

After reviewing the chapter's summary, highlights, and your primary text, discuss the following with members of your study group.

1   How did the frontier act as a "safety valve" for Americans after the Civil War?

2   How did farms begin to resemble factories in the 1880s and 1890s?

3   How did the Grange lead the way in changing the government's role in American society?

4   How did the battle over currency standards define politics after the Civil War?

5   How did the Populist Party reflect deep dissatisfaction among many Americans with their government?

6   How did American Indian policy from 1865 to 1890 complete a "century of dishonor" toward Native Americans?

7   What real differences were there between Democrats and Republicans from 1868 to 1892?

8   Why was "waving the Bloody Shirt" so effective for Republicans after the Civil War?

9   How were trusts a blessing and a curse for America?

10 Did the Gospel of Wealth remove the label of "robber barons" from the industrialists? Explain why or why not.

11 Why were the railroads the first industry to face government regulation?

12 How did the Depression of 1893 reveal major flaws in governmental policies during an economic crisis?

13 How was the nativism of the 1890s a continuation of past attitudes in America?

14 What factors contributed to the "betrayal of blacks" from 1877 to 1900?

15 How did *Plessy v. Ferguson* validate and perpetuate the Jim Crow system?

16 How was the election of 1896 a turning point in American politics?

Essay Skill

Supporting Your Thesis

In writing an answer to an essay prompt, students must offer more than opinions and generalizations about the historical topic. An opinion is a belief or impression that is not based on certainty or knowledge. Opinions are often expressed as vague generalities that treat issues in a global fashion. Students who write this way appear not to have the knowledge and information necessary to deal with a prompt. They will not convince their teacher or an AP reader of the strength of their answer by supporting a thesis with personal opinion or generalizations. (You will recall that a "thesis" is a proposition to be proved.)

In order to score high on both the DBQ and the free-response essays, you must provide specific and appropriate factual information in defending your thesis and supporting your topic sentences within the paper. Often, on the AP examination, students write only opinions and generalizations in support of their thesis and fail to cite concrete evidence that proves their assertions. By using specific information, you establish creditability as someone who understands the importance and significance of the historical problems posed by the prompt. You cannot do this with unsubstantiated opinion and vague generalities.

Look at the essay prompt below, its thesis statement, and the three statements used to support the thesis. The first sentence is factual and provides solid information about the factors that led to the Jim Crow system of inequality. The second statement is a generalization about the period after the war and offers an impression without specific references to the actual events. The third statement is a personal opinion about the behavior of African Americans in the years 1870–1890.

> "For African Americans, the ideals of the Declaration of Independence were an unrealized dream."

Assess the validity of the statement from 1870 to 1900.

Thesis statement: From 1870 to 1900, African Americans were promised equal justice, due process, and voting rights, but neither the North or the South kept this pledge.

Statement 1: The Compromise of 1877 and the removal of northern troops played a major role in the betrayal of African American rights after the Civil War.

Statement 2: The South took rights away from African Americans that were promised by Radical Republicans.

Statement 3: Blacks should have worked harder for their rights after the Civil War.

Practicing the Skill

Look at the two prompts below, their theses, and the three statements to support them. For each prompt, select the strongest statement in support of the thesis and explain why it is the most effective. After discussing your choices with your classmates or with the members of your study group, look at page 226 in the Suggested Responses section for suggested answers and the rationale for the choices.

1. "The industrialists of the last quarter of the nineteenth century were visionaries rather than 'robber barons.'"

Assess the validity of this statement.

Thesis: The industrialists advanced America economically, but their greed gave them a deserved reputation for lawlessness and ruthlessness. (negative thesis statement)

Statement 1: Industrialists such as John D. Rockefeller and Andrew Carnegie did many good things and some bad things, but generally, they helped America become great.

Statement 2: Men such as John D. Rockefeller and Andrew Carnegie should have shared their money with more people, including their workers.

Statement 3: The trusts created by Rockefeller and Carnegie made America competitive internationally, but they exploited their workers and the American public.

The best choice is No._____ because:

_____

_____

_____

2. "While the Populists in the 1890s identified many abuses in American life, they offered unacceptable solutions for correcting them."

Assess the validity of this statement.

Thesis: Farmers in the 1890s realized that America needed to reform, but their call for massive government actions and free silver kept them out of power.

Statement 1: Farmers were really hurting in the 1890s, and the Populists wanted to help them, but they went about it in the wrong way.

Statement 2: The Populist ideas of income taxes, immigration restrictions, and government ownership of utilities were popular with some people but were too radical for most voters.

Statement 3: The Populist Party was really stupid to join up with the Democrats in 1896 because Bryan did not know what he was doing.

The best choice is No._____ because:

_____

_____

_____

Document SKILL

Using Cartoons and Documents Together

In an earlier part of the book, you were introduced to the process of cartoon analysis. At that time, the goal was extracting meaning from a drawing. In this section, you will engage in a more challenging activity—taking information from a cartoon and incorporating it into an essay answer. Remember that cartoons are historical sources just like documents and are commonly used as evidence on DBQ essays. For these reasons, students must be able to determine a cartoon's meaning and use it along with other documents to support a position on a DBQ.

Below are a cartoon and a document about politics in the last decade of the nineteenth century. Both offer opinions about the relative importance of corruption in government as a political issue. In addition to the sources, there is a prompt that asks students to evaluate the role honesty played in the political process of the era and why the issue was important to the electorate. A thesis statement concerning the prompt is proposed, along with a sample paragraph that offers an example of how a cartoon and document can be used in a paragraph as a partial answer for the problem. Notice that in the paragraph, information is drawn from both sources to support the writer's thesis.

Study the information lists, the prompt, the thesis, and the paragraph and discuss them with your classmates or members of your study group. You should focus on how the two sources were used to address the prompt.

"How did politicians live under the shadow of Ulysses Grant's presidency from 1876 to 1896?"

Thesis: The scandals of the Grant administration made honesty in government a dominant political issue for an entire generation.

★ (Sample) Document A

THE "GREAT AMERICAN" GAME OF PUBLIC OFFICE FOR PRIVATE GAIN.
This is not "Protection"; this is very "Free Trade" with the people's money.

★ (Sample) Document B

> *Everybody is talking these days about Tammany men growing rich on graft, but nobody thinks of drawing the distinction between honest graft and dishonest graft. There's all the difference in the world between the two. Yes, many of our men have grown rich in politics. I have myself. I've made a big fortune out of the game and I'm getting richer every day, but I've not gone in for dishonest graft—blackmailing gamblers, saloon-keepers, disorderly people, etc.—and neither has any of the men who have made big fortunes in politics.*
>
> *. . . My party's in power in the city, and it's going to undertake a lot of public improvements. Well, I, tipped off, . . . I see my opportunity and I take it. I go to the place and I buy up all the land I can in the neighborhood. . . . Ain't it perfectly honest to charge a good price and make a profit on my investment and foresight? Of course it is. Well that's honest graft.*
>
> —from George Plunkitt, "How I Got Rich by Honest Graft"

In analyzing the cartoon a student should see that:

- Blaine tried to present himself as the "Plumed Knight," a crusader and a reformer;
- The cartoon is satirizing this view of Blaine;
- Blaine had a history of corruption;
- Blaine was trying to mislead the people;
- He had a fake horse, lance, and breast plate;
- Blaine had taken money from railroads;
- Some saw politics as a game of seeking riches and private interest.

In analyzing the document, a student should see that Plunkitt believed:

- It was okay to use public office for private gain;
- Honest graft did not have specific victims;
- Dishonest graft did hurt specific people;
- Some officials practiced dishonest graft by taking payoffs from saloon keepers and gamblers, etc;
- Using political office to gain advantage and insider information was fine;
- It is the American way to see your opportunities and take them;
- Using insider information is not dishonest; it is using foresight.

Document **SKILL**

★ Sample Paragraph

> After the scandals of the 1870s, the voters demanded honesty from their political leaders. When James Blaine ran in 1884, he was portrayed as faker who tried to fool the people into believing he was a crusader or "Plumed Knight." In fact, he had used his office for private gain. (Doc. A) Moreover, some political bosses tried to justify their misdeeds by saying there was a difference between honest graft, which involved using insider information and did not hurt anyone specifically, and dishonest graft, practiced by those officials who took payoffs from saloon keepers and gamblers. (Doc. B) The voters rejected this distinction and demanded politicians protect the public interest rather than enrich themselves.

Practicing the Skill

Below you will find a prompt, a cartoon, and a document about the election of 1896. As a class, or as part of your study group, complete an information list from each source and write a paragraph that partially addresses the prompt using some outside information and data from the cartoon and the document. At some point, you should look on page 226 in the Suggested Responses section for a suggested list of information.

> In 1896, William McKinley was presented as the solid statesman and William Jennings Bryan as the radical upstart. To what extent was this a fair description of the two men?

★ Document A

★ Document B

> *You come to us and tell us that the great cities are in favor of the gold standard; we reply that the great cities rest upon our broad and fertile prairies. Burn down your cities and leave our farms, and your cities will spring up again as if by magic; but destroy our farms and the grass will grow in the streets of every city in the country . . .*
>
> *. . . If they dare to come out in the open field and defend the gold standard as a good thing, we will fight them to the uttermost. Having behind us the producing masses of this nation and the world supported by the commercial interests, the laboring interests and the toilers everywhere, we will answer their demand for a gold standard by saying to them: You shall not press down upon the brow of labor this crown of thorns, you shall not crucify mankind upon a cross of gold.*
>
> —from William Jennings Bryan,
> speech at Democratic National Convention, 1896

The cartoon shows that:

* _____

* _____

* _____

* _____

The document shows that:

* _____

* _____

* _____

* _____

Your thesis:

_____

_____

Document SKILL

Your paragraph:

_____

_____

_____

_____

_____

_____

_____

_____

_____

_____

_____

_____

Chapter **10**

AMERICA AND THE WORLD

1865–1919

Focus Questions

★ Why did the United States expand overseas in the 1870s and 1880s?

★ How did the United States become a dominant power in the Caribbean and South America after the Civil War?

★ How was the war with Spain in 1898 the culmination of a "new Manifest Destiny" of the 1880s and 1890s?

★ How did the Spanish-American War transform American policy toward South America and the Far East?

★ How did the United States become embroiled in World War I in 1917?

★ Why did the United States Senate reject U.S. membership in the League of Nations and refuse to ratify the Treaty of Versailles?

Summary

For two decades after the Civil War, the nation looked inward. Involved with westward expansion, railroad building, political scandals, and economic dislocation, America was insular and mostly self-contained. Secretary of State **William Seward** did acquire Midway Island and purchase Alaska in 1867, however. Later, the United States took over part of the Samoan Islands (1889) and made an abortive attempt to annex Hawaii (1893). Overall, however, the nation was content to focus on domestic issues.

Expansion in the 1890s

Expansionist ideas began to build in the 1890s. A "New Manifest Destiny" swept the nation. Writers such as historian **John Fiske** and Congregational minister **Josiah Strong** promoted Anglo-Saxon superiority as a force to spread both civilization and Christianity throughout the world. In a different vein, **Alfred Thayer Mahan** linked sea power and expansion to domestic prosperity, national security, and international commerce. These ideas meshed with the upheavals brought on by the Populist movement and the Depression of 1893 to fuel "an outward impulse" for American foreign policy.

By the 1890s, the United States was a regional power focusing its expansionistic energies in the Caribbean area. In 1895, President Grover Cleveland rejuvenated the Monroe Doctrine when he pressured Great Britain to arbitrate a boundary dispute with Venezuela. At the same time, the United States became concerned about the Cuban rebellion against Spain. With fifty million dollars invested in the sugar industry, and appalled by the brutal tactics of **Valeriano Weyler** in attempting to crush the Cuban rebels, the United States demanded Spain end the turmoil on the island or grant Cuba its independence.

The "Splendid Little War"

President **William McKinley** wished to avoid armed intervention in Cuba, but in 1898, the **yellow journalism** of American newspapers was pushing the nation toward war. Further souring relations with Spain were the DeLome letter that criticized McKinley's leadership, and the mysterious destruction of the battleship *Maine* in Havana harbor in February 1898. By April, McKinley gave Spain an ultimatum—end the rebellion, set Cuba free, or face war with America. The Spanish government could not accept these terms, and on April 25, 1898, Congress authorized a declaration of war.

The Spanish-American War was a "splendid little war" for the United States. Lasting from April to August 1898, it cost only 460 American deaths and resulted in the United States acquiring an overseas empire. The war was popular with thousands of volunteers, such as **Theodore Roosevelt**, who happily went to Cuba to fight the Spanish. By December 1898, America and Spain completed the Treaty of Paris, in which Spain freed Cuba and ceded Guam, Puerto Rico, and the Philippine Islands to the United States for twenty million dollars.

Results of the War

The war had a downside, however. While the United States guaranteed Cuba's independence in the **Teller Amendment**, America controlled the island's domestic and foreign policy through the **Platt Amendment** for many years to come. And when the Filipinos, led by **Emilio Aguinaldo**, discovered they had exchanged Spanish colonial rule for American, a four-year rebellion ensued that cost 4,600 American lives and those of over 50,000 Filipinos. Many Americans believed these imperialistic actions violated the nation's principles of liberty, freedom, and justice.

The war changed American foreign policy dramatically. The United States tightened its control of the Caribbean region with Theodore Roosevelt's **Big Stick policy** and his **Roosevelt Corollary** to the Monroe Doctrine. Roosevelt warned Europe that Latin America was not only closed to colonization but that the United States would use its military might to police the region and enforce standards of proper behavior by all nations. His successor, William Taft, supported this approach with **Dollar Diplomacy**, which sought commercial dominance for the United States, minimized European interference, and protected the Panama Canal through America's economic and military power.

In Asia, America faced a different reality and followed a different policy. The United States wanted a piece of the vast China market, yet America was unable to flex its military power to open markets in China. With the other major powers already possessing spheres of influence throughout China, Secretary of State **John Hay** proposed cooperation among the nations. In 1899 and 1900, he issued two Open Door Notes, which called on all nations to maintain equal trading rights in China and respect its territorial integrity as well.

World War I

In 1914, a hundred years of European peace came to an end when Germany and the Central Powers challenged France and England for dominance in Europe. Sparked by the assassination of Franz Ferdinand in the summer of 1914, long-simmering nationalistic disputes and rivalries brought on the first general war in Europe since the time of Napoleon.

The United States declared its traditional policy of neutrality at the outset of the conflict. Within three years, however, America's favorable trade and financial policies towards the allies, Germany's treacherous **Zimmerman Note**, and the Germans' use of submarines as a blockade weapon brought American into the war on the side of the French and English. While President Woodrow Wilson hoped America could work as a neutral to achieve "a peace without victory," Germany's outrages against the United States forced the president on April 2, 1917, to ask Congress to go to war and "make the world safe for democracy."

America and its two million-man army turned the tide in favor of the allies in 1917–1918. Commanded by **John Pershing**, American troops repelled German offensives in the summer of 1918, and on November 11, 1918, Germany surrendered. The human cost of the war was staggering. The United States lost relatively few men (112,000), but the other major combatants suffered 6.4 million deaths in the four-year struggle.

Rejecting the League of Nations

The **Big Four** leaders gathered early in 1919 to settle the war issues. President Wilson wanted a **League of Nations** to preserve world peace. He hoped the treaty would adhere to his **Fourteen Points**, but the French and English demanded that Germany accept blame for causing the war and pay for its cost. The final version of the **Treaty of Versailles** was harsh toward Germany and far different from Wilson's vision, but he hoped the League would correct its punitive shortcomings in time.

Wilson faced a hostile Senate in July 1919, as he sought ratification of the treaty. Republican leaders opposed both the treaty and the League of Nations. **William Borah** and his "irreconcilables" believed the treaty compromised traditional American isolationism and opposed the pact under any circumstances. **Henry Cabot Lodge** and the "reservationists" accepted the League's idea of collective security but demanded more congressional control over America's role within the organization.

President Wilson, for many reasons, refused to compromise with his opponents and embarked on a cross-country campaign to put public pressure on the Senate to accept the treaty without changes. In September 1919, the tour ended tragically when Wilson suffered a paralytic stroke that left him incapacitated for six weeks as the Senate debated the treaty. Neither Wilson nor Lodge would budge in their position, and the Senate rejected the treaty. Wilson's dream of American participation in the League was never realized.

Treaty of Versailles Members of the Versailles Conference (L-R): Vittorio Emanuelle Orlando, Italy; David Lloyd-George, Great Britain; Georges Clemenceau, France; Woodrow Wilson, United States.

HIGH*lights*
of the Period

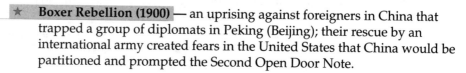

★ **Alfred Thayer Mahan** — naval officer, writer, teacher, and philosopher of the new imperialism of the 1890s; he stressed the need for naval power to drive expansion and establish America's place in the world as a great power.

★ **Big Four** — the leaders who constructed the Treaty of Versailles: Woodrow Wilson, Georges Clemenceau (France), David Lloyd George (Britain), and Vittorio Orlando (Italy)

★ **Big Stick policy** — Theodore Roosevelt's method for achieving American goals in the Caribbean; it featured the threat and use of military force to promote America's commercial supremacy, to limit European intervention in the region, and to protect the Panama Canal.

★ **Boxer Rebellion (1900)** — an uprising against foreigners in China that trapped a group of diplomats in Peking (Beijing); their rescue by an international army created fears in the United States that China would be partitioned and prompted the Second Open Door Note.

★ **Dollar Diplomacy** — President Taft's policy that encouraged American business and financial interests to invest in Latin American countries to achieve U.S. economic and foreign policy goals and maintain control; if problems persisted, the United States reverted to the Big Stick option of the Roosevelt administration, turning to military intervention and employment of force to restore stability and peace.

★ **Emilio Aguinaldo** — Filipino patriot who led a rebellion against both Spain and the United States from 1896 to 1902, seeking independence for the Philippines; his capture in 1901 helped break the resistance to American control of the islands.

★ **Fourteen Points (1918)** — Woodrow Wilson's vision for the world after World War I; it called for free trade, self-determination for all peoples, freedom of the seas, open diplomacy, and a League of Nations. Wilson hoped his Fourteen Points would be the basis for a negotiated settlement to end the war. However, they were not harsh enough on Germany for the other Allies to accept. Only a few of them were incorporated into the treaty.

★ **George Dewey** — naval hero of the Spanish-American War; his fleet defeated the Spanish at Manila Bay and gave the United States a tenuous claim to the Philippine Islands.

★ **Henry Cabot Lodge** — chairman of the Senate Foreign Relations Committee who accepted the Treaty of Versailles and membership in the League but demanded reservations to the League to maintain congressional authority in foreign affairs; Wilson's unwillingness to accept these conditions caused the Senate to reject the treaty.

★ **John Fiske** — historian and expansionist who argued that, with the superiority of its democracy, the United States was destined to spread over "every land on the earth's surface."

★ **John Hay** — secretary of state in the McKinley and Theodore Roosevelt administrations; he was the author of the Open Door Notes, which attempted to protect American interests in China in the early 20th century by asking European countries to pledge equal trading rights in China and the protection of its territory from foreign annexation.

★ **John Pershing** — American commander in France during World War I; his nickname of "Black Jack" resulted from his command of black troops earlier in his career. Before being dispatched to France, Pershing led an American incursion into Mexico in 1916 in a failed attempt to capture Mexican revolutionary Pancho Villa.

★ **Josiah Strong** — expansionist who blended racist and religious reasons to justify American expansion in the 1880s and 1890s; he saw the Anglo-Saxon race as trained by God to expand throughout the world and spread Christianity along the way.

★ *Lusitania* — British passenger liner sunk by a German submarine in May 1915; among the 1,200 deaths were 128 Americans. This was the first major crisis between the United States and Germany and a stepping-stone for American involvement in World War I.

★ **The *Maine*** — U.S. battleship sent to Havana in early 1898 to protect American interests; it blew up mysteriously in February 1898 killing 266 men. American newspapers blamed the Spanish, helping to cause the war. In 1976, it was discovered that the ship blew up accidentally.

★ **Pineapple Republic** — popular name for the government American sugar planters in Hawaii set up in 1894 after they, assisted by the U.S. ambassador there and Marines from a U.S. warship offshore, overthrew the Hawaiian monarch; the rebels immediately sought annexation by the United States, an action supported by many members of Congress. President Cleveland opposed it, and the islands remained independent until 1898, when Congress, with President McKinley's approval, made Hawaii a territory of the United States.

★ **Platt Amendment (1901)** — an amendment added to Cuba's constitution by the Cuban government, after pressure from the United States; it provided that Cuba would make no treaties that compromised its independence or granted concessions to other countries without U.S. approval. The amendment was abrogated in 1934.

★ **Roosevelt Corollary (1903)** — addendum to the Monroe Doctrine issued after the Dominican Republic got into financial trouble with several European nations; the United States assumed the right to intervene in Latin American countries to promote "civilized" behavior and protect American interests.

HIGH*lights*
of the Period

★ **Teller Amendment (1898)** — part of the declaration of war against Spain in which Congress pledged that Cuba would be freed and not annexed by the United States as a result of the conflict.

★ **Theodore Roosevelt** — assistant secretary of the navy, who headed a volunteer regiment in the Spanish-American War; nicknamed the Rough Riders by the press, the First Volunteer Cavalry consisted of Roosevelt's colorful friends from the West and his Harvard days. After the war, Roosevelt "rode" his Rough Riders image to the vice presidency and then the presidency of the United States.

★ **Treaty of Paris (1898)** — ended the Spanish-American War; under its terms, Cuba gained independence from Spain, and the United States acquired Guam, Puerto Rico, and the Philippines. The United States paid Spain twenty million dollars for the Philippines.

★ **Treaty of Versailles (1919)** — ended World War I; it was much harder on Germany than Wilson wanted but not as punitive as France and England desired. It was harsh enough, however, to set stage for Hitler's rise to power in Germany in 1930s.

★ **Valeriano Weyler** — Spanish governor in charge of suppressing the Cuban revolution, 1896–1898; his brutal "reconcentration" tactics earned him the nickname of the "Butcher" in America's yellow press.

★ **William Borah** — led a group of senators who were irreconcilably opposed to joining the League of Nations; he promoted ideals of traditional isolationism and believed the League was "an entangling foreign alliance."

★ **William McKinley** — president of the United States, 1897–1901; a reluctant expansionist, he led America during the Spanish-American War. His assassination in 1901 brought "that damn cowboy" Theodore Roosevelt to the presidency.

★ **William Seward** — secretary of state, 1861–1869; a dedicated expansionist, he purchased Alaska from Russia, acquired Midway Island, and tried to buy the Virgin Islands in 1867.

★ **Yellow journalism** — sensational newspaper stories from Joseph Pulitzer's *New York World* and William Randolph Hearst's *New York Journal* that stirred Americans against Spanish rule in Cuba; this media coverage proved a force for war in 1898.

★ **Zimmerman Note (1917)** — a secret German proposal to Mexico for an alliance against the United States; Germany offered to help Mexico get back territories it lost to the United States in 1848. Britain alerted the Wilson administration to the plan, and Mexico refused the idea.

HIGH*lights* of the Period

Ideas to Ponder

After reviewing the chapter's summary, highlights, and your primary text,
discuss the following with members of your study group.

1   How did the expansionist impulse of the 1890s compare with such ideas and events in the 1840s?

2   How was William Seward the father of the modern American empire?

3   How did the ideas of Frederick Jackson Turner encourage many Americans to look overseas for solutions to domestic problems?

4   Was the Spanish-American War inevitable? Explain your answer.

5   Why were the expansionists of the 1890s able to overcome anti-imperialist sentiment in the nation?

6   How were the Open Door Notes a diplomatic bluff by the United States?

7   Was the Big Stick policy short-sighted in promoting America's long-range interests in South America? Explain your answer.

8   How did the Philippine insurrection expose the flaws in the "New Manifest Destiny" of the 1890s?

9   Why was America's neutrality in the World War I an outdated foreign policy?

10 How could America have avoided war with Germany in 1917?

11 How was Woodrow Wilson a great wartime president but a poor peacemaking one?

12 Why was Woodrow Wilson unable to achieve "a peace without victory" at Versailles?

13 How could Woodrow Wilson have won his battle with the Senate over the treaty and the League of Nations?

14 How was Woodrow Wilson a man twenty years ahead of his time?

15 How was the treatment of black soldiers in the war a mockery to America's claim of strengthening democracy in the world?

Essay Skill

Dealing with All Aspects of the Statement or Question

In writing an answer to an essay prompt, you must address the entire scope of the statement or question. You should include all topics suggested by the prompt and survey the entire chronological period that is defined by the question. For example, a statement that calls for an evaluation of the economic, political, and social causes of American imperialism in the 1890s would require you to write about *all three* areas. Leaving out any one of them would reduce your grade, even if you did a great job on one or two parts of the prompt.

Similarly, if a question asked for an evaluation of United States-Latin American relations from 1898 to 1914 and you wrote brilliantly but only about the events from 1898 to 1902, you would not score high on the question. The grading standards would require you to deal with post–Spanish American war developments as well, and a partial treatment of the period would result in a low grade. A student must deal with every domain and the entire chronological period of an essay prompt in order to ensure a high score.

Practicing the Skill

Below are two essay prompts, their thesis statements, and several topic sentences that could be used to support each thesis statement. The first response is supported and defended by the suggested topic sentences. The second response has missing components and is not adequately developed. As a class or in your study group, examine both responses and discuss why the first response is adequately supported and what is missing in support of the second response. At some point look at page 227 of the Suggested Responses section for a discussion of the strengths and weaknesses of the two responses.

1. "How was the 'New Manifest Destiny' of the late 1800s an answer to the political and economic upheaval of the era?"

   Thesis statement: The turmoil caused by the Populist movement and the Depression of 1893 convinced many Americans that overseas expansion was necessary and justified.

   Topic sentence 1: The ideas of Josiah Strong, Alfred Mahan, and Albert Beveridge reflected the economic and political worries of the 1890s.

   Topic sentence 2: The Populist Party won over one million votes in the election of 1892 as it challenged the political status quo.

   Topic sentence 3: When the Populists called for free silver, they shook up Main Street and Wall Street.

   Topic sentence 4: The Depression of 1893 was the most severe of the nineteenth century, and it frightened both the rich and the poor.

   Topic sentence 5: The depression and the Populist movement convinced many people that overseas expansion would save capitalism and protect America's place in the world.

Essay Skill

2. " The principal reason America entered World War I was British propaganda rather than German actions and mistakes."

Assess the validity of this statement by reviewing events from 1914 to 1917.

Thesis statement: German violations of international law, rather than British propaganda, caused American entry into World War I. (negative thesis here)

Topic sentence 1: When England cut the Atlantic cable, it quickly took control of American public opinion about the war.

Topic sentence 2: Britain used Germany's invasion of Belgium to show the Kaiser's disregard for international law.

Topic sentence 3: German submarine warfare resulted in the deaths of 1,200 people on the British passenger ship *Lusitania*.

Topic sentence 4: German policies rather than English control of information were the main reasons the United States entered World War I.

Document SKILL

Arranging Sources into Categories

While extracting information from documents, charts, and cartoons is very important in the AP process, students must also be able to sort the information they uncover into useful patterns. In other words, you must be able to place sources into categories. A basic, yet important grouping system for information on the AP test is creating categories of support for, or opposition to, the thesis statement you intend to defend. On most DBQs, you will encounter six or seven positive sources and two or three items that challenge or even contradict the thrust of the prompt. Both types of sources must be identified and included when writing an essay answer.

After you have formulated your thesis, listed your outside information, and determined the meaning of the sources, you must place the data into categories of support (pro) or opposition (con). The quickest and most effective technique is to read the thesis carefully, examine each document, and place a plus sign (+) beside all sources that you plan to use in support of your position and a minus (−) along side all those that challenge the thesis. When the labeling is complete, you should make a chart (see the example below) and place the letters of the documents that support the thesis on the plus side (pro) and the letters of contrary documents on the minus side (con). You should list only the letter of the source and not try to write parts of the document into the chart. (Copying documents wastes too much time.) The chart will serve as a graphic organizer for the DBQ that can be expanded as you add outside information that supports or challenges the thesis.

Depending on the prompt, you will likely need to take the categorization process one step further. For example, once the sources have been sorted into pro and con, they may need to be divided into economic, political, and social events, or some specific categories that make the information more meaningful in answering the question. The first place to start categorizing sources, however, is to identify pro and con evidence.

Practicing the Skill

Below is a prompt about expansion in the 1890s, a suggested thesis statement, and four documents used as evidence in the answer. Each document has either a plus sign (+) or a minus sign (−) alongside it to indicate whether it supports or challenges some part of the thesis. In parentheses is a brief explanation of why the source was categorized either as pro or con. Discuss the four documents and their categorization rationale with your classmates or in your study group.

> "By the 1890s, most Americans realized the United States could not cling to its foreign policy past."

Assess the validity of this statement.

> **Thesis statement:** The expansionists of the 1890s realized America must look to the future rather than the past and accept a new international role.

> (This thesis is supported by sources that present the political, economic, and international benefits that expansion offered America. Sources that deal with the isolationist past would challenge the thesis.)

Document **SKILL**

★ (Sample) Document A

> (+) *Hawaii is the central point of the North Pacific. It is in, or near to, the direct track of commerce from all Atlantic ports, whether American or European. . . . It is the key to the whole system. . . . In the possession of the United States it will give us the command of the Pacific.*
>
> —The San Francisco *Evening Bulletin*, January 30, 1893

★ (Sample) Document B

> (−) *I regarded, and still regard [he said] the proposed annexation of these [the Hawaiian] islands as not only opposed to our national policy, but as a perversion of our national mission. The mission of our nation is to build up and make a greater country out of what we have, instead of annexing islands.*
>
> —*Letters of Grover Cleveland*

★ (Sample) Document C

> (−) *. . . The diplomatic service has outgrown its usefulness . . . It is a costly humbug and sham. It is a nurse of snobs. It spoils a few Americans every year, and does no good to anybody. Instead of making ambassadors, Congress should wipe out the whole service.*
>
> —*Public Opinion*, (February 9, 1889)

★ (Sample) Document D

> (+) *Manifest Destiny says, 'Take them[Hawaiian Islands] in.' The American people say, 'Take them in.' Obedient to the voice of the people, I shall cast my vote to take them in, and tomorrow this House of Representatives will by a good round majority say, 'Take them in.'*
>
> —*Congressional Record*, 55 Congress, 2nd session, appendix, p. 549

Document **SKILL**

Pro	Con
Document A	Document B
Document D	Document C

(Document A supports expansion for economic reasons. It describes the commercial benefits the Hawaiian Islands would bring. Document D shows how popular expansion was with the people and how it was a winning political issue. Document B opposes expansion because it goes against America's mission of building internally and avoiding world affairs. Document C opposes involvement in the world as it expresses the idea that the Foreign Service should be disbanded since it had no useful purpose and that the money could be spent more wisely elsewhere.)

Below are a prompt and a thesis statement about the struggle over the Treaty of Versailles. Read the four documents that offer support for the thesis or challenge some part of it, label each one (+) or (−), and place it into the chart provided. After you and your classmates or your study-group members have made your decisions, look on page 227 of the Suggested Responses section for an explanation of how the sources could be categorized.

Assess the role of Woodrow Wilson in preventing America from joining the League of Nations in 1919–1920.

Thesis statement: While Woodrow Wilson's refusal to compromise played a major role in keeping the United States out of the League of Nations, other factors contributed as well.

★ Document A

AMERICANS, AWAKE

( ) *Shall We Bind Ourselves to the War Breeding Covenant?*
   It Impairs American Sovereignty
   Surrenders the Monroe Doctrine!
   Flouts Washington's Warning!
   Entangles us in European and Asiatic Intrigues!
   Sends Our Boys to Fight Throughout the World by Order of a League!
   "The evil thing with a holy name."

   —*Boston Herald,* July 8, 1919

★ Document B

( ) . . . In my opinion . . . the Lodge resolution does not provide for ratification but rather, for the nullification of the treaty. I sincerely hope that the friends and supporters of the treaty will vote against the Lodge resolution of ratification. I understand that the door will probably then be open for a genuine resolution of ratification.

—Woodrow Wilson's letter to the Senate, November 19, 1919

★ Document C

( ) [Article 10] pledges us to guarantee the political independence and the territorial integrity against external aggression of every nation that is a league member. That is, every nation of the earth. We ask no guaranties, we have no endangered frontiers; but we are asked to guarantee the territorial integrity of every nation, practically, in the world—it will be when the League is complete. As it is today we guarantee the territorial integrity and political independence of every part of the far-flung British Empire. . . . We, under the clause of this treaty—it is one of the few that is perfectly clear—under that clause of the treaty we have got to take our army and our navy and go to war with any country which attempts aggression upon the territorial integrity of another member of the league.

—Henry Cabot Lodge speaks in Boston, March 19, 1919

★ Document D

( ) Either we should enter the league fearlessly, accepting the responsibility and not fearing the role of leadership which we now enjoy, contributing our efforts towards establishing a just and permanent peace, or we should retire as gracefully as possible from the great concert of powers by which the world was saved.

—Wilson's letter to the Senate, March 8, 1920

Document SKILL

Pro	Con

Chapter 11

PROGRESSIVE REFORMS AND THE 1920s

1900–1929

Focus Questions

★ How did local, state, and national governments attempt to solve problems of industrialization and urbanization through progressive reforms?

★ How did the 1920s become a struggle between reformers and the defenders of the status quo?

★ How were roles and expectations for women transformed from 1900 to 1929?

★ How did the "New Negro" emerge in America from 1900 to 1929?

★ How did Republican Party policies in the 1920s try to turn political and economic thinking back to the past?

★ How did opposition to immigration evolve into full-fledged discrimination from 1900 to 1929?

Summary

By 1900, America was a troubled nation. The urbanization and industrialization of the late nineteenth century damaged the country's social, economic, and political systems. Business competition all but vanished, governments served only the needs of the wealthy, and millions of people lived in economic deprivation. To combat these problems, progressive reformers stepped forward to change America. Growing out of the Populist Party's platform, the Mugwump revolt, and the Social Gospel movement, these middle-class reformers tried to restore equality and fairness to American society. Although made up primarily of politicians, progressives also included social workers such as **Jane Addams** and writers such as **Ida Tarbell**, **Lincoln Steffens**, and **Upton Sinclair**. These "muckrakers" exposed the injustices of society in order to bring solutions to a wide range of abuses.

Progressive Reformers

Early progressive reform occurred at the municipal and state level. Mayors such as Tom Johnson and Samuel "Golden Rule" Jones began to clean up their cities and make government more responsive to the people. On the state level, Hiram Johnson and **Robert La Follette** instituted direct primaries, initiative, and referendum in their states. As Wisconsin governor, La Follette developed a regulatory plan for railroads and utilities that was a model for the nation.

In Washington, Republican Theodore Roosevelt and Democrat **Woodrow Wilson** led a bipartisan drive to reform the nation. Operating around the 4 Cs of change: control of corporations, conservation of natural resources, citizen protection, and cleaning up government, these presidents harnessed the power of the federal government to correct problems. They created the **Federal Reserve System**, the Federal Trade Commission, and the Department of Commerce and Labor, and encouraged Congress to expand the national parks, to pass the **Pure Food and Drug Act**, and to enact national child labor laws. Overall, the reforms were rather modest, yet the progressives took the first steps to ending the *laissez-faire* philosophy of government and to promoting social justice.

New Freedom vs. New Nationalism

In 1912, Wilson and Roosevelt offered competing visions of progressivism. Wilson espoused "**New Freedom**" as he rhetorically opposed big business and pledged to dismantle abusive trusts. Roosevelt, in contrast, proposed his "**New Nationalism**," which called on the nation to regulate large corporations but accept their existence as part of modern life. In the election, the people chose between these progressive philosophies and President William Howard Taft's program of steady, limited government action. With Taft and Roosevelt dividing the Republican vote, Wilson was elected to the White House despite polling only 42 percent of the popular vote.

The first shots of the World War I all but extinguished progressive reforms. As the nation confronted outrages on the seas and the military preparedness campaign drained resources, the reform fervor faded. When America entered the war in 1917, the nation mobilized for war and much of the unfinished progressive agenda languished until the New Deal of the 1930s.

Urban vs. Rural Values

When World War I ended, Americans were jolted with changes and challenges. By the 1920s, for the first time in history, over 50 percent of the population lived in cities. From the rural point of view, these urban areas were corrupt, sinful, and unhealthy. In addition, progressive reforms and wartime agencies had spawned new bureaucracies, and despite progressive attempts at regulation, trusts continued to dominate economic life. The nineteenth century ideal of the self-made man in control of his destiny had vanished, swallowed up by new economic patterns, social expectations, and living arrangements.

The decade became a battleground between those who accepted change and those who longed for the days of the nineteenth century. Prohibition, the Scopes Trial, and the rebirth of the Ku Klux Klan were skirmishes in this struggle over the direction of American life. The Eighteenth Amendment attempted to restrict the supply of liquor and prevent cities, with their large immigrant populations, from gaining dominance in society. Similarly, the Scopes Trial in 1925 pitted the rural fundamentalists against urban modernists for control over school curriculum. And the emergence of the Ku Klux Klan was, in part, a response by white, rural, Protestants to the rising tide of immigrants, modern women, and the "New Negro."

The Women's Movement

Few groups experienced more changes in the 1920s than women. The efforts of Carrie Chapman Catt, Alice Paul, and other reformers finally convinced the nation to approve the Nineteenth Amendment, which gave women the right to vote. In addition, the number of working women increased over 25 percent during the decade. While most employment was in the traditional areas of teaching and secretarial/retail services, this new economic independence propelled some women to challenge conventional sexual and social roles.

The "New Negro"

Throughout the years 1900–1929, African Americans confronted the Jim Crow system of racial discrimination. Many blacks looked to Booker T.

Washington and his "don't-rock-the-boat" approach to race relations as a means of coping with the injustices. On the other hand, W. E. B. DuBois, Washington's chief rival, called on African Americans, especially "the talented tenth," to agitate for political, social, and economic equality.

World War I and the Great Migration promoted a new attitude among blacks. Four hundred thousand black men served in the war and came home with raised expectations for equality. However, racial clashes during the "Red Summer" of 1919 dashed hopes for better understanding between the races. The migration of southern blacks into northern cities continued after the war. For example, from 1920 to 1930, the black population of New York City doubled, and brought cultural changes as well. In Harlem, writers such as Langston Hughes and Claude McKay wrote about life under Jim Crow. This Harlem Renaissance also featured jazz clubs and theaters that headlined top black entertainers.

When Booker T. Washington died in 1915, DuBois and his allies were unable to fill the leadership void. A new leader, Marcus Garvey, emerged and gained support among urban blacks. Although he was arrested in 1923 and deported in 1927, Garvey's message of racial self-sufficiency, black pride, and pan-Africanism resonated among many black Americans throughout much of decade.

The Red Scare and Normalcy

In the 1920s, America rejected European immigration. Embracing past biases and fearful of Communism, Congress reduced the number of immigrants from 800,000 per year in 1920 to 150,000 by 1929. In addition, A. Mitchell Palmer convinced the country that a Bolshevik revolution was imminent and led a series of raids against suspected radicals before the Red Scare ran its course in the spring of 1920. The hysteria lingered, however, and set the stage for the injustice of the Sacco and Vanzetti case.

Republicans returned to political dominance in the 1920s with presidents Warren Harding and Calvin Coolidge promising to return to "normalcy." Reducing taxes and government regulations, the Republicans tried to emulate the policies of William McKinley. Although scandals during Harding's terms slowed policy direction, Coolidge restored faith in the White House and established the most pro-business administration since the time of Alexander Hamilton.

★ **A. Mitchell Palmer** — attorney general during the height of the Red Scare (1919–1920) who led raids against suspected radicals; reacting to terrorist bombings, fear of Bolshevism, and his own presidential aspirations, Palmer arrested 6,000 people and deported over 500.

★ **Booker T. Washington** — influential black leader; his "Atlanta Compromise" speech (1895) proposed blacks accept social and political segregation in return for economic opportunities in agriculture and vocational areas. He received money from whites and built Tuskegee Institute into a powerful educational and political machine.

★ **Calvin Coolidge** — taciturn, pro-business president (1923–1929) who took over after Harding's death, restored honesty to government, and accelerated the tax cutting and antiregulation policies of his predecessor; his *laissez-faire* policies brought short-term prosperity from 1923 to 1929.

★ **Carrie Chapman Catt** — president of the National American Woman Suffrage Association; Catt led the organization when it achieved passage of the Nineteenth Amendment in 1920 and later organized the League of Women Voters.

★ **Charles Lindbergh** — mail service pilot who became a celebrity when he made the first flight across the Atlantic Ocean in 1927; a symbol of the vanishing individualistic hero of the frontier who was honest, modest, and self-reliant, he later became a leading isolationist.

★ **Eighteenth Amendment (1919)** — prohibited the sale, transportation, and manufacture of alcohol; part of rural America's attempt to blunt the societal influence of the cities, it was called the "Noble Experiment" until it was repealed by the Twenty-first Amendment (1933).

★ **Federal Reserve Act (1913)** — established a national banking system for the first time since the 1830s; designed to combat the "money trust," it created 12 regional banks that regulated interest rates, money supply, and provided an elastic credit system throughout the country.

★ **Great Migration** — movement of southern, rural blacks to northern cities starting around 1915 and continuing through much of the twentieth century; blacks left the South as the cotton economy declined and Jim Crow persisted. Thousands came north for wartime jobs in large cities during World Wars I and II.

★ **Harlem Renaissance** — black artistic movement in New York City in the 1920s, when writers, poets, painters, and musicians came together to express feelings and experiences, especially about the injustices of Jim Crow; leading figures of the movement included Countee Cullen, Claude McKay, Duke Ellington, Zora Neale Hurston, and Langston Hughes.

★ **Ida Tarbell** — crusading journalist who wrote *The History of the Standard Oil Company*, a critical expose that documented John D. Rockefeller's ruthlessness and questionable business tactics.

★ **Industrial Workers of the World (Wobblies)** — revolutionary industrial union founded in 1905 and led by "Big Bill" Haywood that worked to overthrow capitalism; during World War I, the government pressured the group, and by 1919, it was in serious decline.

★ **Jane Addams** — social worker and leader in the settlement house movement; she founded Hull House in 1889, which helped improve the lives of poor immigrants in Chicago, and in 1931 shared the Nobel Peace Prize.

★ **Ku Klux Klan** — Reconstruction-era organization that was revived in 1915 and rose to political power in the mid-1920s when membership reached 4 to 5 million; opposed to blacks, Catholics, Jews, and immigrants, its membership was rural, white, native-born, and Protestant.

★ **Langston Hughes** — leading literary figure of the Harlem Renaissance who wrote verse, essays, and 32 books; he helped define the black experience in America for over four decades.

★ **Lincoln Steffens** — a leading muckraking journalist who exposed political corruption in the cities; best known for his *The Shame of Cities* (1904), he was also a regular contributor to *McClure's* magazine.

★ **Marcus Garvey** — black leader in early 1920s who appealed to urban blacks with his program of racial self-sufficiency/separatism, black pride, and pan-Africanism; his Universal Negro Improvement Association ran into financial trouble, however. He was eventually arrested for mail fraud and deported to his native Jamaica in 1927.

★ **New Nationalism** — Theodore Roosevelt's progressive platform in the election of 1912; building on his presidential "Square Deal," he called for a strong federal government to maintain economic competition and social justice but to accept trusts as an economic fact of life.

★ **Nineteenth Amendment (1920)** — granted women the right to vote; its ratification capped a movement for women's rights that dated to the Seneca Falls Convention of 1848. Although women were voting in state elections in 12 states when the amendment passed, it enabled 8 million women to vote in the presidential election of 1920.

★ **Pure Food and Drug Act (1906)** — law that regulated the food and patent medicine industries; some business leaders called it socialistic meddling by the government.

★ **Red Scare** — period of hysteria after World War I over the possible spread of Communism to the United States; aroused by the Russian Revolution (1917), the large number of Russian immigrants in the United States, and a series of terrorist bombings in 1919, it resulted in the denial of civil liberties, mass arrests and deportations, and passage of the restrictive Immigration Act of 1920.

★ **Robert La Follette** — progressive governor (1900–1904) and senator (1906–1925); he established the "Wisconsin idea" that reformed the state through direct primaries, tax reform, and anticorruption legislation. La Follette was the Progressive Party's presidential nominee in 1924.

★ **Sacco and Vanzetti** — Italian radicals who became symbols of the Red Scare of the 1920s; arrested (1920), tried, and executed (1927) for a robbery/murder, they were believed by many to have been innocent but convicted because of their immigrant status and radical political beliefs.

★ **Scopes Trial (1925)** — "Monkey Trial" over John Scopes's teaching of evolution in his biology classroom in violation of a Tennessee law; it pitted the Bible, fundamentalism, and William Jennings Bryan against evolution, modernism, and Clarence Darrow. Scopes was convicted, but fundamentalism was damaged and discouraged by the trial.

★ **Social Gospel** — movement that began in Protestant churches in the late nineteenth century to apply the teachings of the Bible to the problems of the industrial age; led by Washington Gladden and Walter Rauschenbusch, it aroused the interest of many clergymen in securing social justice for the urban poor. The thinking of Jane Addams, Theodore Roosevelt, Woodrow Wilson, and other secular reformers was influenced by the movement as well.

★ **Tea Pot Dome Scandal** — biggest scandal of Harding's administration; Secretary of Interior Albert Fall illegally leased government oil fields in the West to private oil companies; Fall was later convicted of bribery and became the first Cabinet official to serve prison time (1931–1932).

★ **Upton Sinclair** — socialist muckraker who wrote *The Jungle* (1906) in which he hoped to indict the capitalist system but instead helped convince Congress to pass the Meat Inspection Act (1906), which cleaned up the meat industry.

★ **W. E. B. DuBois** — black intellectual who challenged Booker T. Washington's ideas on combating Jim Crow; he called for the black community to demand immediate equality and was a founding member of the National Association for the Advancement of Color People (NAACP).

★ **Warren Harding** — weak but affable president (1921–1923) who allowed his appointees to loot and cheat the government; after his death, political and personal scandals tarnished his presidency. Harding is rated as a failure as president by most historians.

★ **Woodrow Wilson (New Freedom)** — successful Democratic presidential nominee in 1912 and his progressive program that viewed trusts as evil and called for their destruction rather than their regulation; his social and political philosophy drew heavily on the ideas of Louis Brandeis. As president (1913–1921), Wilson led the nation through World War I.

Ideas to Ponder

After reviewing the chapter's summary, highlights, and your primary text,
discuss the following with members of your study group.

1   How did the Progressive movement borrow most of its program from the Populists?

2   How were Progressivism and Socialism similar, yet different?

3   How did the progressive reformers try to make government more responsive to the people's interest?

4   In your opinion, who was the most successful muckraker? Defend your answer.

5   Did Theodore Roosevelt deserve his nickname of "trustbuster?" Explain why or why not.

6   What strengths and weaknesses did the ideas of Booker T. Washington and W. E. B. DuBois have for dealing with the Jim Crow system?

7   How did Theodore Roosevelt help elect Woodrow Wilson in 1912?

8   Why were the Progressives unable to make greater changes in American society from 1900 to 1914?

9   Did progressive reforms end in the 1920s? If not, cite examples of their continued influence.

10 Why did American business rejoice over Warren Harding and Calvin Coolidge as presidents?

11 How did the American value system change in the 1920s?

12 How did Marcus Garvey address the needs of the "New Negro" in the 1920s?

13 What factors changed the lives of women in the 1920s?

14 How did the rise of the Ku Klux Klan reflect more than racial animosity in the 1920s?

15 How were the passage of the Eighteenth Amendment and the Scopes Trial part of a larger societal struggle in the 1920s?

16 Why did the "noble experiment" fail in the 1920s?

17 How did the Red Scare show America's true feelings toward Europe and immigrants?

18 How did the literature of the 1920s demonstrate the feelings of alienation among both blacks and whites?

Essay Skill

Writing an Introductory Paragraph

An introductory paragraph is vital to a successful essay answer. It introduces the reader to your argument and to your thesis. It provides a road map to follow as you present the direction of your argument. An introductory paragraph will also narrow the focus of the argument and prepare the reader for the ideas that you plan to use in defense of your point of view.

An introductory paragraph has the following elements:

- **A thesis statement**, which should appear early in the paragraph, perhaps as the first sentence; you will recall that a thesis is the position that you intend to take and to defend.

- **The general categories of information** that you plan to cite in proving your thesis; this will be one or two sentences that outline the problem posed by the prompt and how it will be addressed in the body of the essay.

- **A definition of terms** may be necessary for some prompts; for example, if Theodore Roosevelt's liberalism is an issue in a question, you should use the introductory paragraph to establish a definition of liberalism.

- **A transitional sentence** that links the introductory paragraph to the body of the paper.

The following elements do not belong in an introductory paragraph:

- **Specific facts or evidence** that supports the thesis; this information is critical in the essay, but it belongs in the body of the paper. You should remember that the opening paragraph is a general overview of the answer.

- **A statement of intentions**; your intentions should not be expressed. You should never write:

  – "The purpose of this essay is . . ."

  – "In this essay I will . . ."

  Let the facts speak for themselves. If you have a strong thesis and substantial information in support of your position, the reader will be clear on your positions and intentions.

- **An apology**; do not apologize. You should not admit a lack of knowledge or understanding about the prompt. Such an admission can prejudice the reader against your position at the outset of the essay.

- **A conclusion**; do not include a conclusion in the introductory paragraph. You should not try to do too much with the first paragraph. You will have an opportunity at the end of the paper to remind the reader what your thesis was and how it was developed.

Study the prompt below and the paragraph that follows it. Try to identify the elements of a good introductory paragraph before reading the explanation that follows the paragraph. Discuss the paragraph with your classmates or in your study group and make sure that you can identify the key elements of an introductory paragraph.

Theodore Roosevelt was not a true reformer; his presidency failed to make dramatic changes in America.

Assess the validity of this statement from 1901 to 1909.

★ Sample Paragraph

"While not a radical, President Theodore Roosevelt made important reforms in America from 1901 to 1909. During his tenure, Roosevelt expanded presidential powers, regulated trusts, preserved the environment, and protected consumers. All this made the country a better place to live. A review of Roosevelt's presidential years will demonstrate that he changed America and was a genuine reformer."

Explanation

In this introductory paragraph, the writer lays out the clear thesis that Roosevelt was a reformer but not a radical. It also presents the areas that will be discussed in the body of the paper: strengthening the presidency, trust busting, conservation, and consumer protection. Finally, it links the introduction to the rest of paper and again states the thesis that Roosevelt changed America and was a real reformer.

Practicing the Skill

Study the prompt below and write an introductory paragraph that would address it. Make sure to include the elements of a beginning paragraph that were discussed above. After you have completed your paragraph, compare it with those of your classmates or your study group members. At some point you may wish to look on page 227 in the Suggested Responses section for a sample paragraph that has the elements of a strong introductory paragraph for this prompt.

Booker T. Washington was criticized as a leader who failed to stand up for his people, yet in truth he was a pragmatic realist.

Assess the validity of this statement from 1895 to 1915.

Your introductory paragraph:

_____

_____

_____

_____

_____

_____

_____

_____

_____

Document SKILL

Writing a Paragraph from Dissenting Documents

The issue of dealing with contrary or dissenting documents/sources has been discussed at several points earlier in this book. On the DBQ essay, you can expect to confront materials that clash with each other and may challenge your thesis. Usually, out of eight or nine sources, at least two will not support a student's position on a topic. In most cases, the DBQ asks students to account for the transformation of a topic over time. Change produces tension either from people who want to slow it down or from those who wish to see it accelerate. Thus, dissenting sources are often designed to demonstrate a tension around an issue as it changes over time.

Many students ignore these dissenting documents and sources and write their DBQ using only the materials that agree with their thesis. This omission reduces the quality of the essay and lowers a student's grade. While you do not have to use every source to score high on the DBQ, you must include a paragraph toward the end of the essay that deals with dissenting information. This contrary or concession paragraph should not repudiate the thesis of the paper, but it must acknowledge the tension and challenges that dissenting ideas represent. By including this paragraph, you demonstrate that you realize that the topic and related issues are complex and that human events do not unfold without controversy and disagreement.

Look at the prompt below, its thesis, and the two documents that challenge the writer's position. Study the paragraph that was developed from the two documents and discuss it with your classmates or with the members of your study group.

Analyze the attempts of progressive reformers to restore fairness in the American political and economic system from 1900 to 1917. How successful were they in achieving their goals?

Thesis: Through a series of legislative actions, the progressives restored a degree of fairness to the American economic and political system.

★ (Sample) Document A

> *We march because we want to make impossible a repetition of Waco, Memphis, and East St. Louis [anti-Negro riots] by arousing the conscience of the country, and to bring the murderers of our brothers, sisters and innocent children to justice.*
>
> *We march because we deem it a crime to be silent in the face of such barbaric acts.*
>
> *We march because we are thoroughly opposed to Jim Crow cars, segregation, discrimination, disfranchisement, lynching, and the host of evils that are forced on us . . .*
>
> —*Why We March*, Leaflet, July 28, 1917

Document SKILL

★ (Sample) Document B

> *The platform of the Roosevelt Progressive party has much in it with which Socialists are in full agreement but it does not contain any of the vital and fundamental principles of Socialism and is in no sense a Socialist platform. It may perhaps be best described as a platform of progressive capitalism. Its declaration aims at some of the flagrant evils and abuses of capitalism, while the platform as a whole supports and strengthens the existing system, and, doubtless, has the full approval of the steel trust and harvester trust, and like interests which financed Roosevelt's campaign for the nomination. . . .*
>
> —"Eugene V. Debs Says Moose Party Stole Socialist Planks,"
> *Chicago World*, August 15, 1912

★ Sample concession paragraph

While progressive reformers helped the white, middle class, they ignored the plight of African Americans and radical, working-class people. The progressives had no civil rights program, and as late as 1917, black Americans complained that their lives were filled with "segregation, discrimination, disfranchisement, lynching and the host of evils that are forced on us. . . ." In addition, Eugene Debs believed the Progressive platform did not go far enough to help working people; rather, it "supports and strengthens the existing system and doubtless has the full approval of the steel trust and harvester trust. . . ." For these groups, the progressives were too timid to help them improve their lives.

Practicing the Skill

Study the prompt and documents below. When you finish, write a thesis statement for the prompt and then use the two documents to construct a concession paragraph that would challenge or qualify the thesis you wrote. Remember, as you construct your paragraph, you want to qualify your thesis, *not* repudiate it.

Compare your completed thesis and paragraph with those of your classmates or members of your study group. After you have discussed your answers, look at page 228 in the Suggested Responses section for ideas that could be included in an appropriate thesis statement and a concession paragraph.

In the 1920s, most Americans yearned for security and continuity in their lives and relationships.

Assess the validity of this statement by analyzing American values from 1921 to 1929.

Document SKILL

Thesis statement:

_____

_____

★ Document A

> Now my generation is disillusioned, and, I think, to a certain extent, brutalized by the cataclysm which their complacent folly engendered. The acceleration of life for us has been so great that into the last few years have been crowded the experiences and the ideas of a normal lifetime. We have in our unregenerate youth learned the practicality and the cynicism that is safe only in unregenerate old age. We have been forced to become realists overnight, instead of idealists, as was our birthright. We have seen man at his lowest, woman at her lightest, in the terrible moral chaos of Europe.
>
> —John F. Carter Jr. "These Wild Young People,"
> _The Atlantic Monthly_ (September, 1920)

★ Document B

> The basis of freedom of the world is woman's freedom. A free race cannot be born of slave mothers. A woman enchained cannot choose but give a measure of that bondage to her sons and daughters. No woman can call herself free who does not own and control her body. No woman can call herself free until she can choose consciously whether she will or will not be a mother. . . .
>
> Look at it from any standpoint you will, suggest any solution you will, conventional or unconventional, sanctioned by law or in defiance of law, woman is in the same position, fundamentally, until she is able to determine for herself whether she will be a mother and to fix the number of her offspring . . .
>
> —Margaret Sanger, _Woman and the New Race_ (1920)

A concession paragraph:

_____

_____

_____

_____

Chapter 12

THE GREAT DEPRESSION AND WORLD WAR II

1928–1945

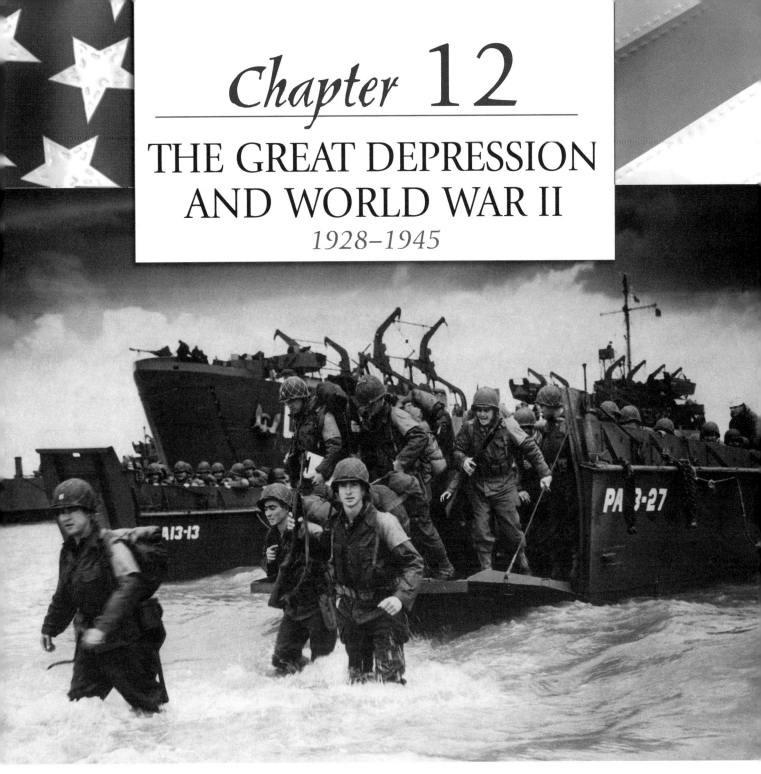

Focus Questions

★ How did the prosperity of the 1920s collapse into the Great Depression of the 1930s?

★ How did Herbert Hoover and Franklin Roosevelt attempt to restore prosperity through political and economic programs?

★ How did the New Deal affect the lives of women and African Americans in the 1930s?

★ How did the major unresolved issues from World War I lead to World War II?

★ How did the United States move from isolationism to internationalism between 1935 and 1945?

★ How did World War II transform American society?

Summary

After six years of Republican prosperity, Herbert Hoover easily won the presidency in 1928 against Al Smith. Although Smith was Catholic and an urban "wet" (he wanted Prohibition repealed), he lost the election because of the good economy, which ended in October 1929, when the stock market crashed, signaling the beginning of hard times. Neither Hoover nor the American people understood, however, that this downturn would become the greatest depression in the nation's history. Beginning as an inventory recession in 1928, conditions snowballed into an economic calamity by 1932. The causes of the Great Depression were numerous and complex: poor distribution of income, manufacturing sector imbalances, inadequate banking regulations, a farmers' depression, ill-timed Federal Reserve actions, and shortsighted trade policies (Hawley-Smoot tariff among them). All this brought the economy to a shuttering standstill. The Gross National Product fell from $104 billion in 1929 to $77 billion in 1932; some 9,000 banks failed; and unemployment reached 25 percent, with many large cities ringed by Hoovervilles, shantytowns of the unemployed.

Hoover and the Depression

Instead of balancing the budget and allowing the business cycle to complete its downward trend, Hoover initiated a series of actions to restore prosperity. He held White House meetings to reassure business leaders and made pronouncements about the soundness of the economy. Moreover, the government ran deficits as Hoover asked Congress to increase spending for public works and to provide assistance to farmers. He also prodded Congress to create the Reconstruction Finance Corporation, which loaned money to banks, railroads, and other large businesses. By past standards, Hoover was very active in fighting the downturn.

Hoover's program failed, however. Conditions continued to worsen even as the deficit hit $500 million in 1932, and Hoover pulled back from his activist stance. He cut spending and tried to balance the budget. Most significantly, he clung to "rugged individualism," a philosophy that would not allow direct government payments to individuals. Millions suffered starvation and deprivation as Hoover preached about the strengths of America's past and its frontier tradition of self-reliance.

The New Deal

The nation repudiated Hoover in 1932 and elected Democrat Franklin D. Roosevelt to the presidency. Although he was uncertain how to solve the Depression, FDR realized the people wanted action, and he offered a New Deal to energize the nation. Drawing on liberal and conservative ideas, including those of his Brain Trust, FDR presided over the most remarkable Hundred Days in American political history. Congress approved thirteen major bills including the creation of the Civilian Conservation Corp, Agricultural Adjustment Administration, and National Recovery Administration. Slowly the country pulled back from the precipice of economic disaster.

Over the next five years, Roosevelt transformed the government and the nation. Although his program did not end the Depression, it provided recovery and restored confidence to the country. Through his three Rs of relief, reform, and recovery, FDR provided direct relief to the people, built roads and bridges, regulated financial institutions, and instituted a limited retirement system for the elderly (Social Security Act).

Friends and Foes

As things improved in the mid 1930s, opposition to Roosevelt's New Deal emerged. The **American Liberty League** claimed Roosevelt's programs were heading toward socialism and communism. Others such as **Huey Long, Charles Coughlin,** and **Francis Townsend** said FDR had not done enough for the poor and elderly. Roosevelt responded to these criticisms with a **Second New Deal** in 1935–1936. Adopting an antibusiness and populist tone, the President promoted legislation that regulated utilities, raised taxes on the rich, implemented Social Security, and assisted organized labor.

After his landslide reelection in 1936, Roosevelt lost his political compass. In 1937, he proposed his politically disastrous **court-packing plan,** which tried to expand the Supreme Court from nine to fifteen justices. This appeared to be a grab for power by FDR, and Congress rejected the idea. Further, economic recovery faltered when Roosevelt reduced spending to balance the budget. During the "Roosevelt recession," four million workers lost their jobs, and by 1938, the New Deal seemed tired and confused.

Neither women nor African Americans found their lives directly changed by the New Deal. Roosevelt did not have programs designed for either group; yet his agenda targeted disadvantaged people, many of whom were women and blacks. The New Deal also indirectly helped blacks as the expanding government bureaucracy employed many African Americans, some in relatively high positions (**Black Cabinet**). Moreover, the president's wife Eleanor was a friend to African Americans and a mentor for many women in the 1930s. She served as a voice for both groups as they struggled for equality.

Isolationism vs. Internationalism

While Roosevelt's main concern in the 1930s was economic recovery, he watched with alarm as the Axis Powers seized territory and prepared for war. Roosevelt was an internationalist, but he was also a realist. He could not act against overseas aggression when 15 percent of Americans were unemployed, and other countries would not stand against Hitler and Hirohito.

Consequently, FDR signed the restrictive **Neutrality Acts** in the mid 1930s, as the nation hoped to avoid foreign entanglements. This mood changed on September 1, 1939, when Germany attacked Poland. Hitler's armies quickly overran Europe. By 1941, America had repealed the Neutrality Acts and extended aid to England. In East Asia, the United States tried to protect China, but after years of economic pressure and haggling, American and Japan reached a diplomatic crisis. Japan decided to break the stalemate by attacking Pearl Harbor, which brought America into World War II.

The Grand Alliance

America, allied with Britain and the Soviet Union, fought the war in two theaters—Europe and Asia. Hitler was the most immediate threat and became the prime target. The Soviets carried the brunt of the fighting until the United States and England established a **second front** in France in June 1944. By May 1945, the Allies overwhelmed Hitler but not before his Nazis destroyed 85 percent of Europe's Jewish population and decimated much of central and eastern Europe. In Asia, the U.S. suffered months of defeats before it began island hopping toward Tokyo. By 1945, America was poised for an invasion of Japan. New president **Harry Truman** hoped to avoid a bloody invasion and ordered the use of two atomic bombs on the cities of Hiroshima and Nagasaki. Both cities were destroyed, along with 200,000 residents. Within days, Japan surrendered.

The Home Front

World War II transformed the American home front. The Depression ended when fifteen million men and women went into the military, and government spending exploded from $9 billion to $100 billion from 1939 to 1945. Women assumed new working and domestic roles, and **A. Philip Randolph** demanded fairer treatment for African Americans. The greatest domestic injustice was the internment of over 100,000 Japanese-Americans during the war. While the Supreme Court upheld this action in 1944, it was a lingering stain on America's civil liberties record.

★ **A. Philip Randolph** — labor and civil rights leader in the 1940s who led the Brotherhood of Sleeping Car Porters; he demanded that FDR create a Fair Employment Practices Commission to investigate job discrimination in war industries. FDR agreed only after Randolph threatened a march on Washington by African Americans.

★ **Agricultural Adjustment Administration (1933)** — New Deal program that paid farmers not to produce crops; it provided farmers with income while reducing crop surpluses and helped stabilize farm production. The Supreme Court declared major parts of this law unconstitutional in 1936, helping lead FDR to his court-packing plan.

★ **Alfred (Al) Smith** — first Catholic ever nominated for president; he lost in 1928 because of the nation's prosperity, but his religion, urban background, and views on Prohibition (he was a "wet") cost him votes as well.

★ **American Liberty League** — a conservative anti–New Deal organization; members included Alfred Smith, John W. Davis, and the Du Pont family. It criticized the "dictatorial" policies of Roosevelt and what it perceived to be his attacks on the free enterprise system.

★ **Atlantic Charter (1941)** — joint statement issued by President Roosevelt and Britain's Prime Minister Winston Churchill of principals and goals for an Allied victory in World War II; it provided for self-determination for all conquered nations, freedom of seas, economic security, and free trade. Later, it became the embodiment of the United Nation's charter.

★ **Black Cabinet** — an informal network of black officeholders in the federal government; led by Mary McLeod Bethune, William Hastie, and Robert Weaver, they pushed for economic and political opportunities for African Americans in the 1930s and 1940s.

★ **Bonus Army (1932)** — group of jobless World War I veterans who came to Washington to lobby Congress for immediate payment of money promised them in 1945; Hoover opposed payment, and when he used the U.S. Army to drive the veterans out of the capital, he was portrayed as cruel and cold-hearted.

★ **Brain(s) Trust** — name applied to college professors from Columbia University such as Rexford Tugwell, Adolf Berle, and Raymond Moley who advised Roosevelt on economic matters early in the New Deal; the Brain Trust took on the role of an "unofficial Cabinet" in the Roosevelt Administration.

★ **Charles Coughlin** — Catholic priest who used his popular radio program to criticize the New Deal; he grew increasingly anti-Roosevelt and anti-Semitic until the Catholic Church pulled him off the air.

HIGH*lights*
of the Period

★ **Court-packing plan** — Roosevelt's proposal in 1937 to "reform" the Supreme Court by appointing an additional justice for every justice over age 70; following the Court's actions in striking down major New Deal laws, FDR came to believe that some justices were out of touch with the nation's needs. Congress believed Roosevelt's proposal endangered the Court's independence and said no.

★ **Fireside chats** — Roosevelt's informal radio addresses throughout his presidency; they gave the people a sense of confidence that he understood their problems and was trying to help solve them. With these "chats," FDR was the first president to use the electronic media to spread his message.

★ **Frances Perkins** — Roosevelt's secretary of labor (1993–1945); the first woman to serve as a federal Cabinet officer, she had a great influence on many New Deal programs, most significantly the Social Security Act.

★ **Francis Townsend** — retired physician who proposed an Old Age Revolving Pension Plan to give every retiree over age 60 $200 per month, provided that the person spend the money each month in order to receive their next payment; the object of Townsend's plan was to help retired workers as well as stimulate spending in order to boost production and end the Depression.

★ **Franklin D. Roosevelt** — president (1933–1945); elected four times, he led the country's recovery from the Depression and to victory in World War II. He died in office, however, just weeks before Germany's surrender. He is generally considered the greatest president since Abraham Lincoln.

★ **Harry Hopkins** — close adviser to Roosevelt and FDR's czar of relief programs; he headed the Federal Emergency Relief Administration, Civil Works Administration, and Works Progress Administration and later undertook diplomatic missions to the USSR.

★ **Harry S. Truman** — vice president who became president when FDR died in April 1945; he was elected on his own in 1948. Truman ordered the use of atomic bombs on Japan to end World War II, set the course of postwar containment of communism in the Cold War, and created a Fair Deal program to carry on the New Deal's domestic agenda.

★ **Hawley-Smoot Tariff (1930)** — raised the duties on imported foreign goods to all-time highs; intended to boost American industry and employment, it actually deepened the Depression when European countries could not repay their loans (World War I war debts) and retaliated against American exports.

★ **Herbert Hoover** — president (1929–1933) who is blamed for the Great Depression; although he tried to use government power to bring on recovery, his inflexibility and refusal to give direct relief doomed his programs and his presidency.

★ **Hoovervilles** — camps and shantytowns of unemployed and homeless on the outskirts of major cities during the early days of the Depression; they were symbols of the failure of Hoover's program and the way the nation held him responsible for the hard times.

★ **Huey Long** — flamboyant Louisiana governor and U.S. senator; he challenged FDR to do more for the poor and needy and proposed a popular "Share-Our-Wealth" program to tax the wealthy in order to provide a guaranteed income for the poor. He was assassinated in 1935.

★ **Hundred Days** — term applied to the first weeks of the Roosevelt Administration, during which Congress passed 13 emergency relief and reform measures that were the backbone of the early New Deal; these included the Civilian Conservation Corp, the Glass Stegal Act (FDIC), Agricultural Adjustment Act, Federal Emergency Relief Act, and the National Industrial Recovery Act.

★ **Lend Lease (1941)** — program authorizing the president to lend or lease equipment to nations whose defense was deemed vital to the U.S. security; it was designed to help a bankrupt Britain continue fighting the Nazis. By 1945, the United States had extended $50 billion in wartime aid to Britain and the Soviet Union.

★ **National Labor Relations Act (1935)** — created a National Labor Relations Board that could compel employers to recognize and bargain with unions; this law helped promote the growth of organized labor in the 1930s and for decades thereafter.

★ **National Recovery Administration (1933)** — agency that created a partnership between business and government to fight the Depression; it allowed major industries to fix prices in return for agreeing to fair practice codes, wage and hour standards, and labor's right to organize. Major parts of the law that created the NRA were declared unconstitutional in 1935.

★ **Neutrality Acts (1935, 1936, 1937)** — series of laws that provided Americans could not ship weapons, loan money, travel on belligerent ships, extend credit, or deliver goods to any belligerent countries; they were high tide of isolationism, and all were repealed between 1939 and 1941.

★ **New Deal (1933–1938)** — Roosevelt's program of domestic reform and relief; the three Rs of Relief, Reform, and Recovery did not end the Depression, but they gave hope and security and made government more responsive to the people in bad economic times.

★ **Pearl Harbor** — United States naval base in Hawaii that was attacked by Japan on December 7, 1941, with serious U.S. losses: 19 ships sunk or destroyed and over 2,000 deaths; the attack brought the United States into World War II.

★ **Reconstruction Finance Corporation (1932)** — Hoover's economic recovery program that provided government loans to businesses, banks, and railroads; it was "pump priming," but it was too little ($300 million) too late to make any real improvement in the economy.

★ **Rugged individualism** — Hoover's philosophy that called on Americans to help each other during the Depression without direct government relief; he feared too much government help would weaken the American character, endanger liberty, and lead to totalitarianism in the United States.

★ **Second Front** — proposed Anglo-American invasion of France to relieve the Soviets, who were fighting a German invasion of the USSR; originally scheduled for 1942, it was not delivered until D-Day in June 1944. This was a divisive issue in Soviet relations with the United States and Britain during the war and after.

★ **Second New Deal (1935–1936)** — name given to a series of proposals that FDR requested and Congress passed to reinvigorate the New Deal as recovery from the Depression began to lag; they were antibusiness in tone and intent and included the Public Utility Holding Company Act, Social Security Act, National Labor Relations Act, and the Wealth Tax Act.

★ **Social Security Act (1935)** — required both workers and their employer to contribute to a federally run pension fund for retired workers; it also provided federal disability and unemployment assistance. Although benefits were meager, it was the first significant government program to provide for retired, disabled, or unemployed Americans.

HIGHlights
of the Period

Ideas to Ponder

After reviewing the chapter's summary, highlights, and your primary text, discuss the following with members of your study group.

1   How did the inventory recession of 1928 become the Great Depression of the 1930s?

2   How was President Hoover's approach to ending the Depression both conservative and liberal?

3   How was the New Deal more of an attitude than a specific plan for ending the Depression?

4   How was Roosevelt's temperament well suited for the problems of the 1930s?

5   How did New Deal programs directly impact the lives of Americans?

6   How did the National Industrial Recovery Act and the Public Utilities Holding Company Act demonstrate Roosevelt's changing attitude towards business in the 1930s?

7   How did political extremists help shape the New Deal programs?

8   Why did the Supreme Court oppose the New Deal from 1933 to 1936? What did Roosevelt do about it?

9   How was 1937 the most difficult year of the Depression for President Roosevelt?

10   How did Roosevelt's actions as president reinforce the charge that he sought dictatorial powers?

11   How did the New Deal ignore the neediest people in the 1930s?

12   How did Roosevelt's New Deal fail to include African Americans and women in its program and yet gain their support?

13   How was the New Deal both a success and a failure?

14   Why was Roosevelt seen as a friend of isolationism in the 1930s?

15   How did World War II change the American home front?

16   Why was the alliance among the United States, Great Britain, and the Soviet Union a fragile one?

17   How did the atom bomb transform the world in 1945?

18   How did World War II change America's place in the community of nations?

Essay Skill

Writing a Concluding Paragraph

A vital, but sometimes overlooked element of a strong essay is the paper's concluding paragraph. Unfortunately, students often do not leave enough time to write a conclusion, which can be extremely helpful in achieving a high score on a free-response essay or on a DBQ. This paragraph should be brief and to the point but provide closure to the paper. It gives the writer one last opportunity to convince the reader of his/her argument and to restate the premise of the paper.

A concluding paragraph should contain:

- A summary of the thesis statement. This should be a paraphrase of the original thesis and not an exact restatement;
- One or two sentences that summarize the salient points used to prove the thesis;
- And in certain cases:
  - A review of the historical significance of the problem posed by the prompt;
  - A solution to the problem posed.

A concluding paragraph should NOT contain:

- New evidence or arguments that were not in the body of the essay;
- A new thesis or point of view that contradicts the original thesis;
- An apology for not doing a better job in writing the essay.

Below are a prompt and a thesis statement concerning an evaluation of the New Deal. In addition, there is a sample paragraph that would conclude the essay and a discussion of its elements. After you have read all the materials, discuss them with your classmates or your study group members, with your discussion focusing on how the paragraph is an effective conclusion to the prompt.

> "The New Deal failed the American people because it did not restore economic prosperity in the 1930s."

Assess the validity of this statement with reference to the years 1933–1938.

> **Thesis:** Although the New Deal did not return the nation to pre-1929 prosperity levels, it successfully reduced suffering, promoted security, and restored faith in the American economic system.

★ Concluding Paragraph

> In summary, the New Deal did not bring about full economic recovery from the Depression in the 1930s; yet it reduced deprivation and provided security for millions of Americans. Moreover, through the three Rs of Relief, Reform, and Recovery, it gave Americans hope and restored their faith in the capitalist system. For these reasons, the New Deal was not a failure; rather, it was a major success.

Essay Skill

Discussion

The paragraph restates the thesis about how the New Deal succeeded and served the American people. (Notice it did not just repeat the original thesis; it rearranged and paraphrased its ideas.) The paragraph reminded the reader that the programs of the three Rs: Relief, Reform and Recovery were the means by which the New Deal helped the country and restored confidence. It is presumed that the body of paper discussed specific programs (e.g., WPA, CCC, AAA, FDIC, Social Security, Wagner Act, etc.). The final sentence brings the thesis home one last time.

Practicing the Skill

Using the prompt and the thesis statement below, write a concluding paragraph that would serve as an effective summary for the thesis and for the main ideas that would support it. Compare your concluding paragraph with those of your classmates or with the members of your study group. After your discussion, turn to page 228 in the Suggested Responses section for some suggested ideas of what elements might be included in this concluding paragraph.

> Examine and evaluate the struggle between the isolationists and internationalists for control of United States foreign policy from 1935 to 1941.
>
> **Thesis:** The isolationists dominated the American foreign policy debate from 1935 to 1939, but as military events in 1940–1941 frightened Americans, the internationalists became increasingly influential.

Concluding Paragraph

_____

_____

_____

_____

_____

_____

_____

_____

Document SKILL

Organizing the Document-Based Question

In the section Tackling the DBQ, several important steps were presented for preparing to write the DBQ. Elsewhere in this book, specific techniques for analyzing sources have been suggested as well. In this section, a graphic organizer will pull those ideas together and make them operational. By following the steps in charts below, you will develop a consistent plan for preparing to write a DBQ.

As you examine the worksheet, several points should be emphasized:

- The worksheet asks you to focus on the issue to be addressed by turning the prompt into a question. If the prompt is already in question form, you will formulate a clarifying question. The main point is for you to zero in clearly on the issue or issues to be addressed in the essay.

- The outside information should include all the facts about **the era under consideration** not just the specific topic within the prompt.

- The outside information should be listed **before looking at the sources**.

- Once the outside information has been listed and the sources summarized, you are ready to answer the question posed at the beginning of the worksheet. This is your thesis statement.

- The outside information and documents should be categorized into pro (support for the thesis) or con (challenge to the thesis). Using the system from Chapter 10, you should use a (+) or (−) to identify each piece of evidence and then place it into the chart at the end of the worksheet.

Practicing the Skill

Below you will find a worksheet that organizes a DBQ. Discuss the various parts of it with your classmates or with the members of your study group. After you complete your discussion, try it out on a sample DBQ. There is a sample DBQ in Chapter 15 of this book that can be used, or you can use a DBQ from a past examination that your teacher has on hand, or you can consult the College Board publication, *Doing the DBQ*. By applying the elements of the worksheet to a DBQ, you will see how the various parts are connected and how this step-by-step process provides a consistent strategy for tackling the DBQ.

Organizing the Document-Based Question

The question to be argued is:

_____

_____

_____

Document SKILL

List outside information about the question:

1. _____

2. _____

3. _____

4. _____

5. _____

6. _____

7. _____

8. _____

9. _____

10. _____

11. _____

12. _____

13. _____

14. _____

Summarize each document below. Use a separate sheet of paper if necessary.

Document A: _____

_____

_____

Document B: _____

_____

_____

Document C: _____

_____

_____

Document D: _____

_____

_____

Document E: _____

_____

_____

Document F: _____

_____

_____

Document G: _____

_____

_____

Document H: _____

_____

_____

Document I: _____

_____

_____

Thesis:

_____

_____

_____

_____

Document **SKILL**

Documents and Facts

Pro (support) for thesis	Con (challenge) to the thesis

Chapter 13

AMERICA WAGES THE COLD WAR

1945–1989

Focus Questions

★ How did the United States and Soviet Union go from World War II allies to Cold War adversaries?

★ How did containment of Soviet power become the cornerstone of American foreign policy from 1945 to 1989?

★ How was containment modified from 1945 to 1989 to fit presidential philosophies and changing world events?

★ How did the Vietnam conflict become America's greatest failure of the Cold War?

★ How did Middle Eastern conflicts complicate America's attempt to contain Communism and maintain peace in the region?

★ How was America's Latin American policy part of the larger containment effort from 1945 to 1989?

Summary

The alliance between the United States and Soviet Union barely survived the final shots of World War II. Neither side relinquished its prewar views of world affairs. The United States maintained an Open Door/Atlantic Charter policy of promoting capitalism and dismantling spheres of influence around the world. The Soviets wanted friendly (Communist) governments on its borders with total control over these nations. Lingering wartime grievances also eroded the alliance. Joseph Stalin retained anger over the lack of a second front during the war, and over the amount of Lend Lease aid offered by the United States. Trouble surfaced at the Yalta Conference and at Potsdam when the Soviets refused to evacuate Poland and other parts of Eastern Europe. Later, President Truman denied Stalin's aid request and adopted a truculent approach towards the Communists. The Soviets clanked down an "Iron Curtain" of repression across Central Europe in violation of most wartime agreements. The United States began to use its financial resources and atomic monopoly to challenge potential Communist threats around the world.

Containment in Europe and Asia

In 1947, the United States decided to contain Soviet expansion. Based on the ideas of George Kennan, this policy recognized the USSR as an aggressive threat to American interests in many parts of the world. Containment became the conceptual framework for America's Cold War strategy. Truman made the concept operational between 1947 and 1950 with the Truman Doctrine, the Marshall Plan, and the North Atlantic Treaty Organization (NATO). Containment began as economic aid and matured into a military alliance to protect Western Europe. It was successful in Europe, with only Czechoslovakia slipping behind the Iron Curtain during the Cold War.

Stopping the spread of Communism in Asia was more problematic. In November 1949, Mao Zedong, a Chinese Communist, won his struggle with Chiang Kai Shek; Chiang and his followers fled to Taiwan and Mao allied with the Soviet Union. In June 1950, Communist-supported North Korea invaded South Korea. Truman responded decisively by sending Douglas MacArthur and hundreds of thousands of American troops to defend the South. The United States, with token assistance from the United Nations, fought a seesaw three-year struggle in Korea. Finally, in July 1953, the fighting ceased with Korea divided again at the 38th parallel but at a cost of 33,000 American lives and with great frustration in the United States over the war's outcome.

New Look Foreign Policy

Dwight Eisenhower, the first Republican president in twenty years, proposed a "new look" foreign policy in 1953. Supported by John Foster Dulles, Eisenhower called for a reduction in military spending and the avoidance of Korean-type military stalemates. The Republicans continued containment, using the threat of massive retaliation to block aggression, covert activities to achieve American goals, and restraint in military interventions. Eisenhower found Soviet leader Nikita Khrushchev willing to accept a period of "peaceful coexistence" with the United States. While rhetorically calling for a rollback of Communism, Dulles accepted the status quo in Europe. Eisenhower used the Central Intelligence Agency (CIA) to overthrow unfriendly governments in Iran and Guatemala and to plan an end to Fidel Castro in Cuba.

Eisenhower's foreign policy record was mixed. He ended the Korean War, avoided involvement in Indochina after Dien Bien Phu, and reduced the defense budget by 16 percent. Yet, he encouraged Ngo Dinh

Diem to repudiate the Geneva agreement and to refuse to hold elections in Vietnam in 1956. Citing the **domino theory**, the President established Vietnam as critical to American security and identified **Ho Chi Minh** and the Communists as the enemy. In short, he deepened America's Asian commitment.

JFK's Foreign Policy

When **John F. Kennedy** became president in 1961, he offered a more aggressive approach to the Cold War, as he proclaimed America "would bear any burden" to protect its interests. He increased defense spending and proposed a "flexible response" in fighting communism. He had trouble quickly as the **Bay of Pigs invasion** failed to remove Castro in April 1961, Khrushchev erected the Berlin Wall, and Diem's regime became increasingly repressive in Vietnam. His greatest crisis occurred in October 1962 when the Soviets put missiles into Cuba (**Cuban Missile Crisis**). Rejecting immediate military action, the President imposed a blockade around Cuba, and after thirteen tense days, the Soviets agreed to remove the missiles.

Vietnam

Vietnam became an increasing problem from 1961 to 1963, as Diem's unpopular regime lost ground to the Viet Cong. By November 1963, Kennedy wanted Diem out and supported a coup to oust him. Despite years of aid and over 16,000 American advisers in the country, South Vietnam fell into chaos. Before the President could react to the crisis, he was assassinated on November 22, 1963.

Lyndon Johnson inherited the Vietnam dilemma and it became his great presidential nightmare. Hoping to honor Kennedy's memory, fearing political repercussions at home, seeing Vietnam as a test of America's will, and believing in the domino theory, Johnson gradually sent 540,000 troops to South Vietnam. Using the **Gulf of Tonkin Resolution** as justification, he Americanized the war and attempted to achieve a political settlement with a confused military response.

By 1968, over 400 Americans per week were dying in Vietnam, and the United States was divided between hawks (supporters of the war) and doves (opponents). When the **Tet Offensive** shocked Americans who

believed victory was at hand and destroyed the political will to continue escalating the war, Johnson's approval rating fell to 35 percent, and within weeks, he decided to retire from politics.

Richard Nixon followed Johnson to the presidency in 1969 and pursued "peace with honor" in Vietnam. Both he and **Henry Kissinger** realized America must leave Vietnam, but they hoped to preserve an appearance of success for the United States. Through Vietnamization, Nixon withdrew American troops, reinforced the South Vietnamese army, and negotiated with North Vietnam. After long diplomatic haggling, a treaty was signed in January 1973. Yet, by 1975, the North had violated the treaty and conquered the South.

Post-Vietnam Foreign Policy

Nixon was more successful with the Soviet Union and China. Reversing his past hardline position with both nations, he opened diplomatic ties with China and negotiated an arms limitation treaty with the Soviets. He used the rivalry between the Soviets and China to achieve détente and to pursue better relations with the communist giants.

After Gerald Ford's presidential interlude, **Jimmy Carter** entered the White House. Basing his policies on morality and human rights, his international approach often seemed confused. He cut off aid to several allies for human rights violations, urged the return of Panama Canal to Panama, and negotiated another arms treaty with the Soviets. His greatest success was the **Camp David Accords**, which established a framework of peace between Israel and Egypt. Despite his good intentions, by 1979 détente was in shambles, fifty-two Americans were held hostage in Iran, and America was frustrated and uncertain about its place in the world.

In 1980, the nation rejected Carter and turned to **Ronald Reagan**, who promised to restore America's confidence and standing in the world. Reagan viewed the Soviet Union as an "evil empire" and embarked on a massive military buildup. He actively supported anticommunist forces in Central America, which resulted in the controversial **Iran-Contra Affair** in 1986–1987, which tarnished his presidency. Although he amassed large deficits, many people credited Reagan's confrontational approach to the Soviet Union with speeding up its demise and ending the Cold War.

★ **Bay of Pigs** — U.S.-supported invasion of Cuba in April 1961; intended to overthrow Communist dictator Fidel Castro, the operation proved a fiasco. Castro's forces killed 114 of the invaders and took nearly 1,200 prisoners. The disaster shook the confidence of the Kennedy administration and encouraged the Soviet Union to become more active in the Americas.

★ **Camp David Accords (1979)** — agreement reached between the leaders of Israel and Egypt after protracted negotiations brokered by President Carter; Israel surrendered land seized in earlier wars and Egypt recognized Israel as a nation. Despite high hopes, it did not lead to a permanent peace in region, however.

★ **Chiang Kai Shek** — ineffective and corrupt leader of China in 1930s and 1940s; he was a wartime ally of the United States, but was unable to stop Communists from seizing power in 1949. Chiang's exile to Taiwan was a major American setback in the early days of the Cold War.

★ **Cuban Missile Crisis** — a confrontation between the United States and the USSR resulting from a Soviet attempt to place long-range nuclear missiles in Cuba (October 1962); Kennedy forced the Soviets to remove them with a blockade and the threat of force. The crisis enhanced Kennedy's standing but led to a Soviet arms buildup.

★ **Dien Bien Phu** — French fortress in northern Vietnam that surrendered in 1954 to the Viet Minh; the defeat caused the French to abandon Indochina and set the stage for the Geneva Conference, which divided the region and led to American involvement in South Vietnam.

★ **Domino Theory** — Eisenhower's metaphor that when one country fell to Communists, its neighbors would then be threatened and collapse one after another like a row of dominoes; this belief became a major rationale for U.S. intervention in Vietnam.

★ **Douglas MacArthur** — World War II hero who led United Nations forces during the Korean War; his outspoken opposition to President Truman's decisions to limit the war cost him his command. He wanted to bomb China, and Truman rejected the idea as too reckless.

★ **Dwight Eisenhower** — World War II hero and president, 1953–1961; his internationalist foreign policy continued Truman's policy of containment but put greater emphasis on military cost-cutting, the threat of nuclear weapons to deter Communist aggression, and Central Intelligence Agency activities to halt communism.

★ **Fidel Castro** — Communist leader of Cuba who led a rebellion against the U.S.-backed dictator and took power in 1959; President Kennedy tried to overthrow him with the Bay of Pigs invasion in 1961 but failed. Castro became closely allied with the Soviet Union, making the Kennedy Administration increasingly concerned about Soviet influence in the Western Hemisphere.

★ **George Kennan** — State Department official who was architect of the containment concept; in his article "The Source of Soviet Conduct" he said the USSR was historically and ideologically driven to expand and that the United States must practice "vigilant containment" to stop this expansion.

★ **Gulf of Tonkin Resolution (1964)** — an authorization by Congress empowering President Johnson "to take all necessary measures" to protect U.S. forces in Vietnam; it was issued following reported attacks on U.S. destroyers off the Vietnam coast. Congress later regretted this action as the Vietnam War escalated, and questions emerged about the legitimacy of the attacks.

★ **Henry Kissinger** — advisor to Presidents Nixon and Ford; he was architect of the Vietnam settlement, the diplomatic opening to China, and détente with the Soviet Union.

★ **Ho Chi Minh** — Communist leader of North Vietnam; he and his Viet Minh/Viet Cong allies fought French and American forces to a standstill in Vietnam, 1946–1973. Considered a nationalist by many, others viewed him as an agent of the Soviet Union and China.

★ **Iran-Contra Affair (1986–1987)** — scandal that erupted after the Reagan administration sold weapons to Iran in hopes of freeing American hostages in Lebanon; money from the arms sales was used to aid the Contras (anti-Communist insurgents) in Nicaragua, even though Congress had prohibited this assistance. Talk of Reagan's impeachment ended when presidential aides took the blame for the illegal activity.

★ **Iran Hostage Crisis (1979–1981)** — incident in which Iranian radicals, with government support, seized 52 Americans from the U.S. embassy and held them for 444 days; ostensibly demanding the return of the deposed Shah to stand trial, the fundamentalist clerics behind the seizure also hoped to punish the United States for other perceived past wrongs.

★ **Jimmy Carter** — president, 1977–1981; he aimed for a foreign policy "as good and great as the American people." His highlight was the Camp David Accords; his low point, the Iran Hostage Crisis. Defeated for reelection after one term, he became very successful as an ex-president.

★ **John Foster Dulles** — Eisenhower's secretary of state, 1953–1959; moralistic in his belief that Communism was evil and must be confronted with "brinkmanship" (the readiness and willingness to go to war) and "massive retaliation" (the threat of using nuclear weapons).

★ **Joseph Stalin** — ruthless leader of Soviet Union from 1925 to 1953; he industrialized the nation and led it in World War II and the early stages of the Cold War.

★ **Lyndon Johnson** — president, 1963–1969; his escalation of the Vietnam War cost him political support and destroyed his presidency. He increased the number of U.S. troops in Vietnam from 16,000 in 1963 to 540,000 in 1968. After the Tet Offensive, he decided to not seek reelection.

HIGH*lights*
of the Period

★ **Mao Zedong** — Communist Chinese leader who won control of China in 1949; a wary ally of the Soviet Union, Mao was an implacable foe of the United States until the 1970s.

★ **Marshall Plan (1947–1954)** — Secretary of State George Marshall's economic aid program to rebuild war-torn Western Europe; it amounted to an enlarged version of the Truman Doctrine, with billions of dollars going to revive European economies and contain Communism.

★ **Massive retaliation** — idea that United States should depend on nuclear weapons to stop Communist aggression; prompted by the frustration of the Korean War stalemate and the desire to save money on military budgets, the concept reduced reliance on conventional forces.

★ **Ngo Dinh Diem** — American ally in South Vietnam from 1954 to 1963; his repressive regime caused the Communist Viet Cong to thrive in the South and required increasing American military aid to stop a Communist takeover. He was killed in a coup in 1963.

★ **Nikita Khrushchev** — Soviet leader, 1954–1964; he was an aggressive revolutionary who hoped to spread Communism into Africa, Asia, and Latin America. Blame for the Cuban Missile Crisis eventually cost him his leadership position in the USSR.

★ **North Atlantic Treaty Organization (NATO) (1949)** — military alliance of the United States, ten Western European countries, and Canada; it was considered a deterrent to Soviet aggression in Europe, with an attack on one NATO nation to be considered as an attack on all members.

★ **Peaceful coexistence (1955–1960)** — period in Soviet-American relations marked by less tension and by personal diplomacy between Khrushchev and Eisenhower; the two leaders recognized that, in a nuclear age, competition between their nations must be peaceful. This thaw in the Cold War was ended by the U-2 spy plane incident over the Soviet Union in 1960.

★ **Richard Nixon** — president, 1969–1974; he extracted the United States from Vietnam slowly, recognized Communist China, and improved relations with the Soviet Union. His foreign policy achievements were overshadowed by the Watergate scandal.

★ **Tet Offensive (January 1968)** — a series of Communist attacks on 44 South Vietnamese cities; although the Viet Cong suffered a major defeat, the attacks ended the American view that the war was winnable and destroyed the nation's will to escalate the war further.

★ **Truman Doctrine (1947)** — the announced policy of President Truman to provide aid to free nations who faced internal or external threats of a Communist takeover; announced in conjunction with a $400 million economic aid package to Greece and Turkey, it was successful in helping those countries put down Communist guerrilla movements and is considered to be the first U.S. action of the Cold War.

★ **Yalta Conference (February 1945)** — meeting of Roosevelt, Stalin, and Winston Churchill to discuss postwar plans and Soviet entry into the war against Japan near the end of World War II; disagreements over the future of Poland surfaced. During the Red Scare of the 1950s, some Americans considered the meeting to have been a sellout to the Soviets.

HIGH*lights* of the Period

Ideas to Ponder

After reviewing the chapter's summary, highlights, and your primary text,
discuss the following with members of your study group.

1. Was the Cold War between the United States and Soviet Union inevitable? Why or why not?

2. How did President Truman establish the cornerstones of American foreign policy for the next forty years?

3. Evaluate containment in Europe and in Asia from 1947 to 1955. What were its successes and failures?

4. How did the Korean conflict change the concept of containment?

5. What lessons did the United States learn from the Korean conflict?

6. How was Eisenhower's "new look" foreign policy a mixture of old and new ideas?

7. In what parts of the world was Eisenhower's foreign policy most successful? The least successful?

8. How did the United States policy toward Indochina/Vietnam from 1945 to 1960 set the stage for the quagmire of the 1960s?

9. Evaluate John Kennedy's policy toward the Soviet Union. Was he just a "cold warrior" with new rhetoric?

10. How were the Bay of Pigs and the Cuban Missile Crisis connected?

11. "The Vietnam War should be called Mr. Kennedy's war rather than Mr. Johnson's." Evaluate this statement.

12. How did the Vietnam War destroy the presidency of Lyndon Johnson?

13. How did Richard Nixon bring a fresh vision to America's place in the world?

14. Evaluate the United States' Middle East policy from 1955 to 1980.

15. What role did the Central Intelligence Agency plan in the Cold War from 1947 to 1975?

16. How did President Carter try to reverse many ideas of Cold War? How successful was he?

17. Why were the American people willing to accept a more active, confrontational approach to world affairs in the 1980s?

18. How did the Reagan administration's zeal to fight Communism in Latin America almost cost the President his job?

Essay Skill

Creating a Rubric for Free-Response Essays

When students complete the Advanced Placement examination in May, the essay section is evaluated by secondary and college teachers, who gather for a week in June to assess the essay answers. In order to ensure validity and reliability of their grades, the readers are trained to use rubric scoring guides to evaluate students' performance. A student who understands the elements of a rubric, how it is constructed, and how it is used in the AP grading process gains important insights into the standards of excellence expected on the test and enhances his/her performance on the essay sections. With an appreciation of the specifics of rubric construction, a student can discover what readers look for as they evaluate student essay answers.

A rubric consists of two elements: a list of the important criteria necessary to demonstrate competency on a specific task and the range or gradation of those criteria in completing the task. The range is usually expressed numerically, with the degree of quality rated from superior to unsatisfactory. Specifically, for AP United States History, a rubric expresses the skills and knowledge that must be demonstrated in writing an essay answer and provides the levels at which those skills/knowledge must be demonstrated in order to achieve superior, above average, average, below average, and poor grades. By analyzing the rubric process, a student answers the question: What do I need to do and know to receive a superior grade on AP United States History prompts? A rubric lists "what counts" in an essay answer. It defines performance expectations and cites the most important components of a superior answer to a prompt.

Below is an excerpt from the rubric used to grade one of the free-response essays on the 1999 AP United States History exam. Examine the various levels of performance that are listed and discuss them with your classmates or with members of your study group. After your discussion, look at the generic observations that are offered about the rubric to see if your analysis was similar to the points mentioned.

"In what ways did economic conditions and developments in the arts and entertainment help create the reputation of the 1920s as the Roaring Twenties?"

The 8–9 essay:

- Contains a clear, well-developed thesis that presents ways that BOTH economic conditions and developments in the arts and entertainment created the reputation of the Roaring Twenties;
- Supports thesis with substantial, relevant information from BOTH areas;
- Discusses BOTH categories but may have some imbalance;
- Emphasizes the link of BOTH categories to the reputation of the Roaring Twenties;
- May contain minor errors.

Essay Skill

The 5–7 essay:

- Presents a thesis that acknowledges BOTH economic conditions and developments in the arts and entertainment and their link to the reputation of the Roaring Twenties;
- Supports thesis with some factual information from BOTH areas. May have information that is not pertinent;
- Addresses BOTH categories but may be imbalanced (uneven treatment);
- Without explanation or elaboration, it acknowledges link of BOTH categories to the reputation of Roaring Twenties, mostly describes conditions and developments;
- May contain errors that do not seriously detract from overall quality of the essay.

The 2–4 essay:

- Contains an unsupported thesis or one that is confused or lacks a thesis;
- Contains information on the 1920s but is mostly unrelated to BOTH categories;
- Does not address BOTH categories;
- May offer links between only ONE category and the reputation of the Roaring Twenties;
- May contain major errors.

The 0–1 essay:

- Provides an incompetent or inappropriate response or is excessively general or vague;
- May simply paraphrase or restate the question;
- Shows little or no understanding of the question;
- May have a few facts but usually has substantial errors.

Observations about the Rubric

- The range of proficiency on the essay is 9–0, with a score of 9 indicating superior achievement and a 0 showing no real effort.
- The criteria for a superior score are:
  - a strong thesis that addresses BOTH parts of the prompt;
  - substantial information for BOTH parts of the prompt;
  - a discussion of BOTH parts of prompt;
  - a strong link established between BOTH parts of the prompt to the reputation of the 1920s;
  - few factual errors.
- The criteria for an average to above-average score are:
  - a thesis that acknowledges BOTH parts of the prompt;
  - some factual information from BOTH areas;
  - BOTH parts of the prompt mentioned in some fashion;
  - linkage of BOTH categories to the reputation of the 1920s acknowledged;
  - several factual errors.

- The criteria for a below-average score are:
  - a confused, weak, or nonexistent thesis;
  - factual information on the 1920s but not related to the topic;
  - does not mention BOTH categories;
  - acknowledges linkage of one category to the reputation issue;
  - contains major errors.

In summary, to score high on this essay prompt, a student would need a strong thesis that included all the elements discussed earlier in the book, substantial factual support that dealt with **all** aspects of the prompt, and an analysis of the relationships of the various elements mentioned in the prompt.

Practicing the Skill

Look at the following prompt on the origins of the Cold War. Fill in the rubric outline provided. When you are done, compare your rubric with those of your classmates or with other members of your study group. At some point, you may wish to look at the sample rubric for this prompt on page 228 of the Suggested Responses section.

"In what ways did TWO of the following events undermine the wartime alliance between the United States and Soviet Union and contribute to the development of the Cold War?"

The Second Front
The Use of the Atomic Bomb
The Yalta Conference

8–9 essay:

- _____
- _____
- _____
- _____
- _____
- _____
- _____

Essay Skill

5–7 essay:

- _____
- _____
- _____
- _____
- _____
- _____
- _____

2–4 essay:

- _____
- _____
- _____
- _____
- _____
- _____
- _____

0–1 essay:

- _____
- _____
- _____
- _____
- _____
- _____
- _____

Document SKILL

Creating a Rubric for a Document-Based Question

The DBQ is also evaluated with a rubric scoring guide. The information concerning the use of rubrics for evaluating free-response essay prompts applies to rubrics for grading a DBQ as well. The one major difference, however, is the need to use sources effectively in order to score high on the DBQ. The rubric for the DBQ must evaluate how well the writer utilizes the various sources available and the degree to which they are integrated into the essay.

Practicing the Skill

Below is the prompt and rubric for the DBQ that appeared on the 2001 AP United States History examination. Study the rubric and discuss it with your classmates or members of your study group. From your discussion, make a list of the most important criterion for scoring in the superior category (8–9) on this prompt. When your list is complete, compare your information with the list on page 229 of the Suggested Responses section.

> What were the Cold War fears of the American people in the aftermath of the Second World War? How successfully did the administration of President Dwight D. Eisenhower address these fears?

Use the documents and your knowledge of the years 1948–1961 to construct your response.

The 8–9 essay:

- Contains a well-developed thesis that **identifies** Cold War fears in the aftermath of World War II and **evaluates** how successfully the Eisenhower administration addressed these fears;
- Discusses **several** Cold War fears 1948–1961 and analyzes the degree of success of the Eisenhower administration in addressing **these fears;**
- Effectively uses a substantial number of documents;
- Supports thesis with substantial and relevant outside information;
- Is clearly organized and well written;
- May contain minor errors.

The 5–7 essay:

- Contains a thesis that **identifies** Cold War fears 1948–1961 and actions taken by the Eisenhower administration;
- Discusses **some** Cold War fears 1948–1961 and some actions taken by Eisenhower administration with regard to Cold War issues; may have limited analysis and may focus considerably more on one part of the question than the other;
- Uses some documents effectively;

Document **SKILL**

- Supports evidence of acceptable organization and writing; language errors do not interfere with comprehension of the essay;
- May contain errors that do not seriously detract from the quality of the essay.

The 2–4 essay:

- Contains a limited, confused, and/or poorly developed thesis;
- Deals with the question in a general manner; simplistic explanation or answers only one part of the question;
- Quotes or briefly cites some documents;
- Contains little outside information or information that is generally inaccurate;
- Has problems in organization;
- May contain major errors.

The 0–1 essay:

- Contains no thesis or a thesis that does not address the question;
- Exhibits inadequate or inaccurate understanding of the question;
- Contains little or no understanding of the documents or ignores them completely;
- Is so poorly organized or written that it inhibits understanding;
- Contains numerous errors, both major and minor.

In your own words, list the criteria necessary for a superior grade on the prompt.

1. _____

2. _____

3. _____

4. _____

5. _____

6. _____

Chapter 14

STRUGGLING FOR THE AMERICAN DREAM
1945–1968

Focus Questions

★ In what way did Presidents Truman, Kennedy, and Johnson operate in the political shadow of Franklin D. Roosevelt?

★ How did President Eisenhower establish "modern Republicanism" in the 1950s as an answer to the New Deal?

★ How and why did America drift into a new Red Scare in the 1950s?

★ How did the Civil Rights Movement gain political and social momentum from 1948 to 1968?

★ How did social and political upheavals make the 1960s the most tumultuous decade of the twentieth century for the American people?

★ How did the Vietnam War undermine Lyndon Johnson's dream of a "Great Society" in America?

Summary

By the end of 1945, Americans feared new economic troubles as the government cut war spending and soldiers returned home looking for work. Depression was not the problem from 1945 to 1947, however. Business boomed, with $140 billion in private savings flowing into the economy, and prices rose 25 percent. In addition to inflation, organized labor, using powers gained in the 1930s, struck for higher wages. There were five thousand strikes in 1946 alone, with major disruptions in many essential industries.

The Fair Deal

Truman tried to address these problems and other concerns with his Fair Deal, a continuation of the reform philosophy of the 1930s. He proposed expanding Social Security, national health insurance, and a limited civil rights program. The country rejected most of his ideas and the Republican-controlled Congress challenged the President with the anti-union Taft-Hartley Act.

In 1948, Truman's domestic program was in tatters, and his political future bleak. No one expected him to win election that year as his party split three ways, with Strom Thurmond attacking his civil rights proposals and Henry Wallace criticizing his hard-line policy toward the Soviet Union. Further, Republicans were confident that Thomas Dewey would lead them to victory. Truman simply went out and "gave the Republicans hell" over their "do-nothing" Congress and their past connection with the Depression. The results shocked the nation as Truman won 303 electoral votes to Dewey's 189. However, he still was unable to enact his reforms during his first full term.

Modern Republicanism

After twenty years of Democrats in the White House and with the Korean War stalemated, the nation elected Dwight Eisenhower president in 1952. The Republicans realized that the core of the New Deal programs was popular and had to be maintained. Eisenhower called for "modern Republicanism," which extended social programs but without deficit spending. He emphasized fiscal discipline, took a pro-business stance toward economic development, and limited federal actions. He did not, however, dismantle the New Deal. Eisenhower extended Social Security, raised the minimum wage, enacted the Federal Highway Act and the National Defense Education Act, and created the Department of Health, Education, and Welfare.

While some saw the 1950s as a time of social and cultural sterility led by "organization men" and "other-directed" people, Eisenhower presided over an era of peace and prosperity. The Gross National Product grew by 25 percent, inflation was 1.4 percent, the nation achieved three balanced budgets, and 25 percent of all the houses ever built were constructed in the 1950s. Eisenhower won reelection in 1956, once again decisively defeating Adali Stevenson. Yet, by 1960, with the shock of *Sputnik* and a lingering recession, Eisenhower's staid policies seemed stale to many.

The Second Red Scare

The issue of internal subversion complicated the presidencies of both Truman and Eisenhower. A second Red Scare swept the country from 1947 to 1960, as fears grew that Americans were spying for the Soviet Union. Fueled by Communist takeovers in Czechoslovakia and China, the Korean stalemate, and the Soviet acquisition of nuclear weapons, many Americans succumbed to this hysteria that ruined thousands of people's lives and careers. Investigated by the House Un-American Activities Committee, Truman's Loyalty Review Board, and ambitious politicians such as Richard Nixon, many Americans' loyalty became suspect. In addition, the high-profile spy trials of Alger Hiss and Julius and Ethel Rosenberg made the charges of espionage extremely believable.

The leader of the Red Scare was Senator Joseph R. McCarthy. From 1950 to 1954, he was the most ruthless and feared Communist hunter in America. Although he uncovered no spies, McCarthy maintained his power until he attacked the Department of Army. In televised hearings, McCarthy showed himself to be unscrupulous and without proof for his reckless charges. His censure in December 1954 and death in 1957 helped end the most egregious phase of the hysteria, although its effects lingered well into the 1960s.

The New Frontier and Great Society

In the early 1960s, President John Kennedy used his youth, glamour, and rhetoric to inspire Americans "to ask what [they] could do for [their] country." His domestic successes were more promise than progress, however. While he proposed a number of New Deal/Fair Deal types of reforms, such as medical care for the elderly, urban renewal, aid to education, and a civil rights bill, his agenda still languished in Congress. On November 22, 1963, he was assassinated.

Lyndon Johnson had the most successful domestic presidential record since Franklin Roosevelt. He used the trauma of Kennedy's death, his own enormous political skills, and Republican disarray to establish his Great Society program. From 1964 to 1967, Johnson convinced Congress to approve Kennedy's stalled agenda of tax cuts, Medicare, and the Civil Rights Act of 1964. In addition, Johnson added an avalanche of achievements of his own. In the mid-1960s, Congress approved 181 out of 200 bills, including the Civil Rights Act of 1965, Head Start, and sixty aid-to-education bills.

His program was doomed by Vietnam, however. As the war became a quagmire, the nation turned against the Great Society. In 1968, his own party revolted against him as Eugene McCarthy and Robert Kennedy challenged his renomination. By the July convention, Johnson had withdrawn from the race, Robert Kennedy had been assassinated, and the party was divided. Hubert Humphrey tried to unite the Democrats, but Republican Richard Nixon and third-party candidate, George Wallace used the discontent over the war and domestic lawlessness to defeat the Democrats.

Civil Rights

After World War II, the Civil Rights Movement flickered to life and became the dominant social movement in the country. Truman initiated the drive when he desegregated the military and proposed a series of government actions to erode the Jim Crow system. He made little progress, however, and antagonized many in his own party in 1948.

President Eisenhower did not support direct government action on behalf of blacks, yet civil rights crowded his domestic agenda. Blacks, energized by the *Brown vs. Board of Education* decision and led by Martin Luther King, pressed the nation for justice. While Eisenhower sent troops to Little Rock and signed the Civil Rights Acts of 1957 and 1960, he failed to use his office to affirm true racial justice.

John and Robert Kennedy were also weak in supporting King's drive for equality. They were deeply affected, however, by the sit-ins, freedom rides, and King's nonviolent protests for equal rights. After several bloody retaliations by southern officials to demonstrations, the president finally proposed a civil rights bill to Congress. King and his supporters marched on Washington in August of 1963 to lobby for its passage.

The Civil Rights Movement's truest friend was President Johnson. He drove Kennedy's civil rights bill through Congress in 1964 and added his own in 1965. In addition, his War on Poverty directly affected thousands of blacks through aid for public housing, education, and job training. By 1966, civil rights topped the nation's social agenda, but violence and division undermined its continuing success. King's nonviolent message came under increasing criticism as urban riots swept the nation. Further, militants such as Malcolm X and advocates of Black Power questioned King's relevance. King's assassination in 1968 brought his martyrdom but fragmented the movement even further. By 1968, a white backlash against militant rhetoric and violence propelled George Wallace to political prominence and further jeopardized racial progress.

★ **Alger Hiss** — State Department official accused in 1948 of spying for the Soviet Union; Richard Nixon became famous for his pursuit of Hiss, which resulted in a perjury conviction and prison for Hiss. Although long seen as a victim of Nixon's ruthless ambition and the Red Scare, recent scholarship suggests that Hiss was indeed a Soviet agent.

★ **Barry Goldwater** — unsuccessful presidential candidate against Lyndon Johnson in 1964; he called for dismantling the New Deal, escalation of the war in Vietnam, and the status quo on civil rights. Many see him as the grandfather of the conservative movement of the 1980s.

★ **Black Power** — rallying cry for many black militants in the 1960s and 1970s; it called for blacks to stand up for their rights, to reject integration, to demand political power, to seek their roots, and to embrace their blackness.

★ *Brown vs. Board of Education* **(1954)** — Supreme Court decision that overturned the *Plessy vs. Ferguson* decision (1896); led by Chief Justice Earl Warren, the Court ruled that "separate but equal" schools for blacks were inherently unequal and thus unconstitutional. The decision energized the Civil Rights Movement in the 1950s and 1960s.

★ **Civil Rights Act of 1964** — proposed by John Kennedy and signed by Lyndon Johnson; it desegregated public accommodations, libraries, parks, and amusements and broadened the powers of federal government to protect individual rights and prevent job discrimination.

★ **Civil Rights Act of 1965** — sometimes called Voting Rights Act, it expanded the federal government's protection of voters and voter registration; it also increased federal authority to investigate voter irregularities and outlawed literacy tests.

★ **Earl Warren** — controversial Chief Justice of the Supreme Court (1953–1969); he led the Court in far-reaching racial, social, and political rulings, including school desegregation and protecting rights of persons accused of crimes.

★ **Fair Deal** — Truman's legislative program; it was largely an extension of the New Deal of the 1930s, and Truman had little success convincing Congress to enact it.

★ **Federal Highway Act (1956)** — largest public works project in United States history; Eisenhower signed the law, which built over 40,000 miles of highways in the United States at a cost of $25 billion and created the interstate highway system.

★ **Freedom rides** — civil rights campaign of the Congress of Racial Equality in which protesters traveled by bus through the South to desegregate bus stations; white violence against them prompted the Kennedy administration to protect them and become more involved in civil rights.

★ **George Wallace** — Alabama governor and third-party candidate for president in 1968 and 1972; he ran on a segregation and law-and-order platform. Paralyzed by an attempted assassination in 1972, he never recovered politically.

★ **House Un-American Activities Committee** — congressional committee formed in the 1930s to investigate perceived threats to democracy; in the 1940s, the committee laid foundation for the Red Scare as it investigated allegations of Communist subversion in Hollywood and pursued Alger Hiss.

★ **Hubert Humphrey** — liberal senator from Minnesota and Lyndon Johnson's vice president who tried to unite the party after the tumultuous 1968 Democratic National Convention in Chicago; he narrowly lost the presidency to Richard Nixon that year.

★ **John Kennedy** — president, 1961–1963, and the youngest president ever elected, as well as the first Catholic to serve; he had a moderately progressive domestic agenda and a hard-line policy against the Soviets. His administration ended when Lee Harvey Oswald assassinated him.

★ **Joseph McCarthy** — junior senator from Wisconsin who charged hundreds of Americans with working for or aiding the Soviet Union during the Cold War; he had no evidence but terrorized people from 1950 to 1954, ruining their lives and careers with his reckless charges until Senate censured him in December 1954.

★ **Julius and Ethel Rosenberg** — an engineer and his wife who were accused, tried, and executed in the early 1950s for running an espionage ring in New York City that gave atomic secrets to the Soviet Union; long considered unjustly accused victims of the Red Scare, recent evidence suggests that Julius was indeed a Soviet agent.

★ **Lyndon Johnson** — president, 1963–1969, who took over for Kennedy and created the Great Society, a reform program unmatched in the twentieth century; however, his Vietnam policy divided the country and his party, and he retired from politics in 1969.

★ **Malcolm X (Little)** — militant black leader associated with the Nation of Islam (Black Muslims); he questioned Martin Luther King's strategy of nonviolence and called on blacks to make an aggressive defense of their rights. He was assassinated by fellow Muslims in 1965.

★ **Martin Luther King, Jr.** — America's greatest civil rights leader, 1955–1968; his nonviolent protests gained national attention and resulted in government protection of African American rights. He was assassinated in 1968 in Memphis, Tennessee.

★ **National Defense Education Act (1958)** — law that authorized the use of federal funds to improve the nation's elementary and high schools; inspired by Cold War fears that the United States was falling behind the Soviet Union in the arms and space race, it was directed at improving science, math, and foreign-language education.

★ **Richard Nixon** — controversial vice president, 1953–1961, and president, 1969–1974, who made his political reputation as an aggressive anti-Communist crusader; his presidency ended with his resignation during the Watergate scandal.

★ **Robert Kennedy** — John Kennedy's brother who served as attorney general and gradually embraced growing civil rights reform; later, as senator from New York, he made a run for the Democratic presidential nomination. An assassin ended his campaign on June 6, 1968.

★ **Rosa Parks** — NAACP member who initiated the Montgomery Bus Boycott in 1955 when she was arrested for violating Jim Crow rules on a bus; her action and the long boycott that followed became an icon of the quest for civil rights and focused national attention on boycott leader Martin Luther King, Jr.

★ **Sit-ins** — protests by black college students, 1960–1961, who took seats at "whites only" lunch counters and refused to leave until served; in 1960 over 50,000 participated in sit-ins across the South. Their success prompted the formation of the Student Non-Violent Coordinating Committee.

★ *Sputnik* — Soviet satellite launched in September 1957; the launch set off a panic that the Communists were winning the space race and were superior in math and science education. It gave impetus for the Nation Defense Education Act of 1958 to improve schools.

★ **Strom Thurmond** — Democratic governor of South Carolina who headed the States' Rights Party (Dixiecrats); he ran for president in 1948 against Truman and his mild civil rights proposals and eventually joined the Republican Party.

★ **Taft-Hartley Act (1946)** — antilabor law passed over Truman's veto; it provided a "cooling off" period wherein the president could force striking workers back to work for 80 days. It also outlawed closed shops and allowed states to pass right-to-work laws.

★ **Thomas Dewey** — twice-defeated Republican candidate for president (1944, 1948); his overconfidence and lackadaisical effort in 1948 allowed Truman to overcome his large lead and pull off the greatest political upset in American history.

★ **Thurgood Marshall** — leading attorney for NAACP in 1940s and 1950s, who headed the team in *Brown vs. the Board of Education* case; later, Lyndon Johnson appointed him the first black justice on the United States Supreme Court.

HIGH*lights*
of the Period

Ideas to Ponder

After reviewing the chapter's summary, highlights, and your primary text,
discuss the following with members of your study group.

1   How did President Truman attempt to continue the philosophy of the New Deal after World War II?

2   How did President Truman achieve the greatest political upset victory in American history in 1948?

3   How did President Truman bring African Americans into the Democratic Party in the 1940s?

4   How did President Eisenhower incorporate the New Deal into his "modern Republicanism"?

5   Why did civil rights become important in America from 1955 to 1965?

6   Why did Americans support Joseph McCarthy's anti-Communist crusade?

7   Why did the Red Scare subside in the late 1950s?

8   In what ways was President Kennedy's administration more style than substance?

9   What caused the tension between Dr. Martin Luther King, Jr., and the Kennedy brothers in the early 1960s?

10 How did events and personalities challenge Martin Luther King's leadership of the Civil Rights Movement after 1963?

11 How did the Great Society make lasting changes in America? Where did it fail and why?

12 How did political assassination alter the history of the 1960s?

13 Why did George Wallace enjoy significant political support in the 1960s?

14 How was Hubert Humphrey a casualty of the Vietnam War in 1968?

15 How did the Warren Court change America's social and political systems from 1954 to 1969?

Essay Skill

Steps in Writing a Free-Response Essay

Throughout this book, you have explored specific skills and strategies to facilitate writing a free-response essay. In this section, those elements are reviewed and summarized into a concise outline.

In writing a free-response essay, you should:

1. identify the critical words in the prompt that indicate:
   - the time period;
   - what process is required (e.g., assess the validity, evaluate, compare/contrast);
   - what content is appropriate as supportive information (e.g., political, social, economic, cultural, intellectual).

2. ask several clarifying questions about the prompt to focus on the issues at hand.

3. decide which prompt or aspects of a prompt to write about by:
   - making a list of possible information AND
   - selecting the prompt or aspects of the prompt with the longest, most detailed list.

4. organize the facts by developing:
   - a network tree OR
   - an outline.

5. write a strong thesis statement that:
   - deals with all aspects of the topic;
   - takes a clear position;
   - provides an organizational framework;
   - addresses the core issues; AND
   - may be positive, negative, or a combination of both.

6. organize facts into categories such as:
   - political, economic, and social (always good bets);
   - chronological periods.

7. be sure to answer the prompt completely by:
   - dealing with all topics suggested AND/OR
   - examining the entire chronological period mentioned.

8. write a strong introductory paragraph that has:
   - a thesis;
   - a general description of the topics to be addressed in the essay;
   - (perhaps) a definition of important terms;
   - a transitional sentence that links the paragraph to the body of the paper.

9. provide paragraphs with topic sentences that support the thesis.

10. write a concluding paragraph that:
    - summarizes the thesis;
    - reviews the significant points from the body of the essay.

Essay Skill

Practicing the Skill

Discuss these ten steps with your classmates or with the members of your study group. It might be helpful for individuals to share which of the steps have been the most difficult for them to master. If there is misunderstandings or confusion about a step, refer to the section in the book that discusses the idea and try to reach agreement about how it should be implemented.

Document SKILL

Steps in Writing a Document-Based Question

In the book, you have examined various ideas and strategies that are helpful in writing a Document-Based Question (DBQ). In this section, the steps for developing a DBQ will be reviewed and summarized. In many ways, writing a DBQ and writing a free-response essay are similar. Both require a thesis, several supporting paragraphs, and a concluding paragraph. The major difference between the two types of essays is the need to integrate documents along with outside information into the DBQ. Also, a strong DBQ should contain a contrary or concession paragraph to account for dissenting documents and data.

In writing a DBQ, you should:

1. read the prompt several times.

2. rephrase the prompt into a question (if it is a statement) or create a clarifying question (if it is already in question form).

3. make a list of all the information about the **era** under consideration. Write this list **BEFORE** looking at the documents. Don't be concerned that the information listed may appear later in the documents. These facts can be eliminated before you start to write your paper, but initially, "drain your brain."

4. summarize each of the sources using some modification of the analytical devices that were introduced throughout the book (e.g., five Ws for documents, TACOS for cartoons, and 3TRG for charts).

5. quickly survey the outside information and the summaries of the sources and construct a thesis statement suggested by the data.

6. sort the sources and outside information into two categories—those that support your thesis (+) and those that challenge it (−).

7. gather these (+)s and (−)s into a chart of supporting and challenging materials.

8. organize the supporting materials into appropriate categories and write the essay. (Remember to include an introductory paragraph and several supporting paragraphs.)

9. survey the (−)/con/challenge side of the chart and write a contrary or concession paragraph to include this information. This paragraph should come just before the concluding paragraph.

10. write a concluding paragraph.

Practicing the Skill

Discuss these ten steps with your classmates or with the members of your study group. A good discussion question might be: which DBQ that you wrote this year was the most difficult, and which part of the process gave you the most trouble? If questions arise about a specific step, return to "Tackling the DBQ" in the introduction or "Organizing the Document-Based Question" in Chapter 12 to review the information and to clear up confusion about the process.

Chapter 15

CRISIS OF CONFIDENCE

1968–1980s

Focus Questions

★ How was Richard Nixon's domestic program a blend of liberal and conservative ideas and policies?

★ How did the Watergate scandal destroy the Nixon presidency?

★ How did the cultural and social upheavals of the 1960s stretch America's social fabric in the 1970s?

★ How did Jimmy Carter's idealism fail to translate into effective presidential policies?

★ How did Ronald Reagan use national dissatisfactions in the late 1970s to launch his "revolution" in the 1980s?

Summary

A postwar baby boom helped ferment a cultural revolution in the 1960s. By 1970, some 50 percent of the population was under age 30, and there was an eight-fold increase in the number of college students since 1950. Influenced by the civil rights struggle and the troubling Vietnam War, many young people questioned the political, social, and economic assumptions of their parents and their government. In 1962, politically active youths formed the **Students for a Democratic Society (SDS)**. Dedicated to participatory democracy, appalled by racial bigotry and America's growing involvement in Vietnam, this group powered many of the protests of the 1960s.

Social Protests

"**Hippies**" were a nonpolitical segment of the youth movement who rejected the activism of the "**New Left**." These nonconformists used drugs, condemned materialism, and generally scorned the values of their middle-class parents. They rejected the sexual beliefs of the past and the bureaucratic practices of large corporations and universities.

Many young women in the 1960s hoped to join the civil rights and antiwar movements but found gender bias among the male leaders. Other women, inspired by the writings of **Betty Friedan**, began to question not only their status in protest movements but their role in American society generally. In 1966, Friedan and others formed the National Organization for Women (NOW), which lobbied for an **Equal Rights Amendment**. By 1970, some 15,000 women belonged to NOW. As the 1970s ended, younger women rallied around the more radical ideas of **Kate Millett** and issued a call for women to band together for an assault on the male power structure.

Nixon's Presidency

Returning from a political wilderness in the 1960s, Richard Nixon became president in 1969. His goals were clear: end the Vietnam War, restore law and order in society, and reestablish Americans' faith in their government. While he was successful in two of the areas, he seriously damaged the country's confidence in the honesty of the government with the **Watergate scandal**.

Nixon took a moderate approach to domestic policy as he demonstrated both liberal and conservative political inclinations. As a conservative, he tried to appoint "strict constructionists" to the Supreme Court and to limit school busing for desegregation. He also abolished the Office of Economic Opportunity, a cornerstone of Johnson's Great Society program. On the other hand, he increased Social Security benefits, created the Environmental Protection Agency, promoted affirmative action in unions, and proposed a "minimum income" for the poor.

Despite several bold initiatives, Nixon was unable to bring economic prosperity to the nation. Inflation was the principle culprit in holding back progress. In his first two years in office, the cost of living increased by 15 percent. In addition, fueled by Vietnam War spending and a 400 percent hike in the price of oil, inflation was 9 percent in 1973 and 12 percent in 1974. Despite devaluing the dollar and imposing wage and price controls, Nixon could not overcome the economic "stagflation" of his presidency.

Although economic problems persisted, Nixon wound down the Vietnam War, quieted domestic unrest, and defused the antiwar protest. Based on these achievements and supported by the "Silent Majority," he easily defeated Democrat **George McGovern** in the 1972 presidential contest.

Watergate

The unraveling of the Nixon presidency began on June 17, 1972, when police caught burglars attempting to bug the Democratic Party headquarters in the Watergate hotel. As the investigation of the crime progressed, it uncovered other break-ins, illegal surveillances, questionable campaign contributions, and other shady activities by the Nixon White House. Rather than allowing these revelations to surface, the president and his aides tried to cover up the Watergate break-in and avoid its political fallout.

Contained until after the November election, the cover-up collapsed when, in March 1973, **James McCord**, one of the so called "plumbers," confessed that he and other burglars had committed perjury and been paid to remain silent. Slowly the scandal spread into the White House, and Nixon's closest aides, **John Mitchell** and **H. R. Haldeman**, were indicted for obstructing justice. Another aide, **John Dean**, accused Nixon himself of being involved. Other officials disclosed that Nixon had a taping system in the Oval Office, and the prosecutors investigating the crime demanded the tapes.

After months of haggling, the Supreme Court ordered the President to surrender the critical tapes. Already under the threat of impeachment for obstructing justice, misusing federal agencies, and defying Congress, Nixon released the "smoking gun" tapes, which revealed he had indeed obstructed justice. On August 9, 1974, rather than face certain impeachment and removal from office, Richard Nixon resigned the presidency.

Vice President **Gerald Ford** entered the White House. He tried to restore the confidence of the country in the government and in the economy. Although a decent man, Ford's pardon of Nixon in September 1974 and his inability to combat the continuing stagflation of the 1970s cost him his election bid in 1976, as Jimmy Carter and the Democrats returned to power.

Carter's Presidency

President Carter promised never to lie to the people (as Johnson and Nixon had done) and to run the govern- ment in a businesslike fashion. Unfortunately, he was inconsistent and unfocused as president. In addition, he was besieged by continuing economic troubles caused by the oil-induced energy crisis. Inflation gained momentum and by 1978–1979, prices were rising 10 percent annually. As the Federal Reserve tried to get inflation under control, interest rates hit an unprecedented 21 percent in 1980, further damaging economic growth. When Carter chastised the nation for its lack of character in these trying times, his popularity fell.

The Reagan Revolution

In 1980, Carter faced a sea of trouble. The economy continued to falter, fellow Democrat Edward Kennedy challenged his renomination, and an attempted rescue of the American hostages in Iran ended in disaster. Under these circumstances, it was not surprising that Republican **Ronald Reagan** defeated Carter in a landslide victory in November.

Reagan promised a new direction for America in 1981. Building on widespread disillusionment with Carter, hostility to government taxing and regulatory policies, and promising to reassert traditional cultural values, the new administration embarked on what some people called the "**Reagan Revolution**." Over the next years, Reagan would cut social spending, reduce income taxes 30 percent, and embark on a massive military buildup to confront the USSR around the globe. In so doing, he created huge budget deficits and an uneven prosperity in the country. On the other hand, he restored America's pride in itself and faith in the presidency. His political legacy remains a hotly debated partisan issue today.

* **Betty Friedan** — author of *The Feminine Mystique* (1963), which raised the issue of a woman's place in society and how deadening suburban "happiness" could be for women; her ideas sparked the women's movement to life in the 1960s.

* **Equal Rights Amendment (ERA)** — proposed amendment to the U.S. Constitution passed by Congress and submitted to the states for ratification in 1971; outlawing discrimination based on gender, it was at first seen as a great victory by women's-rights groups. The amendment fell 3 states short of the 38 required for ratification. However, many states have adopted similar amendments to their state constitutions.

* **George McGovern** — unsuccessful Democratic candidate for president in 1972; he called for immediate withdrawal from Vietnam and a guaranteed income for the poor. When his vice presidential choice got into trouble, he waffled in his defense, which cost him further with the electorate.

* **Gerald Ford** — president, 1974–1977, who served without being elected either president or vice president; appointed vice president under the terms of the Twenty-Fifth Amendment when Spiro Agnew resigned, he assumed the presidency when Nixon resigned.

* **H. R. Haldeman** — a key aide to President Nixon who ordered the CIA and FBI not to probe too deeply into the Watergate break-in; he helped provide money to keep the burglars quiet and was later sentenced to prison for his role in Watergate.

* **Hippies** — members of the youthful counterculture that dominated many college campuses in the 1960s; rather than promoting a political agenda, they challenged conventional sexual standards, rejected traditional economic values, and encouraged the use of drugs.

* **James McCord** — one of the "plumbers" who worked for the White House to plug "leaks" to the media; he committed illegal break-ins and surveillances. His revelations in 1973 that he was being paid to keep quiet began the unraveling of the Watergate cover-up.

* **John Dean** — White House aide who participated in the Watergate cover-up; in a plea bargain, he testified that President Nixon knew and participated in the cover-up. Many did not believe his testimony until the White House tapes surfaced.

* **John Mitchell** — Nixon's first attorney general and his close friend and adviser; many people believe he ordered the Watergate break-in. He participated in the cover-up and served nineteen months in prison for his role.

* **Kate Millett** — author of *Sexual Politics* (1969), a book that energized the more radical elements in the women's liberation movement with its confrontational messages about the male-dominated power structure in American society.

★ **New Left** — label for the political radicals of the 1960s; influenced by "Old Left" of the 1930s, which had criticized capitalism and supported successes of Communism, the New Left supported civil rights and opposed American foreign policy, especially in Vietnam.

★ **National Organization for Women (NOW)** — founded by Betty Friedan and others in 1966; it focused on women's rights in the workplace, fought against legal and economic discrimination against women, and lobbied for the Equal Rights Amendment.

★ **Organization of Petroleum Exporting Countries (OPEC)** — cartel of oil-exporting nations, which used oil as a weapon to alter America's Middle East policy; it organized a series of oil boycotts that roiled the United States economy throughout the 1970s.

★ **Reagan Revolution** — the policies of the first Reagan administration, which increased defense spending, reduced social programs, and cut taxes; they were based on "supply side" theory of growing the economy by cutting government interference and taxes.

★ **Ronald Reagan** — president, 1981–1989, who led a conservative movement against détente with the Soviet Union and the growth of the federal government; some people credit him with America's victory in the Cold War while others fault his insensitive social agenda and irresponsible fiscal policies.

★ **Saturday Night Massacre (October 1973)** — name given to an incident in which Nixon ordered Attorney General Elliot Richardson to fire Archibald Cox, the special prosecutor who was relentlessly investigating Watergate; Richardson refused and resigned along with his deputy, who also refused to carry out Nixon's order. A subordinate then fired Cox. The incident created a firestorm of protest in the country.

★ **Silent Majority** — label Nixon gave to middle-class Americans who supported him, obeyed the laws, and wanted "peace with honor" in Vietnam; he contrasted this group with students and civil rights activists who disrupted the country with protests in the late 1960s and early 1970s.

★ **Spiro Agnew** — vice president, 1969–1973, and a vocal critic of antiwar and civil rights opponents of the Nixon administration; he resigned the vice presidency in 1973 when it was discovered he had accepted bribes as governor of Maryland and as vice president.

★ **Stagflation** — name given the economic condition throughout most of the 1970s in which prices rose rapidly (inflation) but without economic growth (stagnation). Unemployment rose along with inflation. In large part, these conditions were the economic consequences of rising oil prices.

★ **Students for a Democratic Society (SDS) (1962)** — radical political organization founded by Tom Hayden and others; it set forth its ideals in the Port Huron Statement: government should promote equality, fairness, and be responsive to people. It was probably the most important student protest group of the 1960s.

★ **Warren Burger** — Chief Justice of the Supreme Court, 1969–1986; although considered more conservative in leadership than Earl Warren, his court upheld school busing, a woman's right to an abortion, and ordered Nixon to surrender the Watergate tapes.

★ **Watergate scandal** — name applied to a series of events that began when the Nixon White House tried to place illegal phone taps on Democrats in June 1972; the burglars were caught, and rather than accept the legal and political fallout, Nixon and his aides obstructed the investigation, which cost him his office and sent several of his top aides to prison.

★ **Woodstock** — a three-day rock music festival (August 15–17, 1969) held on a farm in New York's Sullivan County; attended by some 300,000 young people, this remarkable and unusually peaceful event is considered the high point of the counterculture in the 1960s and 1970s.

HIGH*lights*
of the Period

Ideas to Ponder

After reviewing the chapter's summary, highlights, and your primary text,
discuss the following with members of your study group.

1   How did the rise of the New Left and the counterculture reflect generational differences in America in the 1960s?

2   How did the Civil Rights Movement and Vietnam War provide the impetus for a new feminist movement in the 1960s and 1970s?

3   How could the cultural and political turmoil of the 1960s have been avoided?

4   How well did the political label "liberal" fit the presidency of Richard Nixon? Explain.

5   How did the domestic challenges faced by President Nixon drive his political agenda?

6   Why didn't President Nixon tell the truth about Watergate?

7   Why didn't President Nixon destroy the White House tapes?

8   If Watergate had not occurred, how might the history of the 1970s have been different?

9   Why did Gerald Ford lose the election of 1976?

10 How did the energy crisis of the 1970s undermine the presidencies of Nixon, Ford, and Carter?

11 How did President Carter fail the American people?

12 Would President Carter have won the election of 1980 if the hostages had been freed in Iran? Why or why not?

13 "Ronald Reagan was one of America's greatest presidents." Evaluate this statement.

Essay Skill

Writing a Free-Response Essay

Below are three prompts about United States history from the 1790s to the 1960s. Select one of the three prompts and write a free-response essay answer about it. Use the planning procedures and strategies recommended earlier in the book and allot 35 minutes for writing your answer. When you have completed your essay, look at page 230 in the Suggested Responses section for suggested themes and specific information that might appear in your answer. Each one of the three prompts is summarized in the Suggested Responses section, so **if you do not peek at the other two essays**, you can repeat this process two more times before the Advanced Placement examination and test your knowledge of each of the three periods of history.

Practicing the Skill

1. "While the Federalists saw America's economic future clearly, they badly misread its political possibilities."

Assess the validity of this statement by reviewing the economic and political ideas and policies of the Federalist party from 1789 to 1801.

2. "In the Gilded Age, the two political parties failed the American people. The Republicans abandoned earlier principles and the Democrats would not change with the times."

Evaluate this statement by discussing how the parties dealt with TWO of the following issues from 1868 to 1896.

    Currency reform
    Honesty in government
    Civil rights

3. "Many American social and political problems in the 1950s grew into major crises for the nation in the 1960s."

Assess the validity of this statement by discussing TWO of the following topics from 1950 to 1970.

    The Vietnam conflict
    The Civil Rights Movement
    United States–Cuban relations

_____

_____

_____

_____

_____

Essay Skill

Essay Skill

Document SKILL

Writing a Document-Based Essay

Below is a Document-Based Question about the 1960s. Using the planning techniques suggested earlier in the book, write an essay response to the prompt. When you have completed your answer (allot yourself 15 minutes for preparation and 40–45 minutes to write), compare your response with a suggested set of themes, document use, and outside information on page 230 of the Suggested Responses section.

Practicing the Skill

The following question requires you to write an essay that uses Documents A–J AND your knowledge of the period mentioned.

> Evaluate the impact of the war in Vietnam on American society from 1961 to 1970. To what extent did the war challenge America to redefine its political and social beliefs?

★ Document A

> *The deteriorating situation in South Viet-Nam requires attention to the nature and scope of the United States national interests in that country. The loss of South Viet-Nam to Communism would involve the transfer of a nation of 20 million people from the free world to the Communism block. The loss of South Viet-Nam would make pointless any further discussion about the importance of Southeast Asia to the free world. . . . The United States should commit itself to the clear objective of preventing the fall of South Viet-Nam to Communist [sic]. . . . We should be prepared to introduce United States combat forces if that should become necessary for success. Dependent upon the circumstances, it may also be necessary for United States forces to strike at the source of the aggression in North Viet-Nam.*
>
> —Excerpts, Dean Rusk and Robert McNamara's Report to President Kennedy, November 11, 1961

Document SKILL

★ Document B

> *Unlike youth in other countries we are used to moral leadership being exercised and moral dimensions being clarified by our elders. But today, for us, not even the liberal and socialist preachments of the past seem adequate to the forms of the present . . . We oppose the depersonalization that reduces human beings to the status of things. . . . As a social system we seek the establishment of a democracy of individual participation, governed by two central aims: that the individual share in those social decisions determining the quality and direction of life, that society be organized to encourage independence in men and provide the media for their common participation.*
>
> *It is imperative that the means of violence be abolished and the institutions—local, national, international—that encourage non-violence as a condition of conflict be developed. [Thousands of students] move actively and directly against racial injustices, the threat of war, violations of the individual rights of conscience, and, less frequently, against economic manipulation. . . .*
>
> —Excerpts, Port Huron Statement, June 1962 (Tom Hayden)

★ Document C

Vietnam War protesters outside the White House, November 30, 1965

★ Document D

> *We will stay because a just nation cannot leave to the cruelties of its enemies a people who have staked their lives and independence on America's solemn pledge—a pledge which has grown through the commitments of three American Presidents. . . . To yield to force in Viet-Nam would weaken that confidence, would undermine the independence of many lands, and would whet the appetite of aggression. We would have to fight in one land, and then we would have to fight in another—or abandon much of Asia to the domination of Communists.*
>
> —Lyndon Johnson's State of Union Address, January 12, 1966

★ Document E

The Strategists Bill Mauldin, *The Sun-Times* (Chicago), 1966

Document SKILL

★ Document F

> *The official war aims . . . , as I understand them are to defeat what is regarded as North Vietnamese aggression, to demonstrate the futility of what the communists call "wars of national liberation," and to create conditions under which the South Vietnamese people will be able freely to determine their own future. . . . What I do doubt . . . is the ability of the United States to achieve these aims by the means being used. I do not question the power of our weapons and the efficiency of our logistics; . . . What I do question is the ability of the United States, or France or any Western nation, to go into a[n] . . . undeveloped Asian nation and create . . . democracy where there is no tradition of it and honest government where corruption is almost a way of life.*
>
> *The cause of our difficulties in southeast Asia is not a deficiency of power but an excess of the wrong kind of power which results in a feeling of impotence when it fails to achieve the desired ends. . . . We are trying to remake Vietnamese society, a task which certainly cannot be accomplished by force and which probably cannot be accomplished by any means available to outsiders. . . .*
>
> —Senator J. William Fulbright, *The Arrogance of Power*, 1966

★ Document G

> *A few years ago there was a shining moment. . . . It seemed as if there was a real promise of hope for the poor—both black and white—through the poverty program. There were experiments, hopes, new beginnings. Then came the buildup in Vietnam and I watched the program broken and eviscerated as if it were some idle political plaything of a society gone mad about war, and I knew that America would never invest the necessary funds or energies in rehabilitation of its poor so long as adventures like Vietnam continued to draw men and skills and money . . . So I was increasingly compelled to see the war as an enemy of the poor and to attack it as such . . . it became clear to me that the war was doing far more than devastating the hopes of the poor at home. It was sending their sons and their brothers and their husbands to fight and to die in extraordinary high proportions relative to the rest of the population. . . .*
>
> —Speech, Dr. Martin Luther King, Jr., New York City, April 4, 1967

★ Document H

Table. Outlays of the Federal Government by Major Functions 1961–1970 (in millions)

Year	Total Outlays	Defense	(% of Total)	Health	(%)	Education	(%)
1961	97.7	47.3	48.4%	.8	.8%	1.2	1.0%
1962	106.8	51.0	47.7	1.1	1.0	1.4	1.3
1963	111.3	52.5	47.1	1.3	1.1	1.5	1.3
1964	118.5	53.5	45.1	1.7	1.4	1.7	1.4
1965	118.4	49.5	41.8	1.7	1.4	2.2	1.8
1966	134.6	56.7	42.1	2.5	1.8	4.2	3.1
1967	158.5	70.0	44.2	6.6	4.1	5.8	3.6
1968	178.8	80.5	45.0	9.6	5.3	6.7	3.7
1969	184.5	81.2	44.0	11.6	6.2	6.5	3.5
1970	196.5	80.2	41.0	12.9	6.5	7.2	3.6

Source: *Historical Statistics of the United States Colonial Times to 1970*

★ Document I

> . . . We can have honest debate about whether we should have entered the war. We can have honest debate about the past conduct of the war. But the urgent question today is what to do now that we are there . . . We have ruled out attempting to impose a purely military solution on the battlefield.
>
> We have ruled out either a one-sided withdrawal from Viet-Nam or the acceptance in Paris of terms that would amount to a disguised defeat . . . If Hanoi were to succeed in taking over South Viet-Nam by force—even after the power of the United States had been engaged—it would greatly strengthen those leaders who scorn negotiation, who advocate aggression, who minimize the risks of confrontation. It would bring peace now, but it would enormously increase the danger of a bigger war later.
>
> We have no objection to reunification, if that turns out to be what the people of South Viet-Nam and the people of the North Viet-Nam want; we ask only that the decision reflect the free choice of the people concerned. . . .
>
> —President Nixon's Report on Vietnam, May 14, 1969

Document **SKILL**

★ Document J

I am a child of Amerika . . .
I dodged the draft.
I went to Oberlin College for a year, graduated from the University of
Cincinnati, spent 1 ½ years in Israel and started graduate school at Berkeley
I dropped out.
I dropped out of the White Race and the Amerikan nation.
I dig being free.
I like getting high.
I don't own a suit or tie.
I live for the revolution.
I'm a yippie.
I am an orphan of Amerika.

—Excerpts, Jerry Rubin, "Self-Portrait of a Child of Amerika," 1970

Organizing the Document-Based Question

The question to be argued is:

_____

_____

_____

List outside information about the question:

1. _____
2. _____
3. _____
4. _____
5. _____
6. _____
7. _____
8. _____
9. _____
10. _____
11. _____
12. _____
13. _____
14. _____
15. _____
16. _____
17. _____
18. _____

Document SKILL

Summarize each document below. Use a separate sheet of paper if necessary.

Document A: _____

_____

_____

Document B: _____

_____

_____

Document C: _____

_____

_____

Document D: _____

_____

_____

Document E: _____

_____

_____

Document F: _____

_____

_____

Document G: _____

_____

_____

Document H: _____

_____

_____

Document I: _____

_____

_____

Document J: _____

_____

_____

Thesis:

_____

_____

_____

_____

Document **SKILL**

Documents and Facts

Pro (support) for the thesis	Con (challenge) to the thesis

Writing the Document-Based Question

Document SKILL

Chapter 1

Identifying Critical Words in an Essay Question

Time Period: Seventeenth century 1600–1699

What to do: Determine the accuracy of the statement about tobacco's impact.

Content: social and economic issues

Determining What Documents Mean

★ Document A

When: 1639, shortly after the founding of colony

Who: residents of Windsor, Hartford, and Wethersfield (probably written by Thomas Hooker and John Haynes—two prominent members of the colony)

What: Good governments write down their rules, the general assembly will meet twice a year, and the governor can only serve two years and must be a member of a church congregation.

Where: the other colonists and officeholders, both current and future

★ Document B

When: 1742, about seventy years after the colony was settled

Who: Eliza Lucas, a prominent and successful indigo farmer

What: Life is good in South Carolina; opportunities are numerous for those who will work.

Where: her brother

Chapter 2

Focus on the Question: What Is It Asking?

1. British policy from 1763 to 1776 was "a history of repeated injuries and usurpations" designed to establish "an absolute tyranny" over the colonies.

   Ask:

   a. What injuries and usurpations were done to the Americans?

   b. Was England's goal an absolute tyranny?

   c. If not, what were England's goals?

   d. Why did the colonists think this?

2. How was the colonial social and economic structure affected by the Revolution's ideology?

Ask:

a. What was the Revolution's ideology?

b. How did the social structure change?

c. What economic changes did the Revolution bring on?

d. What factors prevented greater social and economic changes?

Determining Credibility: Whom Do You Believe?

In Set 1, the Fessenden document has the most credibility because it is an eyewitness account written only four days after the battle. In addition, as an observer, he had a vantage point to see what went on. He also offered the testimony under oath. Granted, he may not have been completely objective because he may have favored the colonial side, but the second source has even more problems. It was written many years after the fact, and the author was a British soldier, so he would definitely have had a partisan view.

In Set 2, the source by John Dickinson had the most credibility. It was written by one of the participants of the Revolution and was drafted at the height of the imperial crisis. The first document is a secondary source written in the 1950s. While it offers a nice summary and perspective, we must give more credence to a primary source written at the time of the event.

Chapter 3

Making Inferences from Documents

a. The Alien and Sedition Acts are just and necessary.

b. Foreigners were not welcome in America in the 1790s.

c. America needed to protect itself from foreigners.

d. If you were loyal, you would not be affected by the acts.

e. Only the dishonest and lawless challenged the acts.

f. Freedom is not unlimited.

g. Unstrained freedom could endanger the country.

Chapter 4

Putting Your Answer into a Graphic Organizer

Suggested network tree:

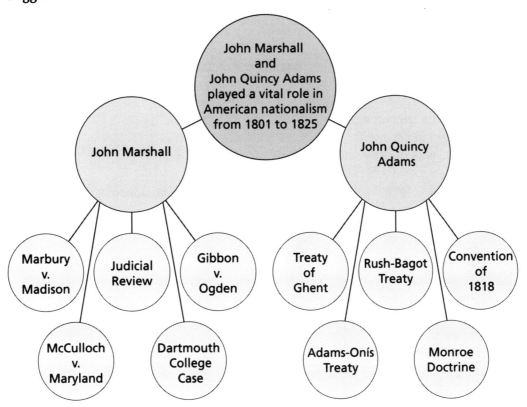

Chapter 5

Organizing Your Answer: Writing an Outline

A. Whig beliefs
  1. Economic
     a. supported the Bank
     b. high tariffs
     c. internal improvements at government expense
  2. Political
     a. opposed a strong executive
     b. executive usurpation
     c. elitist in views
     d. less regard for the agrarian population
     e. less regard for South and West
     f. pushing for an active government in an era of egalitarianism
B. Whig policies
  1. Failed to implement the American System
     a. Clay was too aggressive with Congress and Presidents
     b. Harrison's death
     c. out of step with times—people looking to shrink size of the government
  2. Much of program blocked by John Tyler
     a. vetoed National Bank twice
     b. would not raise tariff
     c. alienated Whigs—not renominated
  3. Henry Clay stood in the way of cooperation between executive and legislative branches
     a. strong personality with little respect for chief executives
     b. Tyler was a very strong stubborn leader
     c. Tyler was states' righter, and Clay's nationalistic position offended him
C. Seeds of failure
  1. Really based on opposition to Jackson
     a. Whigs were opposed to Jackson's use of the veto
     b. Jackson died in 1845
     c. by 1849, the influence of Jacksonians (Van Buren and Polk) was diminished
  2. Program had economic appeal but out of step politically
     a. help with growing Market Revolution
     b. saw future was in manufacturing not agriculture
     c. saw an expanding role for government when the mood was reduction of government's role
     d. increasingly, politics was about slavery, not the American System
  3. Henry Clay always working against presidential candidate
     a. Clay failed three times as a presidential candidate
     b. long career in politics, made many enemies
     c. always believed he was smarter and more popular than the president

Dealing with Documents That Contradict Each Other

The two speeches by Calhoun demonstrate his journey from nationalist to sectionalist. In document A, he rejects the idea that internal improvements be left to the states. He wants the national government to undertake the expense and responsibility of building roads and canals. Eleven years later, he speaks for a besieged South Carolina expressing a state's right to nullify federal law. He reversed himself, going from a nationalist to a sectionalist.

Your paragraph should mention that as Secretary of War and until the early 1820s, he favored a large role of the federal government even at the expense of the states. He believed internal improvements were critical to national defense and well-being. Further, you should acknowledge that he was not always a voice of discord and sectionalism; rather, he acquired that role as South Carolina's economic future declined and as his chances for the presidency dimmed.

Chapter 6

Writing a Strong Thesis Statement

Statement 3 is the strongest thesis to use to answer the question. It is on topic, it takes a position, it provides a structural framework, and it deals with all aspects of the topic (i.e., political, social, and economic differences).

The other two statements are lacking in some way in addressing the four elements of a strong thesis.

Analyzing Charts

1. 1810–1860

2. women's ages and child-bearing patterns

3. The overall number of women was growing rapidly; they were having fewer babies, and they were living longer.

4. Consistent trend regarding population figures; with child-bearing numbers dropping from 1810 to 1850 and then going up 1850–1860.

5. Women's population increased as fewer died. Maybe fewer births allowed women better health and longer lives. The trend up in 1850s may reflect more young immigrant women coming into the nation and having more babies.

6. yes, fewer births, better health, less danger to women's health, so they lived longer

7. women and their families

8. a stretch to say doctors and midwives who delivered fewer babies

9. Women's lives seemed to be improving as they had more control over their bodies, lived longer, and were a significant component of America's growing population.

Chapter 7

Writing a Positive or Negative Thesis Statement

1. **Question:** How did southern actions and demands convince the North that a slave power conspiracy existed?

    Positive Thesis: The South, through its attempt to extend slavery and to repeal the Missouri Compromise, supported Northern contentions that a slave power was conspiring against them and their way of life.

2. **Question:** Would stronger American action have resulted in British concessions in Oregon?

    Negative Thesis: Rather than cowardly, President Polk's Oregon policy was prudent and based on a realistic assessment of America's national interest in 1846.

3. **Question:** Did the land acquired in 1848 help or hurt American development?

    Positive/Negative Thesis: While the land acquired in 1848 caused sectional turmoil and conflict, it also provided valuable economic and national security benefits for the United States for many years to come.

Analyzing Political Cartoons

1. 1844

2. The election of 1844

3. anonymous, but probably a Whig because it presents the Whig Party in a better light

4. Henry Clay, James Polk, Thomas Hart Benton, Andrew Jackson, John C. Calhoun

5. Polk and Clay are trying to gain the laurels of the presidency of the United States in 1844.

6. Confusing statements by the Democrats as they push Polk toward the presidency; Polk seems unhappy with the "encouragement." Clay, on the other hand is very comfortable about the campaign.

7. The labels within the cartoon do support the caption because they are both climbing toward the presidency.

8. The laurel wreath of the presidency; the mop may mean the Democrats need to clean up their act. Jackson's cane indicates his age.

9. Clay is doing well in his unified campaign and nearing victory. The Democrats are far behind and are divided in their message and advice to their candidate, who is doing poorly.

10. The cartoon clearly supports the Whigs and is critical of the Democrats who would oppose its message.

TACOS

Answers 1, 3, 5, 8, and 9

Chapter 8

Creating Categories to Answer Essay Questions

1. Categories:

   1. The political leaders (blundering generation)

   2. The events 1845–1860

   3. The secessionist crisis 1860–1861

2. Categories:

   1. Lincoln's goals 1861–1863

   2. Lincoln's goals 1863–1865

   3. The ideals of the Declaration of Independence

   4. Constitutional principles related to slavery and civil rights

3. Categories:

   1. Radical's intended economic, political, and social goals

   2. Actual lasting changes made

   3. Reasons for the gap between intent and reality

4. Categories:

   1. Southern military leadership

   2. Southern political leadership

   3. Consequences of the gap between military and political leadership

5. Categories:

   1. Ideas of popular sovereignty

   2. Ideas of compact theory

   3. How they contributed to secession

Using Charts and Documents Together

From Document A, students might see:

- The South was dependent on the North for manufactured goods;
- The South was agrarian and rural;
- The South lacked artistic achievements;
- The North was outdistancing the South in population;
- Immigrants would not settle in the South;
- Southern population was not very diverse;
- The North controlled the money the South needed.

From Document B, students might see:

- The Northeastern states in 1860 had 10 times the manufacturing population of the South;
- The Northeastern manufacturing population grew 27% from 1850 to 1860;
- The South's manufacturing population grew 15% 1850–1860;
- The North Central manufacturing population grew faster than both the North and South;
- The South had only about 1 in 12 people living in a city in 1860;
- The North had about 1 in 3 people living in a city;
- By 1860, the South was far less industrialized or urbanized than the Northern states.

Chapter 9

Supporting Your Thesis

Prompt 1

The best choice is **Statement 3**. It has specific information about how the industrialists made America competitive with other countries, but it also suggests how they abused Americans at home. **Statement 1** is too general and vague to develop the thesis. **Statement 2** is an opinion about the industrialists and is not backed up with facts or proof.

Prompt 2

The best choice is **Statement 2**. It makes reference to several planks of the Omaha platform and supports the thesis in a concrete manner. **Statement 1** is too general and does not really defend the thesis with concrete information. **Statement 3** is an opinion.

Using Cartoons and Documents Together

In analyzing the cartoon, a student should see that:

- McKinley was Civil War veteran;
- Outside information: Republicans still waving the bloody shirt;
- McKinley was a grown up, mature;
- Bryan was immature;
- Outside information: Bryan only 36 at time of election;
- Bryan had little experience;
- Bryan is playing a rattle (noisy), a dig at his inflammatory speeches.

In analyzing the document, a student should see:

- Bryan is sowing discord between the classes;
- He sees division between cities and rural areas;
- Lots of us vs. them;
- Gold vs. silver;
- Talks of fights, struggle, confrontations;
- Sees rural people as persecuted by cities and the gold standard;
- Sees rural areas as superior to the cities;
- Fighting the rising tide of urbanization;
- Bryan is challenging the status quo.

Chapter 10

Dealing with All Aspects of the Statement or Question

Prompt 1

The topic sentences address the main topics of the prompt: the ideas of the "New Manifest Destiny" will be explained in sentence (1); sentences (2) and (3) deal with the political and economic impact of the Populist; and sentence (4) suggests the economic dislocation from the Depression of 1893. The final sentence suggests how the depression and the Populist were connected with the expansion ideology of the 1890s.

Prompt 2

Prompt 2 is not fully supported because the topic sentences do not indicate the writer will go beyond the events of 1914–1915. The student does not appear likely to use information beyond the sinking of the *Lusitania* in May 1915. Notice that the question asked the student to assess the validity of the statement by reviewing the events from 1914 to 1917. The topic sentences suggest the analysis will not deal with the complete chronological period under consideration.

Arranging Sources into Categories

The prompt and thesis statement would be supported by documents that indicate Wilson played a significant role in defeating the Treaty in 1919–1920. These sources would highlight his refusal to compromise with his opponents. Documents B and D are examples of these sources. In **Document B**, Wilson tells his supporters to vote against the treaty when it included the Lodge reservations. In **Document D**, he suggests that the American people must choose between the League as he wants it or withdraw from contact with the allies. (Again no room for compromise.)

Documents A and C suggest that Wilson was not completely at fault in the rejection of the League. **Document A** shows how deep isolationist feelings flowed in America after the war. **Document C** highlights Senator Lodge's role in using the reservationists to the treaty to block its ratification.

Your chart should look like:

Pro	Con
Document B	Document A
Document D	Document C

Chapter 11

Writing an Introductory Paragraph

Sample introductory paragraph on Booker T. Washington's realism.

At first Booker T. Washington was realistic in his approach to fighting Jim Crow, but his philosophy failed to change with the times. Washington's advice to accept social and political segregation in return for economic opportunities made sense for a while, but by the early 1900s, he was outdated. In the new century, the aggressive views of W. E. B. DuBois gained credence. A review of the debate between DuBois and Washington will demonstrate that Washington's realism lost its relevance in the early 1900s.

Writing a Paragraph from Dissenting Documents

A thesis should indicate:

- The 1920s were a battleground over values;
- Older, conservative people wanted security and continuity in their lives;
- Young people and women challenged generational and sexual ideas.

The concession paragraph should demonstrate that in contrast to mainstream America, the younger generation:

- was disillusioned;
- was cynical about the future;
- saw the impact of the Great War negatively.

And that women challenged sexual attitudes by:

- wanting more control of their bodies;
- practicing birth control;
- choosing when and whether to become mothers.

Chapter 12

Writing a Concluding Paragraph

In summary:

- (Restatement of thesis) Events of the 1930s favored the isolationists, but when Hitler conquered Europe, the internationalists became more powerful;
- Because of economic troubles, the country wanted to stay out of European affairs;
- The Neutrality Acts demonstrated the power of the isolationists;
- As the Nazis conquered Europe, Americans became anxious, repealed the Neutrality Acts, and began Lend Lease;
- The struggle between the isolationists and internationalists was a seesaw battle strongly influenced by world events.

Chapter 13

Creating a Rubric for Free-Response Essays

8–9 essay:

- contains a clear, well-written thesis that presents the way that BOTH events undermined unity and caused the Cold War;
- provides an analysis how BOTH events led to the division between the two nations;
- supports thesis/analysis with substantial relevant information about BOTH topics;
- clearly links the BOTH events to undermining unity and causing Cold War;
- has minor errors.

5–7 essay:

- has a general thesis that acknowledges that BOTH events undermined and brought on the Cold War;
- describes the BOTH events and generally suggests how they led to division;
- supports thesis with some relevant information about BOTH topics;
- vaguely links the events to undermining unity and causing Cold War;
- has several errors.

2–4 essay:

- has unfocused thesis or none at all;
- describes ONE event;
- has little factual information or may be off topic;
- does not link events to undermining unity and causing the Cold War;
- has major errors.

0–1 essay:

- has no thesis;
- describes events that are off topic;
- little relevant information;
- makes no attempt at linkage of event;
- has many substantial factual errors.

Creating a Rubric for a Document-Based Question

List of Criteria

1. Well developed thesis that identifies and evaluates how Eisenhower addressed Cold War fears.
2. A discussion and analysis of several (more than 2) fears and how well Eisenhower dealt with them.
3. Use of substantial documents/sources.
4. Use of substantial relevant outside facts.
5. Well written, organized.
6. Few minor errors.

Chapter 14

Chapter 14 does not require any responses, only discussion amongst your study group.

Chapter 15

Writing a Free-Response Essay

Possible themes and information about writing prompts.

Prompt 1

Themes

- Federalists realized America would not be agrarian forever
- Federalists developed policies that promoted mercantile, nonfarming segment of society
- Federalists realized that America needed a strong financial foundation to compete internationally
- Federalists looked to English society for their political model
- Federalists never envisioned "the common man" participating fully in government
- Federalists had little tolerance for freedom of expression
- Federalists realized that the Articles of Confederation were undermined because they could not maintain order
- Federalists had repressive, somewhat authoritarian traditions
- Federalists favored property requirement to limited poor participation in government
- Federalists expected political authority always to flow from the top

Possible Information

- Hamilton's financial plan
  - creation of National Bank
  - tariff
  - tax on whiskey and other items
  - Hamilton's "Report on Manufactures" (1791)
  - protect American industries
  - work toward self-sufficiency
- Hamilton's "Report on the Public Credit"
  - redeem bonds at face value
  - creation of national debt (assumption of state debts)
  - establish full faith and credit of the United States
- Repressive measures politically
  - Whiskey Rebellion 1794
  - about 5000–6000 farmers in western Pennsylvania refused to pay whiskey tax.
  - attacked collectors, destroyed property
  - compared tax to Stamp Act of 1775
  - Washington personally led (briefly) "the Watermelon Army" that put rebellion down
  - about 12,000 soldiers called, cost 3 years of revenue to crush it
  - Washington saw rebellion as foreign inspired (Jacobins in France)
  - 150 arrested
  - Jeffersonians called it overkill

- Alien and Sedition Acts
  - 1798
  - perceived threat from France
  - Alien Acts
    - Alien Enemies Act—president could deport or imprison the subjects of opposing powers in time of war
    - Alien Act—president could deport aliens if he decided they were dangerous to the United States
    - Naturalization Act—increased the length of time to be naturalized citizen from 5 to 14 years
  - Sedition Act
    - outlawed writing, printing, or uttering "false, scandalous and malicious statements" against the government or president
    - two years in prison, $2,000 fine
    - 15 arrested, 10 convicted
    - violated First Amendment
    - gave rise to the Virginia and Kentucky Resolutions

Prompt 2

Themes

- Republicans had been the party of emancipation and equal rights
- Men such as Abraham Lincoln, Thaddeus Stevens, and Charles Sumner helped end slavery and promote racial equality.
- Republicans were the party of the 13th, 14th, and 15th Amendments and the Civil Rights Act of 1875.
- In Gilded Age, Republicans were party of Stalwarts, Grantism
- Neither party accepted expanding money supply significantly. A great hardship on debtors.
- Democrats maintained their states' rights outlook from before the war.
- Democrats sought to limit power of the central government.
- Democrats in South would not accept African Americans as equals.
- Democrats involved in political scandals when they achieved control
- Both parties took large amounts of money from special interests.
- Both parties used and supported the spoils system.

Possible Information

- Civil Rights
  - Republicans abandoned the cause
  - leadership died: Lincoln in 1865, Stevens in 1868, Sumner in 1874
  - Compromise of 1877
  - nation wanted sectional reconciliation

- Democrats maintained prewar bias and attitudes
  - Ku Klux Klan activities in South
  - expected no interference from Washington after 1877
  - sought to restrict federal power on all levels
  - created Jim Crow system throughout the South
  - neutralized the 15th Amendment with poll taxes, literacy tests, and grandfather clauses
- Neither party spoke out against Supreme Court's actions
  - *Slaughterhouse Case*
  - *Cruikshank v. United States*
  - *U.S. v. Singleton*
  - *Plessy v. Ferguson*
  - rulings reduced reach of the 14th Amendment and eventually put government's approval on Jim Crow
  - neither party challenged the poll taxes, literacy tests, or grandfather clauses
- Honesty in Government
  - both parties had major scandals
  - Republicans
    - Grantism
    - Credit Mobilier
    - Whiskey Ring
    - impeachment of William Belknap
    - struggle between Stalwarts and Half Breeds
    - one estimate that under Grant government lost $95 million in stolen taxes annually
  - Democrats
    - Tweed Ring in New York City
    - Richard Croker later in New York headed Tammany Hall
    - various scandals in southern Reconstruction government
  - both parties depended on spoils system (number of government jobs tripled from 1865 to 1891)
  - both parties took large cash donations from Big Business
- Currency reform
  - contraction of money supply after Civil War—$450 million in greenback currency retired
  - farm price index fell by 33% from 1868 to 1896
  - neither party supported expanding money supply beyond gold, seen as sound money
  - formation of third parties such as Greenback-Labor and Populist because the two major parties would not address the issue
  - battle of the standards: gold for rich eastern business interest and silver for poor western agrarian interest

Prompt 3
Vietnam

Themes

- United States became involved in Vietnam slowly
- After World War II hoped to combat colonialism and were lukewarm to French activities in Indochina
- By early 1950s, Communism was greatest concern, and we helped France in Indochina by 1954 paying 80% of the cost of their war
- In 1954, USA replaced France as protector of Southeast Asia against Communism
- Ngo Diem became a shaky ally after U.S. supported his decision not to hold elections in 1956
- Diem was corrupt and unpopular and lost support of his people
- Diem was unable to maintain control without American economic aid
- Diem's overthrow in 1963 resulted in political chaos in the South
- President Johnson increased troops, economic aid, and started to bomb North Vietnam
- Tet offensive was a psychological blow that stopped America's escalation of war
- War divided nation and the Democratic Party

Possible Information

- Dien Bein Phu
- The Geneva Conference 1954
- Ho Chi Minh
- John Foster Dulles
- Dwight D. Eisenhower
- Domino theory
- Viet Cong
- Ngo Diem
- John Kennedy
- Flexible response
- Coup of 1963
- Lyndon Johnson
- Gulf of Tonkin Resolution
- Students for a Democratic Society
- Operation Rolling Thunder
- Tet offensive
- 1960—1,000 Americans in Vietnam; 1963—16,000; 1967—540,000

Civil Rights

Themes

- Courts led way in energizing civil rights in 1950s
- Montgomery bus boycott made Martin Luther King a national figure
- Eisenhower was a reluctant supporter of the movement
- Students led way with sit-ins and freedom rides
- Kennedys were cautious on civil rights; they often clashed with King
- King's nonviolent protest grabbed the attention and conscience of the nation
- Lyndon Johnson was a great advocate for civil rights
- By 1965, King was under attack and pressure from more militant voices
- The urban rioting caused a white backlash in late 1960s

Possible Information

- Rosa Parks
- *Brown vs. Board of Education*
- Martin Luther King
- Little Rock crisis
- Civil Rights Acts of 1957, 1960
- Wiretaps on King by Kennedy brothers
- Sit-ins
- Freedom rides
- James Meredith
- Selma/Birmingham
- March on Washington
- Civil Rights Acts of 1964, 1965
- War on Poverty
- Malcolm X
- Black Power movement
- King's assassination
- George Wallace
- 1964–1968 riots from Watts to Washington, D.C.: 200 killed, 40,000 arrested

U.S. Cuban Relations

Themes

- Caribbean had lingering resentment towards U.S. because of Big Stick/Dollar Diplomacy era
- Castro was anti-American and opposed to Batista
- Castro was not a clear Marxist in the 1950s
- Bay of Pigs was an American attempt to overthrow Castro
- After invasion failed, Robert Kennedy became obsessed with Castro's removal
- After invasion failed, Castro wanted protection

- Khrushchev saw an opportunity to change the balance of power in the Cold War by putting missiles in Cuba
- U.S. discovered the missiles and demanded their removal
- U.S./USSR resolved the crisis peacefully
- Castro continued to be a threat to American interests in Caribbean and Central America

Possible Information

- Castro's role model: Jose Marti—1890s revolutionary against Spanish
- Big Stick Policy
- Dollar Diplomacy
- Fulgencio Bautista (seized power in 1952)
- Fidel Castro
- 1957–1958 CIA sent Castro $50,000 but too late
- Castro nationalized $850 million in U.S. property
- April 1961, Bay of Pigs (1,400 captured)
- Central Intelligence Agency (Guatemala coup 1954)
- John and Robert Kennedy
- Operation Mongoose ($50 million dollars and 400 agents working to overthrow Castro)
- Nikita Khrushchev
- 1962, USSR had 42,000 troops in Cuba, tried to put 40 missiles on island
- Bombing vs. blockade
- Crisis cost Khrushchev his job two years later
- Triggered an arms race between the U.S. and USSR

Writing a Document-Based Question

Themes, document use and outside information for the DBQ

Themes

- The war called into question the domino theory and America's ability to transform other countries in its own image
- Vietnam shook America's faith in itself
- Vietnam made Americans question the truthfulness of their government
- Vietnam got young people involved in changing political policies
- Vietnam and civil rights transformed many young people into activists who did not accept the values of their parents, corporations, or the government
- Vietnam derailed the civil rights movement as spending priorities changed and young, poor blacks were sent to fight
- The war raised the issue of "guns v. butter"
- Many young people lost faith in the government and society in the 1960s
- Protests spawned an alternative lifestyle among many with drugs and casual sex
- Protests went beyond politics to include career choice, dress, and hairstyles

Document Use

Document A: Expresses main belief about Vietnam in 1961: vital to American security, democracy vs. Communism, domino theory in play, use military option to gain American goals.

Document B: Young people saw their differences with past. They believed they could transform society. Rejected racial bias, war. Idealism that drove the civil rights movement and antiwar movement. Clearly questioned past role for young.

Document C: Students became early critics of war. Protest and no longer a silent generation of students like their older brothers and sisters or parents. Connect with Document B.

Document D: Johnson still talked of America keeping its word and domino theory, believed victory was very possible in Vietnam. Connect with Document A. Continuation of traditional Cold War ideas.

Document E: Media began to see that American strategy was flawed in Vietnam. Connect to other protest Document C.

Document F: Congress also saw flaws in America's Vietnam policy. Tried to do too much. Leaders were not aware of limits and could not match means with ends. Questioned America's post World War II ability to transform world.

Document G: Vietnam divided old allies. King believed the war took valuable resources from War on Poverty and civil rights battle. Also raised the racial and class issue about the draft. War began to split the Great Society coalition.

Document H: Statistics can be used several ways: proof that King was right about how resources were being drained from domestic issues to fight war. (From 1965 to 1968, defense spending increased by $31 million; health by only $11.2 million; and education by $5.0 million) On the other hand, in the same period, spending for these areas was up over fourfold. This document could be used in a concession paragraph to demonstrate that Johnson tried to keep his commitments in Vietnam and also to the war, which caused inflation later on.

Document I: Nixon still accepted that America cannot lose face, but he had given up on achieving a military victory and seemed less concerned about spread of Communism. Hinted at domino theory. Contrast this document with documents A and D, in which America was confident and saw Vietnam as part of America's worldwide commitment to stop the spread of Communism. Some ideas could be used in concession paragraph to show how America did cling to some of its Cold War beliefs about Communism and its place in the world.

Document J: Demonstrates the impact of war, protest on the most radical nonpolitical members of the counterculture. Cynical view of America dedicated to dropping out and using drugs. Contrast it with Document B and the idealism of the early 1960s.

Possible Outside Information

Domino theory	containment	Ngo Dinh Diem	appeasement
Gulf of Tonkin Resolution	Tet offensive	Rolling Thunder	Ho Chi Minh
Viet Cong	baby boom	March on Pentagon	Great Society
War on Poverty	Woodstock	Civil Rights Acts	hippies
Eugene McCarthy	Robert Kennedy	Martin Luther King	New Left
counterculture	Bob Dylan		
	Students for a Democratic Society		
	Student Non-Violent Coordinating Committee		
	Free Speech Movement		

100 MILESTONE DOCUMENTS

The following is a list of 100 milestone documents, compiled by the National Archives and Records Administration and drawn primarily from its nationwide holdings. The documents chronicle United States history from 1776 to 1965.

1. Lee Resolution (1776)
2. Declaration of Independence (1776)
3. Articles of Confederation (1777)
4. Treaty of Alliance with France (1778)
5. Original Design of the Great Seal of the United States (1782)
6. Treaty of Paris (1783)
7. Virginia Plan (1787)
8. Northwest Ordinance (1787)
9. Constitution of the United States (1787)
10. Federalist Papers, No. 10 and No. 51 (1787–1788)
11. President George Washington's First Inaugural Speech (1789)
12. Federal Judiciary Act (1789)
13. Bill of Rights (1791)
14. Patent for Cotton Gin (1794)
15. President George Washington's Farewell Address (1796)
16. Alien and Sedition Acts (1798)
17. Jefferson's Secret Message to Congress Regarding the Lewis and Clark Expedition (1803)
18. Louisiana Purchase Treaty (1803)
19. Marbury v. Madison (1803)
20. Treaty of Ghent (1814)
21. McCulloch v. Maryland (1819)

22. Missouri Compromise (1820)

23. Monroe Doctrine (1823)

24. Gibbons v. Ogden (1824)

25. President Andrew Jackson's Message to Congress "On Indian Removal" (1830)

26. Treaty of Guadalupe Hidalgo (1848)

27. Compromise of 1850 (1850)

28. Kansas-Nebraska Act (1854)

29. Dred Scott v. Sanford (1857)

30. Telegram Announcing the Surrender of Fort Sumter (1861)

31. Homestead Act (1862)

32. Pacific Railway Act (1862)

33. Morrill Act (1862)

34. Emancipation Proclamation (1863)

35. War Department General Order 143: Creation of the U.S. Colored Troops (1863)

36. Gettysburg Address (1863)

37. Wade-Davis Bill (1864)

38. President Abraham Lincoln's Second Inaugural Address (1865)

39. Articles of Agreement Relating to the Surrender of the Army of Northern Virginia (1865)

40. 13th Amendment to the U.S. Constitution: Abolition of Slavery (1865)

41. Check for the Purchase of Alaska (1868)

42. Treaty of Fort Laramie (1868)

43. 14th Amendment to the U.S. Constitution: Civil Rights (1868)

44. 15th Amendment to the U.S. Constitution: Voting Rights (1870)

45. Act Establishing Yellowstone National Park (1872)

46. Thomas Edison's Patent Application for the Light Bulb (1880)

47. Chinese Exclusion Act (1882)

48. Pendleton Act (1883)

49. Interstate Commerce Act (1887)

50. Dawes Act (1887)

51. Sherman Anti-Trust Act (1890)

52. Plessy v. Ferguson (1896)

53. De Lôme Letter (1898)

86. Senate Resolution 301: Censure of Senator Joseph McCarthy (1954)

87. Brown v. Board of Education (1954)

88. National Interstate and Defense Highways Act (1956)

89. Executive Order 10730: Desegregation of Central High School (1957)

90. President Dwight D. Eisenhower's Farewell Address (1961)

91. President John F. Kennedy's Inaugural Address (1961)

92. Executive Order 10924: Establishment of the Peace Corps (1961)

93. Transcript of John Glenn's Official Communication with the Command Center (1962)

94. Aerial Photograph of Missiles in Cuba (1962)

95. Test Ban Treaty (1963)

96. Official Program for the March on Washington (1963)

97. Civil Rights Act (1964)

98. Tonkin Gulf Resolution (1964)

99. Social Security Act Amendments (1965)

100. Voting Rights Act (1965)

SELECTED SOURCES AND REFERENCES

Below are several sources that will help you strengthen and reinforce your AP skills and knowledge. All these sources are useful in developing debates, supporting written arguments, completing classroom assignments, deepening your understanding of specific topics, and constructing your own DBQs. Also consult the bibliography at the end of each chapter in your primary textbook for a list of reference materials that will help you develop in-depth knowledge of specific topics.

Books

Davidson, James West, and Mark Hamilton Lytle. *After the Fact: The Art of Historical Detection*. New York: McGraw-Hill, 1999.

> This book gives a student "two for the price of one." It provides historical information about major topics such as the Salem Witch Trials, John Brown's Raid, and Watergate at the same time it provides guidance on historical skills such as the problem of selecting evidence, using psychohistory, conducting oral history, and determining points of view.

Dollar, Charles M., and Gary W. Reichard, ed. *American Issues: A Documentary Reader*. New York: McGraw-Hill, 2002.

> This reader is a collection of primary and secondary sources that are chronologically arranged, so it can be used with any textbook. The primary sources are informative and could be valuable in constructing student-made DBQs. The secondary sources offer provocative points of view of the events and topics in the chapter.

Finkenbine, Roy E. *Sources of the African-American Past: Primary Sources in American History*. Rye, New York: Pearson Longman Publishing, 2003.

> A comprehensive survey of sources from the African-American perspective that includes speeches, letters, poetry, and essays by prominent black leaders. It is a very useful source in the area of social and cultural history.

Madaras, Larry, and James M. SoRelle, ed. *Taking Sides: Clashing Views on Controversial Issues in American History*. Guilford, Connecticut: Duskin Publishing Group, 2000.

This two-volume reader provides contrasting points of views on major issues and events from 1607 to the 1990s. By offering contrasting positions, the book is an excellent source for classroom debates and for strengthening historical arguments. The book deals with all the major topics of the survey.

McClellan, Jim R. *Changing Interpretations of America's Past*. Guilford, Connecticut: Dushkin Publishing Group, 1994.

This book of primary and secondary readings deals with all the major topics in the survey course. It has first impressions (primary sources) of an event, which are useful for adding depth to your knowledge and could be valuable in assembling student-made DBQs. The second impressions are secondary sources that add a historiographic slant to various topics.

Monk, Linda R., ed. *Ordinary Americans: U.S. History Through the Eyes of Everyday People*. Washington: Close Up Publishing, 1994.

This set of primary readings has a unique perspective. All the views are from "regular people" who see historical events through the eyes of unheralded individuals who are trying to earn a living and raise their families. An excellent source for viewing history from the "bottom up."

Ruiz, Vicki L., and Ellen DuBois, eds. *Unequal Sisters: A Multicultural Reader in U.S. Women's History*. New York: Routledge Publishing, 2000.

This reader examines women's roles in American history from a variety of ethnic and racial perspectives. It is an excellent source for social history and the role of some of the forgotten players of history.

Spoehr, Luther, and Alan Fraker. *Doing the DBQ*. New York: The College Board, 1995.

This book has all the DBQs from 1973 to 1994. It is not only a great place to look at the topics that have been used for DBQs, but it offers comments on each DBQ with specific guidance about the type of analysis of the documents and outside information that would be necessary for a successful answer to the question.

Internet Sources

http://www.lcweb.loc.gov/

The American Memory project of the Library of Congress has over seven million digital items. It is an outstanding source for papers, debates, and DBQs.

http://www.historyteacher.net

A good source for documents and cartoons and information about the United States history course in general.

http://www.ku.edu/history/VL/USA

A good source for documents in many areas of American history. The sources are divided by topic to help you find specific areas of interest.

http://www.unc.edu/depts/diplomat

Sources in American Diplomatic History.

http://www.smithsonianeducation.org/educators/

The Smithsonian Institution has many good sources and ideas for teachers and students. Their publication *Artifacts and Analysis* is described on the site and is an interesting source for using museum artifacts to build a DBQ.

http://www.gilderlehrman.org

The Gilder Lehrman Collection is a wonderful source of primary documents and ideas for using them.

http://www.archives.gov/digital_classroom/index.html

The National Archives has many primary sources and ideas for using them.

http://www.indiana.edu/~liblilly/cartoon/cartoons.html

Good source for cartoons on the first half of the survey course.

http://www.archives.gov/exhibit_hall/picturing_the_century/index.html

National Archives site with some interesting photos from the twentieth century.

Credits and Sources

Photos and Art: Cover images, Artbase, Inc. p. 15, North Wind Picture Archives; p. 16, Reuters/Archive Photo; p. 18, North Wind Picture Archives; pp. 19, 20, 27, 30, 31, 32, 39, 42, 43, 44, 53, 54, 56, 57, 58, 65, 66, 68, North Wind Picture Archives; p. 69, Bettmann/Corbis; p. 77, Hulton Archive/Getty Images; p. 78, North Wind Picture Archives; p. 80, Hulton-Deutsch Collection/Corbis; p. 81, North Wind Picture Archives; p. 82, MPI/Getty Images; p. 89, Bettmann/Corbis; pp. 90, 92, 93, 94, North Wind Picture Archives; p. 100, New York Public Library; pp. 103, 104, 106, 107, 108, North Wind Picture Archives; p. 109, National Archives; p. 119, North Wind Picture Archives; p. 122, Hulton-Deutsch Collection/Corbis; pp. 123, 124, North Wind Picture Archives; p. 128, "The 'Great American' Game of Public Office for Private Gain" by Thomas Nast, from Harper's Weekly, August 9, 1884; p. 130, "The Deadly Parallel" from Harper's Weekly, 1896; p. 133, Corbis; p. 135, Bettmann/Corbis; pp. 136, 137, 138, North Wind Picture Archives; p. 147, Corbis; p. 150 (top), Hulton Archives/Getty Images; p. 150 (bottom), New York Times/Getty Images; p. 151, MPI/Getty Images; p. 152, Stock Montage, Getty Images; p. 159, Hulton Archives/Getty Images; p. 162, MPI/Getty Images; p. 163 (top), Marie Hansen/Time Life Pictures/Getty Images; p. 163 (bottom), Fox Photos/Getty Images; p. 164 (top), Hulton Archives/Getty Images, p. 164 (bottom), Time Life Pictures/US Navy/Getty Images; p. 173, Howard Sochurek/Time Life Pictures/Getty Images; p. 176 (top), Margaret Bourke-White/Time Life Pictures/Getty Images; p. 176 (bottom), New York Times Company/Getty Images; p. 177 (top), Time Inc./Time Life Pictures/Getty Images; p. 177 (bottom), MPI/Getty Images; p. 178, Mark Kauffman/Time Life Pictures/Getty Images; p. 187, AFP/Getty Images; p. 190, Blank Archives/Getty Images; p. 191 (top), Keystone Features/Getty Images; p. 191 (bottom), Burt Shavitz/Pix Inc./Time Life Pictures/Getty Images; p. 192, Michael Rougier/Time Life Pictures/Getty Images; p. 197, Mark Wilson/Getty Images; p. 200 (top), Neil Boenzi/New York Times/Getty Images; p. 200 (bottom), Bill Eppridge/Time Life Pictures/Getty Images; p. 201 (top), Robert Sherbow/Time Life Pictures/Getty Images, p. 201 (bottom), Dirck Halstead/Time Life Pictures/Getty Images; p. 208, Hulton-Deutsch Collection/Corbis; p. 209, Bill Mauldin, *The Sun-Times* (Chicago)

Documents: p. 24, excerpt from *Memoirs of the Historical Society of Pennsylvania (Philadelphia, 1858)*, source: Robert E. Burns, Lee R. Boyer, James R. Felton, Philip Gleason, John J. Lyon, James O'Neill, Charles J. Tull, *Episodes in American History: An Inquiry Approach*, Lexington, Massachusetts: Ginn and Company, 1973, p. 110; p. 25, *Fundamental Orders of Connecticut*, January 14, 1639, source: Bernard Feder, *Viewpoints: USA*. New York: American Book Company, 1967, pp. 5–6; p. 26, *Eliza Lucas, Journal and Letters*, 1742, source: *Sources in American History: A Book of Readings*, Chicago: Harcourt Brace Jovanovich Publishers, 1986, p. 28; p. 37 (top), Thomas Fessenden, a colonial onlooker at Lexington, April 23, 1775; p. 37 (bottom), Ensign Jeremy Lister, British officer, writing in 1832, source: Peter Bennett, *What Happened on Lexington Green*, Menlo Park: Addison-Wesley Publishing Company, 1970, pp. 9, 17–18; p. 38 (top), John R. Alden, *The American Revolution*, 1775–1783, source: New York, Harper, 1954, p. 8; p. 38 (bottom), John Dickinson, *Letters from a Farmer in Pennsylvania*, 1767, source: Ashbrook Center Web site; p. 51, The Northwest Ordinance of 1787, source: Bernard Feder, *Viewpoints: USA*, New York: American Book Company, 1967, pp. 39–40; p. 52, excerpt from *The Life of Timothy Pickering, Vol. III*, edited by Charles W. Upham, 1873, source: Bernard Feder, *Viewpoints: USA*, New York: American Book Company, 1967, pp. 73–74; p. 62, Felix Grundy, *Annals of Congress*, 12th Congress, 1811, source: Bernard Feder, *Viewpoints: USA*, New York: American Book Company, 1967, p. 94; p. 63, John Quincy Adams, *Memoirs*, Philadelphia, 1875, source: Bernard Feder, *Viewpoints: USA*, New York: American Book Company, 1967, pp. 100–101; p. 74, J. S. Buckingham, *America, Historical, Statistic and Descriptive*, source: New York: Harper and Brothers, 1841; p. 75, Harriet Hanson Robinson, *Loom and Spindle: Life Among the Early Mill Girls*, 1898, source: *Sources in American History*, Orlando: Harcourt Brace Jovanovich, 1986, p. 125; p. 76 (top), John Calhoun, *Works*, February 1817, source: Bernard Feder, *Viewpoints: USA*, New York: American Book Company, 1967, p. 142; p. 76 (bottom), *South Carolina's Exposition and Protest*, December 19, 1828, source: Bernard Feder, *Viewpoints: USA*, New York: American Book Company, 1967, p. 145; p. 87, source: *Historical Statistics of the United States Colonial Times to 1970*, p. 16; p. 114, source: Adapted from John Hope Franklin, *RECONSTRUCTION AFTER THE CIVIL WAR*, the University of Chicago Press, Copyright © 1961. Reprinted by permission of the University of Chicago Press; p. 115, James S. Pike, *The Prostrate South*, New York: Appleton-Century-Crofts, 1874, pp. 10, 14–15, 17–21, source: Allan O. Kownslar and Donald B. Frizzle, *Discovering American History*, New York: Holt, Rinehart and Winston, Inc., 1967, pp. 505–506; p. 116 (top), Hinton Helper, *The Impending Crisis*, New York: Burdich Brothers, 1857, p. 21; p. 116 (bottom) source: Adapted from Edwin Fenton, *A New History of the United States: An Inquiry Approach*, New York: Holt, Rinehart and Winston, Inc., 1969, pp. 304–305; p. 129, excerpt from George Plunkitt, "How I Got Rich by Honest Graft" found in *PLUNKITT OF TAMMANY HALL: A SERIES OF VERY PLAIN TALKS ON VERY PRACTICAL POLITICS*, pp. 3–8, edited by William L. Riordan, published by Alfred A. Knopf, 1948; p. 131, excerpt from William Jennings Bryan speech at the Democratic Convention, 1896, source: Pauline Maier, Merritt Roe Smith, Alexander Keyssar, Daniel J. Kevles, source: Inventing America, documents (CD-ROM, Chapter 20); p. 143 (Document A), excerpt from The San Francisco *Evening Bulletin*, January 30, 1893, source: Julius Pratt, *Expansionists of 1898*, Chicago: Quadrangle Paperbacks, 1964 edition, p. 147; p. 143 (Document B), excerpt from Letters of Grover Cleveland, pp. 491–492, source: Julius Pratt, *Expansionists of 1898*, Chicago: Quadrangle Paperbacks, 1964, p. 209; p. 143 (Document C), *Public Opinion*, VI, 367 (February 9, 1889), source: Thomas Bailey, *A Diplomatic History of the American People*, 10th edition. Englewood Cliffs: Prentice-Hall, Inc., 1980, p. 391; p. 143 (Document D), from *Congressional Record*, 55th Congress, 2nd session, appendix, p. 549, source: Thomas Bailey, *A Diplomatic History of the American People*, 10th edition. Englewood Cliffs: Prentice-Hall, Inc., 1980, p. 434; p. 144, from *Boston Herald*, July 8, 1919; p. 145 (Document B), Woodrow Wilson's letter to the Senate, November 19, 1919; p. 145 (Document C), Henry Cabot Lodge speaks in Boston, March 19, 1919; p. 145 (Document D), Wilson's letter to the Senate, March 8, 1920; p. 156, *Why We March*, Leaflet, July 28, 1917, source: William Katz (ed.), *Eyewitness: The Negro in American History*, New York: Pitman Publishing Company, 1969, p. 393; p. 157, "Eugene V. Debs Says Moose Party Stole Socialist Planks" *Chicago World*, August 15, 1912; p. 158 (top), John F. Carter Jr. "These Wild Young People" *The Atlantic Monthly* (September, 1920), 302–303, source: Robert Burns, *Episodes in American History: An Inquiry Approach* (Lexington, Massachusetts: Ginn and Company, 1973), pp. 49–50; p. 158 (bottom), Margaret Sanger, Woman and the New Race (1920), source: Linda Monk (ed.) *Ordinary Americans: US History Through the Eyes of Everyday People*, Washington: Close Up Publishing, 1994, p. 177; p. 207, excerpts from Dean Rusk and Robert McNamara's Report to President Kennedy, November 11, 1961, source: Neil Sheehan, *The Pentagon Papers*, New York: Bantam Book, 1971, pp. 150–153; p. 208, excerpts from Port Huron Statement, June 1962, (Tom Hayden), source: Website of Institute of Advanced Technology in the Humanities; p. 209, excerpt from Lyndon Johnson's State of the Union Address, January 12, 1966, Department of State Publication 8011, pp. 9–10, source: Bernard Feder, *Viewpoints: USA*, New York: American Book Company, 1967, pp. 320–321; p. 210 (top), Senator J. William Fulbright, *The Arrogance of Power*, 1966, from Paterson, Thomas G., *Major Problems in American Foreign Policy*, Third Edition, Vol. 2, Copyright © 1989 by D.C. Heath and Company. Used by permission of Houghton Mifflin Company; p. 210 (bottom), excerpt from *I Have a Dream: Writings and Speeches that Changed the World* by Martin Luther King, edited by James M. Washington. Harper San Francisco, 1992; p. 211 (top), *Historical Statistics of the United States Colonial Times to 1970*, source: Washington, DC: US Department of Commerce. p. 1,116; p. 211 (bottom), excerpt from President Nixon's Report on Vietnam, May 14, 1969, source: George Kahn and John Lewis, *The United States in Vietnam*, New York: A Delta Book, 1969, pp. 517–519; p. 212, excerpt from *Self-Portrait of a Child in Amerika*, by Jerry Rubin, Copyright © 1970